God's
Vitamin "C"

for the Spirit™ *of* MEN

Compiled by
D. Larry Miller

STARBURST PUBLISHERS

P. O. Box 4123, Lancaster, Pennsylvania 17604

D. Larry Miller has been a policeman for 25 years. Currently, he is a police sergeant with the Huntington Beach Police Department, California. Larry is a member of the National Speakers Association (NSA) and he speaks to church and business groups about leadership, management and marriage. With his wife, author and speaker Kathy Collard Miller, he speaks extensively across the nation and internationally about the needs husbands and wives bring into marriage, and the cyclical stages of love. Along with Kathy, he is the compiler of the bestselling God's Vitamin "C" for the Spirit series.

He can be reached for scheduling speaking engagements at P. O. Box 1058, Placentia, California 92670 (714) 993-2654.

To schedule Author appearances write:
Author Appearances, Starburst Promotions, P. O. Box 4123
Lancaster, Pennsylvania 17604 or call (717) 293-0939

Credits:
Cover by David Marty Design
Unless otherwise noted, or paraphrased by the author, all Scripture quotations are from the King James Version of The Holy Bible.

To the best of its ability, Starburst Publishers has strived to find the source of all material. If there has been an oversight, please contact us and we will make any correction deemed necessary in future printings. We also declare that to the best of our knowledge all material (quoted or not) contained herein is accurate, and we shall not be held liable for the same.

First Printing, September 1996

ISBN: 0-914984-81-0
Library of Congress Catalog Number 96-68838
Printed in the United States of America

Table of Contents

Success—267

God's Vitamin "C" for the Spirit of MEN is a collection of inspirational Stories, Quotes, Cartoons, and Scriptures by many of your favorite Christian speakers and writers. It will motivate your life and inspire your spirit. You will find them to be both heart-tugging and thought-provoking.

Be sure to read *God's Chewable Vitamin "C" for the Spirit of DADs: A Dose of Godly Character, One Bite at a Time*—a collection of Quotes and Scriptures from many of the same speakers and writers found in *God's Vitamin "C" for the Spirit of MEN.*

This is another in the series of *God's Vitamin "C" for the Spirit*™ books published by Starburst Publishers. All are available at your local bookstore.

1

Christian Living

I am crucified with Christ; nevertheless I live; yet not I, but Christ liveth in me: and the life which I now live in the flesh I live by the faith of the Son of God, who loved me, and gave himself for me.

Galatians 2:20

The Messiah Is Among You

I remember an old Hasidic Jewish tale about a rabbi and an abbot of a monastery who often took walks with each other in the woods. Each of them looked forward to these special times. Each found in the other a sympathetic listener to the problems faced daily in carrying out his respective religious responsibilities.

One day the abbot confessed that there had been a rash of conflicts in the monastery. He told how the monks had become petty and were constantly being mean to each other. "As a matter of fact," said the abbot, "unless something changes, I fear the fellowship of the monastery will fall apart and no one will want to come and be a part of our community."

"This is very strange news," responded the rabbi, "especially since it is widely rumored that one of your monks is the Messiah."

When the abbot returned to his monastery, he reported to the brothers the incredible thing the rabbi had told him. Everyone was abuzz about this news and everyone wondered which of them might be the holy one. Each looked upon the other with an inquisitive manner. Each wondered whether the brother he met in the daily round of work could be the Christ, living among them.

It is said that in the days that followed, all bickering and complaining ceased. Furthermore, the spiritual life of the monks was quickly raised to a brilliantly high level. And word of the love and of the quality of life at the monastery spread far and wide. Instead of declining, the fellowship of the brothers grew in number and increased in spiritual depth. And all of this happened because of a rumor that suggested, "the Messiah is among you!"

—Tony Campolo

Playing The Game For Someone Else

As head football coach of the University of Colorado Buffaloes, I have an intense desire to beat our arch-rival, Nebraska. Unfortunately, when we were facing them in 1991, we were aware that we had not beat Lincoln for twenty-three years. So, on the Thursday night before the Friday game I called the team together in one room. I explained to them that I had heard somewhere that people spend 86 percent of their time thinking about themselves and only 14 percent thinking about others. I told them that if they can stop thinking about themselves and start thinking about others, they'll have a new energy source available to them. With that in mind I said, "Men, I've ordered sixty footballs and we're going to put the final score of Saturday's game on these balls. On Monday, we're going to send each ball to a person you've designated in advance. Here's what I'm asking you to do. By midnight tonight (Thursday night), I'm requiring any guy who wants to get on that airplane to Nebraska to dedicate this game to someone other than himself. I want you to call that person and tell them that they ought to watch you on every play. If they can't be at the game, then they should watch it on television. Tell them you are going to show how much you love them; that you're going to play with all your heart, and you are playing this game for them. It might be your mom or dad. I want you to call tonight. Then, I want you to demonstrate that love on Saturday."

Do you remember what happened in that game? The Colorado Buffaloes broke a twenty-three year losing streak in Lincoln and won the game 27–12.

Christian men all over our nation and around the world are suffering because they feel they are on a losing streak and can't break the pattern. The Adversary has us where he wants us—feeling defeated. It need not be that way.

—**Bill McCartney**

Chocolate Milk

Our son was telling me how chocolate milk makes him dizzy.

I almost said, "So don't drink it." But I didn't. Instead, I said, "How can chocolate milk make you dizzy?"

He said, "well, watch."

He squirted a glob of Hershey's chocolate syrup into his mouth, took a mouthful of milk, and then shook his head back and forth to mix it up.

"No wonder you're dizzy," I said.

Then I asked him why he didn't just mix it in a glass like everyone else does.

"Because I don't waste any by mixing more than I can drink."

I complimented him on his practicality, but his method didn't impress me very much. He wasn't waiting for my blessings, however. He seemed to like his creativity—except for the dizzy part—and thought it suited him pretty well.

That's when we both shook our heads. I shook mine because I didn't understand. He shook his because he was having more chocolate milk.

That's also when I realized that sometimes shaking my head is the best thing to do—especially when something is beyond my control.

And if all else fails, I've heard chocolate milk will help.

—Paul Budd

"How Much Does It Cost?"

"What are all these clothes doing on the floor?" I asked my wife as I walked through the front door after work. Sitting on the floor surrounded by piles of baby clothes was my wife, Debbie, and my year-and-a-half old daughter, Sophie.

Debbie looked up and smiled. "I'm sorting through Sophie's clothes. A lot of these can be reused and I think we should give them away."

Sophie tugged on my pant legs and held up a denim jumper for me to see. I scooped her up into my arms and kissed her on her cheek. She giggled.

Debbie began telling me how she had seen a woman selling baby clothes across the street. It reminded her of how God provided our daughter's clothes. All her clothes had been given to her by family and friends. Some were old, some new, but all were in good condition. Debbie felt led to give them away and bless others just like we had been blessed. She figured if we had another child, God would provide again. I thought it was a good idea. I was also excited about telling people about Jesus as we gave away the clothes.

The next Monday, which was President's Day, we loaded up the clothes, and laid them out on the grassy area across the street. I hung up a sign on a nearby tree which said, "Free Baby Clothes."

Some women came by and inquired, "¿Cuanto cuesta?" (How much does it cost?) as one of them held up a denim outfit.

"It's free. Es gratis." I said in Spanish.

"¿Gratis?" she replied with a puzzled look. "¿Porque?" (Why?) she asked.

In my broken Spanish I tried to explain to her that we were giving them away for Jesus and that Jesus loved her. She seemed to understand and smiled. After choosing a few more items, she thanked us and went on her way.

As Sophie arranged and rearranged her clothes on the grass,

Debbie and I continued to answer the questions of the people who walked by. Although most people were happy to select free clothing for their children, some people did not bother to stop when they saw the sign. Some women tried to pay us something for their selections. When they realized why we would not take any money, they smiled and thanked us. One woman asked if she could take several clothes for cousins she had in Mexico. Debbie told her to take as many as she needed.

Later in the day, my wife took Sophie home for her nap. I stayed to give away the rest of the clothes. Four young Mexican boys between the ages of eight and eleven came by and examined the clothes.

"Why are you giving the clothes away for free?" asked one of the boys.

"My wife and I are trying to obey Jesus and give to the poor. What are your names?" I said boldly.

"My name is Alberto," said the tallest. "This is Felix, John and Matthew," he said pointing to the others.

"Do you believe in Jesus?" I questioned.

"Yes." Albert and Felix replied.

"Well, then you are all 'hermanos en Cristo' " (brothers in Christ), I said smiling. "It's really important that we learn to love each other. Jesus wants us to love one another, especially our brothers in Christ."

After they left, I gathered the clothes and returned home.

Later that evening Debbie and I reflected on our experience. We shared how blessed we both felt to give away what had been given to us.

"You know?" I said, "In a way, those clothes are like salvation. Salvation is free. Some people don't want it because it is free. It's difficult for them to receive."

"And some people, like the women who wanted to pay us, want to give something in exchange for it," Debbie replied. "And the woman who took lots of clothes for her family in Mexico is like someone who is eager to share the free gift of salvation that she's received."

"The boys I spoke to might be symbolic of how God calls us into a relationship with the Giver," I said. "Sometimes we are satisfied with what God gives us and fail to become followers of Jesus."

As we sat in the quiet of our living room, we smiled at one another as we felt the deep peace of the Lord's presence. We were reminded again to share what Jesus had given us and expect Him to lead us through the ordinary events of our days.

—Craig A. Nell

Still Believing?

The story is told of a public school teacher who opposed the Christian faith. At the beginning of the year, the teacher announced that by the end of the year none of his students would believe in God.

However, one boy let it be known that, not only did he believe in God, but he knew God personally. That boy became a special target of the teacher's attacks.

The teacher didn't use lead-pipe tactics. He just went about subtly undermining faith when the opportunity presented itself. In a "nice" way, he kept putting the Christian student on the spot. All year long this continued.

On the last day of school, the teacher reminded the class of what he had said at the beginning. "But Christian, here, still believes. Is that right?" The boy nodded his head vigorously. "Well, we are going to settle this God business right now," the teacher said. He took an egg from his desk drawer, walked around the desk to stand before the class, held the egg above the floor and said, "I am about to drop this egg. But before I do, Christian, here, is going to pray that it won't break. We'll see whether or not there is a God!"

There was absolute silence in the room as the boy began to pray. "Dear Lord," he said, "when teacher drops that egg, I pray that it will shatter into a thousand pieces . . . and teacher will drop dead!"

The students gasped. Had you been near the front of the room, you could have seen an almost imperceptible tightening of the teacher's grip on the egg. Slowly he walked back behind his desk, opened a drawer, and carefully deposited the egg inside. Then he announced, "class dismissed."

I love to tell that story. Audiences love it, too. I don't know whether it's true or not, but it sure gives "what-for" to the opposition. Ha! That teacher's faith in his unbelief wasn't nearly as strong as he wanted everyone to think. In fact, his attempts to destroy the faith of others were mostly due to his need to shore up his own weak faith in atheism. He was trying to believe that there is no God.

—**Stanley Baldwin**

Be The Best

It was not meant that every man
should rise to leadership—
Not every man can build a bridge
Or into stardom slip—
He might not be an executive
Or even own a store—
But he can be his finest self
And strive for something more—
If we can't be a blazing sun
Perhaps we can be a star—
At least each one can try
to be—the best—
whatever we are!

Hard Of Hearing

Whenever we visit my wife's longtime friend, it's an adventure. That's because she has three little girls with far too much energy, and because I can't always communicate with the girls.

Part of the problem is mine. I don't think I'm hearing as well as I used to. The other problem is with the girls. Sometimes I think they are speaking another language—especially the two youngest.

Last Friday we visited our friend and her daughters again. As usual, they had saved up their energy for me. And as usual, we didn't communicate very well.

After a while I noticed that the youngest girl and her sister seemed to understand each other. And what sounded like noise to me was communication to them.

So the next time the youngest girl yelled something at me, I asked her sister, "Do you understand what she said?"

She nodded her head, yes.

"How can you understand your sister?" I persisted.

This time I heard fine when she said, "Because I love her."

After that, I was able to communicate with the girls a little better. Once I learned that love can sometimes help our hearing.

—**Paul Budd**

The Toss Of A Coin

My roommate, Don, and I were both single but attended different churches. One Friday night Don asked me, "How would you like to attend my church's 'singles get-together' at the nearby house of a fine Christian lady?"

"Sure, why not?" I replied, happy to get out of the house for the night.

I enjoyed myself among the 50-60 adult singles, all from the Single Parent Fellowship (SPF) group of Don's church. But I never did meet the hostess—that "fine Christian lady" as Don put it.

While living in Boise, Idaho after my divorce, I spent a lot of time reading an old, tattered Living Bible. One night, as I was reading from Proverbs while lying on my bed, one verse literally jumped out at me: *We toss the coin, but it is the Lord who controls the decision* (Proverbs 33:16).

While reading, I was thinking about Sandy, a girl with whom I had an ongoing on-again-off-again romance. Sandy lived in California, but we had kept in contact with each other via the telephone. When I saw that verse, I wondered if we would ever marry. I took a coin from my pocket and said to myself, "OK, Lord, are Sandy and I ever going to marry? If the coin comes down heads, we will, and if it comes down tails, we won't."

I tossed the coin into the air, and it came down *tails*. "No, Lord," I said, "that's not the right answer. Let's go two out of three." I tossed the coin into the air again, and it came down *tails*. A third time—*tails*. And a fourth time. "Well, this is just a bunch of 'hokey' anyway," I said.

Then my eyes glanced across the room at a *Lookout* magazine lying on the floor. On the back cover was an advertisement for a book by Susan F. Titus entitled *Parables for Young Teens*. "Well Lord," I said, tossing the coin up again, "who am I going to marry, Susan F. Titus?" The coin landed heads up. "Well," I said to myself, "that just goes to prove that this is a bunch of 'hokey.' I don't even know Susan F. Titus." The incident was soon forgotten.

After that Friday night party, I occasionally attended Don's SPF church group. I soon met a woman there named Susan. One night, as a group of us were laughing and talking, Susan said, "One thing that I miss from my previous marriage is the baseball tickets to the California Angels."

It happened that I shared California Angel season tickets to a box seat with a friend. I said, "Susan, I've got Angel tickets. Maybe we can go some time."

I meant this offer only as a friend, but Susan misunderstood. She cleared her throat a few times then said quietly, "I would like to, but I'm currently dating someone."

"Well," I said glibly, "If you ever change your mind, let me know."

Several months later, on a Friday night, I telephoned Sandy, and she told me she was going to marry someone else. I was in shock. I "knew" that someday Sandy and I would be married. I never felt more alone than I did that night.

The following Sunday, Susan and I were walking from the church sanctuary to the parking lot when she stopped me and said, "Dick,". . .

"Yeah?"

"Remember what you said about my telling you if I ever wanted to go out with you?"

"Yeah!"

"Well, I'd like to."

"OK."

We had lunch the following Wednesday, and on our next date I brought a pizza to Susan's house so we could watch the winter Olympics. I was stunned when I walked into Susan's house and realized that it was the same house where Don took me for a get together not too long before on a Friday evening!

It didn't take long for Susan and I to become known in SPF as an "item" and then we became engaged. One day, while helping to carry some of Susan's son's things upstairs to his room,

I noticed two framed posters hanging on the hall wall, one which read, *Parables for Young Teens*, authored by Susan F. Titus. As I stared open-mouthed at the poster, a chill started at the top of my head and swept down to the bottom of my feet.

"Did you write that?" I asked incredulously, as Susan carried a box by me to Richard's room.

"Yes," she answered as she swept past, "why else would I have it hanging on my wall?"

I could not believe my eyes. "This is just too much," I said to myself. Later, on our honeymoon to the Caribbean, I told Susan the story that I have just told you. "But don't ever tell anyone," I said, "they'll never believe it."

—Richard A. Osborn

Nice Day At Golf

The story goes that Moses and Jesus Christ were on the first tee when an old man walked over and asked if he could join their golf game. Moses and Jesus smiled at each other, then assured the man that he was welcome to play.

Moses hit the ball first. His ball went toward the water hazard, but the waters parted before the ball could get wet, and it hit the now-dry surface and rolled onto the green.

Jesus smiled at Moses and said, "Nice shot." Then he stepped up to the tee and struck his first ball. Once again, the ball landed in the water hazard, but instead of dropping to the depths, the ball walked across the water until it reached the green.

Now Moses complimented Jesus. "Nice shot," he said.

Finally, it was the old man's turn. He approached the tee, and swung at the ball with all his might.

Moses and Jesus exchanged smiles. Then, a squirrel appeared. It picked up the ball in its mouth and proceeded to run down the fairway. Suddenly, a giant bird plunged from the sky and picked up the squirrel. Then a roar of thunder came forth, and a bolt of lightning shot from the sky, striking the bird. The bird screamed in pain, dropping the squirrel to the ground. Upon impact, the squirrel spit out the ball which landed at the very edge of the hole. Finally, a great gust of wind came from nowhere, and gently directed the ball into the hole.

Moses looked at Jesus, and Jesus looked at the old man and said, "Nice shot, DAD."

—Eric Scott Kaplan

How God Used My Pain

It was April of 1979 and I was hospitalized with the worst pain of my life. I was well-acquainted with kidney stones. Previously, I had "given birth" to seven stones, so having another one was not news. This time I was in no real pain to begin with, but my doctor had discovered the stone during an exam when he noticed that my kidney was enlarged. Surgery was the only option, and after much prayer, I went under the knife.

After a couple of days in the hospital, I was still in a great deal of pain. Some discomfort is normal following surgery; however, my pain was worsening as the days went on. The strength and frequency of the shots increased until I was being given morphine shots every four hours.

In the middle of all of this pain, I frequently asked the Lord, "Why won't you heal me? Why do I have to go through all this pain?" I couldn't see any purpose in it.

Yet, several times God was able to turn my eyes off myself long enough to begin talking to the other patient in the room, an older man whose name was John. He was a diabetic and had to have his toes amputated. John was not a Christian, but his wife, Opal, was a very strong believer. John and I began discussing spiritual things. I shared with him how he needed to accept Jesus Christ as his own personal savior. I normally don't do a lot of direct witnessing like this, but when you are in a lot of pain, you tend to focus on the really important things in life. I remember asking one of the nurses about her salvation as well.

The complications from John's diabetes grew worse. He thrashed around in his bed as his own pain became excruciating. I remember a pastor coming in to pray for John's physical and spiritual health. He gave John an opportunity to accept Christ, but at that point, I did not know John's response. They moved John out of my room a day or so later.

My own pain was getting worse as well. Sometimes when Opal

would come into the room she would pray for me and hold my hand for a while. That small act of kindness meant a great deal to me in my condition. During this time, one of my co-workers came to visit me and noticed that my coloring was not good. He went back to the office and told people he was not sure if I would be coming back or if I would even live. As my anxiety grew, I finally called my in-laws to come down from Northern California. I wanted them to be here with my wife, Karin, who was seven months pregnant, in case I didn't make it. They arrived shortly and were a big encouragement to both of us.

Finally my doctor determined that something was radically wrong. I was a relatively healthy young man of 29 and should have recovered in the few days I had been in the hospital. The doctor did some X-rays, but this was more difficult than you might think. I was writhing in pain so much that it was almost impossible for me to lie still enough for the X-rays to be taken. They discovered that some of my body waste was leaking back into my system and this was causing the incredible pain. I went in for a second surgery to correct the problem. This time, as I awakened in the recovery room, I felt sure that everything was back in the right place.

After I returned home, Karin and I went to visit Opal. She shared with us that John had died before I was even released from the hospital. She also said that John had accepted Christ before he died. Opal was very grateful to me for sharing with John. I expressed my appreciation to her for her comforting me when I was hurting so badly.

As I look back on this episode, I realize that I need to be available to be used by God no matter where I am. He can bless others through me and comfort me—even in the middle of incredible pain.

—Dave Fite

God's In Charge!

As a teenager, I began to fall away from God and get involved in drugs and other forms of deception. I was leading more than a double life; I was a "chameleon." I tried to live up to the expectations of whomever I was with. I didn't know who I was!

Then on January 3, 1993, when I was a junior in high school, my life changed forever. After church I had dinner with some friends. On the way to play pool, we decided to race double the speed limit on the freeway. Suddenly, I noticed a car about ten feet in front of me. I swerved to avoid it and lost control. The next thing I knew I was lying in a hospital bed.

As doctors did routine tests to check for a possible concussion, they discovered I had a brain tumor. They suspected it had been part of my body since birth and began growing at puberty. The pressure in my brain had been gradually increasing and it could have shot up and killed me at any moment. The accident actually saved my life.

After brain surgery, I was in a coma for ten days. When I awoke from the coma, I couldn't move any of my muscles and needed help to breathe. As I lay there, unable to communicate, I cried out in my mind, "Why is this happening to me?" but no one could hear me. I felt so frustrated and confused. "Am I going to get better?" I kept asking the Lord. He didn't seem to answer. But I did sense His strength as an army of prayer warriors supported me.

The next four months in rehabilitation were like a nightmare. I knew what people were saying to me, but I couldn't respond. I felt like I was trapped in someone else's body, but I couldn't remember what had happened. My family told me that I had been in a very serious car accident where my car rolled four times up a freeway overpass. Thankfully, the only visible injury that I received was a small cut over my left eye. My friend in the passenger seat only bruised his knee cap even though the car came to rest upside down on the hood and his leg!

When I heard this, it was the turning point of my life. I realized that God had been in control during the accident, in the surgery, and throughout my whole life. He seemed to say, "Don't worry, I have a plan for you."

During surgery, doctors were forced to remove part of my cerebellum, which destroyed almost all of the connections between my brain and my muscles. Doctors didn't know how much I would recover. On April 4 a psychologist concluded, "Karl's thinking is not normal. Damage is more extensive than we thought."

I began multiple therapies to rebuild these connections. I never realized how important and complicated these tasks were until I couldn't do them. I did hundreds of exercises so I could eat, talk, walk, and have control over my body. In March, I ate my first meal since the surgery. I also said my first word, "home," which is where I wanted to go. The exercises for my balance included parallel bars in a pool and eventually land. After that I began walking short distances with a walker. In late April, I walked fifty feet from the gym to my room and back. On June 2, 1993, while only speaking a few words I was released from the hospital in a wheelchair.

When I came home I didn't expect life to be easy. I continued my therapies that summer and had a home teacher. On June 17, I finally took six unassisted steps. However, everything was a very slow process. Sometimes I wanted to give up. "Lord, I can't do it anymore," I cried. I even considered suicide. But when I thought about how that would let down the many people who were praying for me, I couldn't do it. I worked harder than I ever had before, and when I saw the improvements I was making I realized that it was worth the work. Although sometimes I got discouraged, I would turn to Philippians 4:13 over and over. I can do *everything* with Jesus' help.

In June of 1994 I graduated from high school, with my class. Now I'm in college, majoring in Psychology. I am looking forward to being able to surf again.

I still have some problems with balance and coordination, but

God was in control throughout it all and still is. I can see now that God tried many ways to bring me back to Him. I wouldn't listen. But I didn't ignore the car accident and brain tumor. I'm glad He didn't give up on me!

—**Karl Joy**

ATHLETE'S CREED

REAL WINNERS have learned . . .

- The most important goal, whether you win or lose, is to do your best.
- Not to quit, no matter how hard the the going gets.
- Not to blame others, for you will lose the respect of friends, coaches, and yourself.
- To always play fair and by the rules, for that is the real essence of sportsmanship.
- That God is the one who gave you your abilities, and to always, be thankful for His gifts.

—**Mark Batson**

I'm Immortal

"Remember doctor, it's the left one," I said.

The doctor smiled at my comment as he walked alongside the gurney taking me to the operating room. As we rolled along, I reflected on the events of the last few days, my mind in something of a whirl.

It was Saturday morning, May 13, 1989, eight months since I had retired from practice after thirty eight years as an optometrist. I was looking forward to some retirement years, but for the past several weeks I had been having increasing signs of kidney dysfunction, culminating on Friday morning with a complete blockage of my bladder. X-rays the previous week had showed a suspicious area in my left kidney, and my doctor said, "You'd better go home and get a toothbrush and check in at the hospital—even without a cat scan, I'm 99% sure we're dealing with cancer, and the sooner we get that kidney out the better."

My heart skipped a beat as I thought of the prospect of surgery without any backup blood. I am a low-grade hemophiliac with a history of serious bleeding after any kind of surgery, even tooth extractions. Almost thirty years earlier, a blood fraction had been isolated which had been used successfully in a couple of tooth extractions for me, but that was before the age of AIDS. Now, that material was too risky.

Two years earlier, I had a coronary artery bypass graft, for which a new product, called desmopressin, or DDAVP, had been used. This being a synthetic product, prepared in the pharmaceutical laboratory, there was no danger of contamination. To be sure, however, over a period of several weeks I had donated several units of my own blood, called autologous donation. During the bypass surgery some of this blood was used—but not all of it.

Since autologous blood is to be used only for the donor, many of the tests which are done for routine donations are simply not done. (What you give is what you get.) Therefore, blood bank policy does not allow the use of autologous blood for anyone except the donor. The blood is kept in cold storage, but not frozen. Once the surgery is over, the blood bank simply discards any that has not been used.

When I heard the doctor's words, "Cancer . . . surgery . . . tomorrow morning," my first thought was, "Why couldn't I have had warning so I could build up a stock of autologous blood?"

My second thought was, "As long as God has something for me to do, I'm immortal. If He doesn't have anything for me to do, why stick around?"

As my wife and I drove home from the doctor's office, we were absorbed in prayer and concern. Sure, we both had faith in a God Who hears and answers prayer. But we knew of plenty of times when it had appeared that His answer was, "No." We were reminded again of the extraordinary fragility of life.

The day's mail had been delivered by the time we arrived at our home after the doctor's appointment that Friday. We couldn't believe our eyes when we saw a card from the blood bank, which said something like: "We have just discovered that we inadvertently froze a unit of the autologous blood you donated for yourself in September, 1987. If you would like us to continue to keep it in frozen storage, please remit the following fee. If you choose not to have us do this, we will dispose of it."

I got on the phone immediately and called the blood bank to tell them that they would be hearing from the doctor about what to do with the blood. Then I called his office and they were able to arrange to have the blood at the hospital the following morning. The surgery was concluded without complications, and the pathology report verified the doctor's diagnosis.

Thinking back over these events, I was reminded of Matthew 6:8, . . . *your Father knows what you need before you ask Him* (NIV).

—**Richard J. Lindholtz**

God Fixed Our Model "T"

The first "miracle" I can remember occurred in the challengingly remote but beautifully rugged Ozark Mountains. During my childhood, my parents would frequently pack up us kids and venture back over the mountains from our Missouri home to revisit their roots in Arkansas. We would bravely attempt to scale the Ozarks in our ancient model "T" Ford sedan.

In the 1920's roads were poorly engineered, very few cars braved those primitive trails. The inclines were sometimes too steep for our model "T." On those occasions, passengers would disembark; then the old Ford would be turned around and readied to climb the mountain—in reverse. Everyone would push and pray, grunt and groan—it always worked.

On one of those early excursions, we were stranded for some time after the motor sputtered and failed. Since there was no self-starter on the old "T," my father wore himself out turning the crank. Then he tinkered with the spark plugs, carburetor and whatever else was exposed under the hood. All to no avail. The trusted Ford had died. And that was that!

At last, in obvious desperation, Pop announced that only God could help us. There was no Auto Club to call. It was time to plead in prayer: "Dear Lord, please heal this broken-down car."

Dramatically acting on his sincere petition to the Heavenly Father, Pop walked around once more to the hand crank while the family watched in suspense as he yanked sharply to spin the motor. We cheered as the Ford vibrated with power.

No pushing that day. Forward or reverse. No grunting and groaning. Just praying. And then wondering in amazement.

Over a lifetime I have followed my father's example: crank as hard as you can. Add prayer! And keep on cranking!

—D. Leroy Sanders

Sudden Pressure

"Any chance you could bring me a load of gravel for the driveway today?" Ken asked as he filled my truck with gas.

"We're leaving on vacation right after lunch," I reminded him. "That's why I came down to your station for a fill up."

I had been in the excavation business for the past 10 years. Some people call us "dirt-movers." We haul and move sand, gravel, dirt and the like.

"I was hoping you might take care of this one dump-load before you left," Ken said. "Cars have been kicking up so much dust, I'm always having to sneeze."

Before I could answer I remembered the conversation I had yesterday with my pastor. "Gene," he said to me, "the problem with you is that you seem to resist at every turn. You want everything to go your way."

"That's where you're wrong," I retorted. "I tried things my way for 47 years. Only place it got me was jail. Why do you think I decided to give my life to God three years ago?"

"But you still won't give Him a chance to change your heart, Gene."

"Hey, I'm trying to do what He wants me to, but you won't see me kneeling at any altar becoming one of those 'religious fanatics.'"

Placing his hand on my shoulder, he responded, "Watch out when you start trying to tell God what to do with your life. You're like someone holding a Daily Planner. You look at the available slots in your day and fit God into the most convenient space. Quit fighting, Gene . . . that was your old way of living . . . quit fighting."

As Ken tapped his finger on the hood of my car waiting my response, the pastor's words rang in my mind. "Quit fighting, Gene . . . quit fighting."

Maybe this was my chance to prove my pastor wrong. The answer came with no more thought. "Sure, I'll get the load and be back when I can."

Now I could leave on vacation with a clear conscience. I was pleased to think I didn't even have to "lose myself" in that "religious" stuff to do it.

"What can I do for you, Gene?" Ed at the quarry asked when I pulled in.

"Just need 6 yards of gravel for Ken's driveway."

"I thought you were leaving town today," he responded.

I smiled proudly, "I am, but thought I'd help Ken before I left." How could Ed help but admire my new thoughtful attitude?

"Back'er up over there, and you'll be all set," Ed said. "Oh, and have a great trip."

"We will!" I responded with assurance. "I have it all planned!"

It's planned my way; what could my pastor say about that? I was certain God didn't care to plan my vacations.

I rolled down the window to feel the sea breeze as I drove back to the station in the little town of Cambria, on the California Coast. The beautiful weather helped to encourage my vacation mood. The clear turquoise surf glistened as the sun struck each crest. The waves gently rolled in on the rough, rocky shoreline. *God, your touch in my rocky life has been somewhat like that ocean. Am I really fighting you?*

I arrived at Ken's and backed my 1974 International dump truck in the driveway. Then I engaged the hydraulic system, and the truck bed rose to deliver the gravel. Approximately a third of the way up, the cable broke. With gears disengaged, the truck bed stopped in midair—locked in place.

Turning off the engine, I jumped down from the driver's seat and ran around the front of the truck to the passenger's side. I knew that if I manually engaged the gears it would enable the hydraulic system to continue lifting the truck bed. I leaned my head on the truck frame to view the gears below. The gravel-laden bed was held securely approximately three feet above my head.

Without warning, the truck bed lowered slowly and silently. I was caught! As my mouth pressed against the truck frame I could feel my teeth piercing through my lips. Eight tons of pressure fell across the back of my head and shoulders, squeezing me like a pair of giant scissors against the sharp steel of the truck's frame. There was no time for fear, panic, questions, or planning a way of escape. I was dying.

I'm comin' home, Lord! If You have other plans, You'd better do something about it right now.

As I silently uttered that prayer, my neck snapped. The crackling sounds I heard were my vertebrae popping into alignment. I found myself standing three feet from my truck, looking at the place where, only the moment before, I was being squeezed to death. Blood dripped off my chin. The sudden pressure of swelling lips confirmed I was still alive. As I touched my back, I felt two layers of shirt sliced as if by a razor. No skin was broken but I could feel a warm trickle down my back from a half-inch depression.

Was it an angel who pushed me from the descending vise grip of death, or the mighty hand of God who pulled me to this standing position? The only thing I knew as I stood staring at the truck was that my head should be gone. *I should be dead!*

Bill, a close friend who worked at the station ran toward me from the cab. With his voice shaking, he announced, "I didn't know you were under the truck! Are you hurt?"

I mumbled, "I seem fine." Pressure from my swelling lips made it hard to speak.

"I saw the bed was stuck. I thought you'd want the hydraulics released, so I pushed the lever. I was only trying to help." Color left his face as he confirmed my thoughts. "I almost killed you—you should be dead!"

Not knowing what to do next I suggested, "Guess I better unload this gravel." Bill looked at me again, then hurried off.

I slid under the truck on my back to engage the gears, wincing as the dirt and gravel ground into my injured back. Gears now repaired, I shuffled to the cab.

Reaching to wipe my forehead I caught sight of my blood-stained sleeve. Mounting the cab I felt my rapid heartbeat as my lips pulsed with pressure. The engine noise broke the silence. *I should be dead.* The truck bed raised, dumping gravel on the driveway. *I should be dead*, reverberated through my brain over and over again.

I drove back to the truck yard and parked the truck, sitting in silence for some time. Opening the door, I fell to my knees. God only knows how long I knelt at this altar fashioned of brittle weeds.

"Oh God, I don't want to fight You anymore. You saved me! I can't imagine why . . . but, I know Your plans are better than mine. Go ahead . . . make *all* my plans from now on."

As I drove home to tell my wife, I wondered which miracle to share first—that God had spared my life or that He had changed my heart. One thing I knew, the only plan I had now was to let God be my Daily Planner.

—Gene DeShores

The Bible And The TV Guide

On the table side-by-side,
The Holy Bible and the TV Guide.
One is well-worn, but cherished with pride
(Not the Bible, but the TV Guide).

One is used daily to help folks decide
No! It isn't the Bible, it's the TV Guide.
As pages are turned, what shall they see?
Oh what does it matter, turn on the TV

Then confusion reigns, they can't all agree
On what they shall watch on the old TV
So they open the book in which they confide.
No! It isn't the Bible, it's the TV Guide.

The Word of God is seldom read,
Maybe a verse 'ere they fall into bed.
Exhausted and sleepy and tired as can be,
Not from reading the Bible . . . from watching TV

So, then back to the table, side-by-side
Is the Holy Bible and the TV Guide.
No time for prayer, no time for the Word,
The plan of salvation is seldom heard
Forgiveness of sin so full and free,
Is found in the Bible, not on TV

—**Unknown**

Forgiven

The group of us sat on the swimming dock. It was a bachelor party for the first of my hometown friends getting married the next weekend. We'd come north to Lake Wallenpaupack in the Pennsylvania Poconos where my grandmother owned a lakeside cottage. My friend Jon casually asked my father if he had a knife in the motorboat. My Dad pulled out a cut-in-half plastic milk container from under the driver's seat and set it on the dock. After riffling through the contents, he pitched a brown-handled tri-bladed knife onto the dock.

"That good enough?"

It certainly was. But my mouth momentarily dropped in horror.

Jon picked up the knife and gazed at it curiously. I knew instantly why he scrutinized it so carefully. The knife had once belonged to him. Years ago when we were youngsters he had lost it. Or should I say, I had stolen it.

In juxtaposition to that searing moment, was another stark fact: two days previous I had become a Christian. For the first time in my life I felt free and forgiven for years of mini- and maxi-wrongdoings. In less than twenty-four hours I shed years of guilt, fear, worry, and self-loathing, and found cleansing in Christ.

But there was something else about that forgiveness I didn't understand until that moment as I stared at the knife.

I said to Jon, "Do you recognize that knife?"

He shrugged. "I'm not sure."

I said, "You should. It was yours. I stole it from you when we were kids."

The dock became still as a morning glare. Jon wouldn't look at me. I could feel everyone staring at me in amazement.

I went on, "I'm sorry I did that. It was wrong. You can have the knife back."

Jon waved his hand. "It's all right. Don't worry about it." Then he turned to me, "Man, Littleton, you are a little too honest!"

I started to protest, but he added, "Hey, it's good. I wish I could be that way."

We went on to other subjects.

Later, as I reflected on what had happened, I realized that because I was forgiven and set free, I no longer feared exposure. I could face my sin and say, "Yes, I sinned. I believe God has forgiven me. But now, will you forgive me?"

Only the Christian has the freedom to admit he's guilty. The game is up. There's no more use in hiding it or covering it.

—Mark R. Littleton

2

Faith & Trust

Trust in the Lord with all thine heart; and lean not unto thine own understanding. In all thy ways acknowledge him; and he shall direct thy paths.

Proverbs 3:5-6

Just Wait!

Look at all God has for us if we will just stay true to our first love. If you want to be an overcomer and share these rewards, you are going to have to go all the way with Jesus Christ. You say, "But it's so hard, and I'm not getting any credit right now."

Let me tell you about Henry Morrison, a missionary to Africa. He was coming home from Africa on a ship which was also carrying Theodore Roosevelt. When the ship docked in New York, thousands of people were there to greet Roosevelt. But no one was cheering for Morrison.

Henry Morrison had served the Lord for forty years in Africa. As he watched the crowds greet Theodore Roosevelt, he became dejected to think he had served all those years and yet no one was there to greet him.

Morrison said that as he walked down the gangplank in a depressed mood, a voice whispered to him, "Henry, don't worry. You are not home yet." Then he said he saw a vision of multiplied thousands of Africans standing at the gates of heaven, those who he had reached for Christ, applauding him as he entered the pearly gates.

So if people are not recognizing you down here, if you are not getting any applause right now, don't worry. You are not home yet. Remember what Christ has waiting for you.

—Tony Evans

God Repaired Me
When Bubba Broke Down

The week had been full of annoying little glitches. My wife, Katie, and I had just moved into our first new home, and the air-conditioning system was not working. For three days I'd had a nagging headache, and was extremely tired and sort of grouchy. This was totally out of character for me. Then my four-wheel drive vehicle, Bubba, broke down. Katie and I worked different shifts at the post office. I either had to find someone to ride with or disturb Katie's sleep so she could pick me up each morning.

When the repairman said it could take as long as two weeks just to get the parts, I decided to rent a car, even though the rental rates would strain our budget. Then Thomas, a jovial kind of guy I'd spoken to but never really gotten to know, offered to drive me to and from work, even though it was several miles out of his way. At first, I considered declining his offer. I didn't want to inflict my bad mood on him. In addition, riding with Thomas would cause me to lose overtime, because his section did not put in the extra hours like mine did.

As I walked over to Thomas to decline his offer, an almost imperceptible feeling caused me to change my mind and accept.

Shortly after arriving home, the repair shop owner called to tell me the part would have to be shipped from California, thus costing more than anticipated. I considered calling Thomas and canceling the riding arrangement, so I could get the extra overtime, but again I had a feeling that this was not what I should do.

For the next couple of days I enjoyed riding with Thomas. Then on Friday, as we were rounding a curve about a mile from my house, I grabbed my head and slumped over in my seat. The world went black. Thomas sped to my house and pulled up in the driveway with the horn blaring. Katie rushed out of the house, took one look at me, and ran back inside to call 9-1-1.

I remember waking up in the hospital emergency room. Katie was standing near the bed. Her eyes were red from weeping, and her hair was disheveled. I thought how odd it was that this normally fastidious woman should be out in public looking like that. I said, "Hi, Honey." She came to my side and took my hand. Then I drifted off to sleep again.

My memories of the next few days are very hazy. There was talk of an operation. The words ruptured aneurysm filtered into one brief moment of consciousness. My son appeared at my side—while my mind told me he was supposed to be thousands of miles away in California.

Three days after I was admitted to the hospital I was stable enough to undergo an operation to repair a major rupture of an aneurysm on the right side of my brain. When I was finally lucid enough to be aware of my surroundings and understand the severity of what had happened, I learned what had been going on, and I began to understand what God was doing for me. My sister's church in California had prayed for me, as had churches in several other states. The surgeon told me that considering the severity of the aneurysm, I was lucky to have made it through the three days it took to stabilize me, and even luckier to have survived the surgery. I told the doctor luck had nothing to do with it.

The whole situation was perfectly clear. God had allowed Bubba to break down. Had I been behind the wheel, I would never have survived an accident on the curve where Thomas was driving when the aneurysm burst. God had put Thomas in the right place at the right time. God planted the thoughts in my mind that caused me to forego renting a car and accept the offer from Thomas.

God is the Great Physician, and He can perform life-saving miracles. My faith in God is far stronger, and my gratitude is boundless.

—Jack Martin

Weathering Life's Storms

Over the past three years I have come to appreciate the complexity of life's storms in a new way as I have had to come to grips with a storm of illness in my own life. Even as the world was undergoing enormous political changes in the Fall of 1989 and 1990, I began to experience changes of my own.

My first concern was a slight tremor in my hands, which I attributed to my tiring schedule. Before long, however, I experienced some difficulty in walking long distances or in doing simple things, like stepping up to a platform to deliver a sermon. So I went to the Mayo Clinic for tests. There, the doctors informed me that I was suffering from an early and mild form of Parkinson's disease. Needless to say, that wasn't the kind of news I wanted to hear. But even though the diagnosis came as a surprise, I decided I wasn't going to overreact. I wanted to take things slowly, follow the treatment the doctors prescribed, and see if I could overcome this condition.

Over the past twenty years or so I have had to deal with all sorts of illnesses, some serious, many relatively minor. This has been a new experience for me, but I am glad to report that I am doing fine. I have been told to slow down a little, and my doctors are satisfied with my progress.

By its very nature, the Christian faith involves a certain amount of blood, sweat, and tears. Jesus calls us to be disciples—regardless of the circumstances. When we come to Him, He takes away one set of problems—the burdens of sin, guilt, isolation, hopelessness, and separation from God—and He says to us, *Take my yoke upon you and learn from me* (Matthew 11:29). It is not a yoke that is too heavy for us to bear, for Christ Himself bears it with us. He says, *My yoke is easy and my burden is light* (Matthew 11:30). Nevertheless, He calls us to follow Him, regardless of the cost. He never promises that our path will always be smooth. No life is without its own set of problems. When I decided to give my life to Jesus Christ as a young man, it was not because I believed He would take away all my pain. No, I trusted Him because He promised me eternal life. I believed He would always be with me and give me the strength to cope with the difficulties of this life. I may not have understood all of it at the time, but I believed that in the long run Jesus would help me live a victorious life. And He has done that and more.

Corrie ten Boom used to say, "The worst can happen but the best remains." That is a wonderful message, because we all have to endure storms in our lives. When any preacher or teacher of the Word oversells either the material or the spiritual benefits of the Christian life, I believe he is contributing to the work of the horseman who deceives. There is nothing on earth to compare with new life in Jesus Christ, but it will not always be easy, and as I have said, I am learning more of that truth each day.

—Billy Graham

Mad Max, Devil Dog

As a police sergeant for the Huntington Beach Police Department in Huntington Beach, California, I frequently have the opportunity of supervising canine teams. When one of our K-9 Unit dogs, Max, was acquired by Jack, his handler, Jack brought him into the station to get acquainted with the other policemen. An officer named Ron walked up to Jack and asked, "Hey, you got your new dog. Can I pet him?"

"Sure," Jack replied.

Ron began rubbing the top of Max's head and scratched him behind his ears. When he started rubbing under Max's chin, Max bit Ron on the hand.

"AWWW!" Ron called out, as he jerked his hand away. "I thought I could pet your dog!"

Jack shot back, "Yeah, but I guess not under his chin."

That's how Max's reputation started. He was an ugly Belgium-breed Malanoid who seemingly hated everyone, except Jack. His chest was massive and muscular; his head chiseled and angular like a pit bull. But worst of all, his evil-looking big yellow eyes gave him an intimidating look. By the time Max's tour as a police dog ended, he had apprehended many criminals and also bit four policemen. Soon, everyone referred to him as Mad Max, the Devil Dog. He was a police dog with an attitude.

Besides biting policemen, Max performed other dysfunctional behaviors like urinating and leaving "little gifts" on the report room floor. Soon, Max was banished from the station. When Jack was inside during briefing, Max had to stay in the car.

If anyone approached Mad Max's police car, he barked incessantly and spun around in the back of the unit, incensed that someone dared come near his domain. Everyone kept their distance.

During the four months that Jack and Mad Max were assigned to my squad, I took it as a personal challenge to make Max obey.

One day when we were out in the field, I approached Jack's police car and Mad Max went berserk again. I commanded him, "Max, lay down!" He continued to bark. For almost a full minute, I firmly told him repeatedly, "Max, lay down!"

Finally, Max began to reluctantly obey. When he finally lay down on the platform in the back of the unit, his barking had turned into a low growl, seemingly unhappy that someone had gotten the better of him. It was as if he were saying, "I hate you."

One day I rolled along with several officers, including Jack and Mad Max to a burglary alarm. When we arrived we saw that the glass door was shattered and as far as we knew, the suspect was still inside.

I deployed the men around the building as Jack readied Max for an entry and search. As we congregated outside the door, standing by the shards of glass on the ground, Jack placed a blue blanket over the glass to protect Max's paws. I directed Jack and Mad Max along with another officer to enter the store and search for the suspect. Jack commented to the other officer, "Stay close to me as we go in. Max has a tendency to circle around quickly and might attack you if you're not right behind me."

The back-up officer glanced immediately at me and seemed to plead with his eyes, "Sarge, why me?"

As the men stood poised to enter the store, Jack called into the building, "This is the police. If you don't come out we're sending the dog in after you." Jack gave Mad Max the signal to bark heartily as an incentive—but no one's voice answered back.

Jack released Mad Max into the store. Mad Max made a mad dash through the door and immediately turned around and attacked the blanket laying over the glass. He growled and chomped on the blanket with a frenzy.

"No, Max, No!" Jack screamed at him. "Not the blanket. Go into the store!"

As several of us stood nearby we couldn't believe what we were seeing. The burglary was a serious situation but I couldn't help it. I began giggling, then laughing. Soon all of us were nearly rolling with laughter on the parking lot. Jack didn't think it was so funny and kept trying to get Mad Max to give up on the blanket.

Eventually Mad Max stopped his rampage on the blanket and began his search for the burglar. Fortunately for the suspect, he had left before we arrived. After the search, Jack came sheepishly over to us with Max close beside him. As we tried to stifle our laughter, we told him, "Don't worry, Jack. Our lips are sealed."

Jack looked at us and rolled his eyes. "Oh, yeah. Sure."

Within a few hours, everyone knew about Mad Max's escapade.

Six months later, the same scenario occurred. A blanket had again been thrown on top of broken shards of glass and Mad Max attacked the blanket.

Sometimes I see a little of Mad Max in my own life. Too often I angrily crouch at God's instructions and discipline in my life. Sometimes I find myself impulsively jumping for that blanket of fun before me when I have a much more important job just beyond my reach. My memories of Max encourage me to come gratefully before my Master to receive His instructions.

—**D. Larry Miller**

The Great Outdoors-Man

The "Great Outdoors" used to be a childhood love of mine. Through the years I have grown to realize that bugs aren't fun, dirt feels "yucky," fish go in the water you're swimming in, and you need lots of matches and gallons of lighter fluid to start a nice campfire. In recent years, however, that "Great Outdoor Itch" had taken hold of me, and I waited anxiously for the opportunity to oil that itch by going camping, fishing, and/or hunting for a week or two. This year, on Mother's Day, my opportunity came. God granted my wish, supplied my need, and protected this fragile city boy. Though it didn't last a week, this one glorious day will have soothed the outdoors-man's itch for quite awhile. This is an account of that day.

It is slightly hard to see, possibly just the angle of the sunshine, even though the sky is painted with only two or three clouds to give the sky texture. I can feel a crisp northern breeze sifting through my hair and a sweet whisper that tickles my ears. Nature, along with a few man-made items, surrounds me to remind me of God's great artistic hands. My heart beats effortlessly as His peace calms my spirit. I slow my breath to silence it, and listen for a voice to move my soul.

With confidence, I moved along my path of choice, and for a total of three-and-a-half hours I traveled this road. Diligently, I checked the sights of the well-oiled machine I was using. For miles I could see through its powerful sights. It allowed me to see almost anything that moved. I was awake. I was alert. I was in control. No! God was in control, and I feared nothing!

Then, in the bat of an eye she appeared out of nowhere! Twenty-five feet away—a beautiful, unblemished, well-groomed deer! No time to think. What's this? She's moving right into my path and in the dead-center of my sights. She's huge. It'll be a miracle if I miss this one! Stop moving so she doesn't panic!

"BANG!" I nailed her, knocking her to the ground like a sack of potatoes. She rolled like a tumbleweed in the wind.

My spirit is no longer calm. My heartbeat is the loudest thing I hear, and my no-longer-silent breath runs a close second.

My first deer! Oh, the adrenaline! The anticipation! The tension! The exhilaration! The awe! The excitement!

OHHHH! The anxiousness! The awful embarrassment! The sudden withdrawal from a major adrenaline rush!

Yeah! It is my first deer, all right! However, Mother's Day does not occur in the middle of deer season. The deer was smack dab in the middle of my "sights" in which most people call a wind-shield! Yes, the well-oiled machine happens to be what used to be my car. The crisp northern breeze . . . it was from the car vents. The sweet whisper tickling my ears . . . Angela, my significant and best friend. The voice to move my soul . . . that was here as well. And that "path of choice" I had mentioned earlier, that path has a proper name—State Highway 35.

Oh yeah! The angle of the sun was definitely a factor in the slightly-impaired sight in the midst of a clear sky. I believe the angle would be anywhere between a vertical 180 to 360—in other words, "somewhere else in the world." Here in LaCrosse, Wisconsin, we call it *night*. It was eleven o'clock at night to be exact. Angela and I were on our way home from a couple of our friends' graduation party two hours away, and we had only one more hour of driving before we could sleep in our own beds to rest from the busy day. The mile-marker deer was a momentary set-back.

On the bright side, God did provide and protect us in this incident. In spite of the large size of the deer, no damages had been made to the engine itself—no radiator nor oil leaks, no obvious change in the performance of the car. The major dam-ages occurred to only the deer, one high-beam headlight, and the hood of my car. Angela and I survived without injury. No other cars were around, so no one else got hurt.

I am so thankful to the Lord for His protection. God has

reminded me that all these things are temporal. The value of the car is nothing, compared to the value of our lives.

As for now, "Me hunter!" Just call me "Elmer Fudd." Next deer season, you'll see me with a new fluorescent orange outfit, hunters license on my back, and a nice shotgun in hand. One more deer on the dinner table means one less possibility of killing one with my car.

—**Michael Vincent Obar**

Our Son Came Home

The phone rang. It was Father's Day and our youngest son, Dale, was calling long distance to wish me a happy Father's Day! This would be an unforgettable Father's Day. After chatting a while, he told my wife, Virginia, and I that he had accepted Christ as his personal Savior only five days before. We were thrilled beyond words, for we had prayed for his salvation for ten long years. There was little sleep that night as we continued to praise God for His goodness to us in bringing Dale "home."

Dale was our third son, the middle child of five, all born in the span of five and one-half years. At a very early age, we dedicated all of our children to God and taught them Christian principles.

But Dale began making wrong choices at an early age. There were, of course, the usual childhood conflicts. But in his teen years he began to drink alcoholic beverages and smoke marijuana. By the time Dale was in high school, things were nearly unbearable at times. There were many times during those years that we were at the end of our strength and understanding. But faith in God gave us the courage to go on.

After Dale graduated from high school, he moved to an apartment with friends so that he would be able to enjoy his life-style without our rules. Shortly after that, we felt God leading us to another job, 200 miles away. We had to leave our son in God's hands! All we could do was pray and keep communication lines open. We began to pray that God would send someone across his path who would have a real impact on his life and be able to win him to Christ.

Following a series of circumstances, including my wife Virginia's healing from cancer, Dale indicated that he was thinking of becoming a Christian, but was not ready yet. We answered his many questions and kept praying. Soon, he was laid off from work and, having too much time on his hands, he decided to take guitar lessons. Of course, we feared he would now get involved in a rock group, but we held onto God's promise and kept praying.

During the next few months, his guitar teacher, who was also on drugs, became a Christian and began to witness to Dale. Dale saw his teacher's life change and watched as God worked miracles to save his marriage. Dale began to think of how rotten his own life was. He had a lovely wife, a nice home, two cars, money in the bank, but he was not happy!

Our second son, Bob, lived in the same town at that time and had been praying and fasting for Dale's salvation. Bob had begun to spend time with Dale. One night on his way home from Bob's home, Dale began to reflect on his past life and the life he was now living. Bob had just that evening approached him about making a commitment to Christ. He thought about his other brother, Duane, who had just taken his first pastoral assignment. He was reminded how Duane had never had much of this world's goods in the years of his college training, and yet was always happy. Dale reflected on the money he was spending to feed his bad habits, and by the time he reached home, he was crying. He went directly to his bedroom, knelt by his bed, and asked God for forgiveness. Dale was wonderfully saved! God delivered him from all of his bad habits. He is living proof that God does hear and answer prayer!

A year later, Dale mailed us the following poem:

I thank the Lord daily for the love that I have,
which He's poured out upon me from Heaven above.
That besides His blessings that He constantly gives,
He grew me in love as a child of His.
Unworthy am I to have grown in such love,
but to have never acknowledged it stemmed from my home.
Unworthy am I to have been taught by such ones,
as the parents God gave me who were constant and one.
I look at the teaching that you gave me to learn,
and now I understand how God's love had shown through,
because I saw His love manifest in you two.

Now I see how unworthy am I,
to have sat and listened and yet turned aside.
But I thank my God truly for opening the eyes of one
who was nearsighted and blind.
I love you both dearly beloved of God,
who nurtured and fed me with love from the Son.
And as I look back on the life that I lived,
it is not without thanksgiving that you raised me as His.

Your Son in God,
    Dale

—**David H. Baty**

A Case In Chile

A missionary pastor to a group of extremely poor peasants in Chile did everything he could to minister to their needs. He revealed what he considered to be the full counsel of the Lord, teaching the Bible as the Word of God and leading them into many significant and deep understandings. But one day the Lord spoke as clearly as if He had been standing face to face with him. "You have not declared My whole truth to these people," He said.

"But Lord," the missionary replied, "I don't understand. I've taught them about justification by faith, forgiveness of sins, baptism in the Holy Spirit, miracles, and walking in Your power. I've taught them about the church, history, and doctrine. I've taught them about holy living and the Second Coming.

"What, my Lord, have I failed to teach them?"

He waited a moment. The voice was very clear. "You have not declared My tithe to them."

The missionary was stunned. "But Lord, these are very poor people! They hardly have enough to live. I can't ask them to tithe. They have nothing."

Again, a silent moment. "You must declare to them My tithe."

He was a faithful, obedient man. And the debate ended.

The next Sunday morning, with heavy heart he stepped into the pulpit of the little rustic church in that poor, backward community, took a deep breath, and began.

"My beloved brethren," he said, looking into the open, up-lifted faces of his flock, "God has shown me that I haven't been faithful in declaring to you His whole counsel. There is something you have not been doing that I must tell you about. You have not been tithing to the Lord."

And he began a trek through the Scriptures with them that lasted nearly an hour. He explained everything, including the Malachi portions urging that the Lord be proven on the matter.

The next Sunday, it was their turn. In they came, obedient to the Word. They didn't have money, so they brought eggs, chickens, leather goods, woven articles, and all manner of things from their poor peasant homes. The altar area was heaped high.

The missionary felt badly about taking the gifts, but he too was faithful, so he sold some and used the money for the work of the church. He distributed some of the gifts to the destitute in the neighborhood and kept some for his own sustenance, in lieu of income.

The same thing happened Sunday after Sunday. The people tithed.

It wasn't long before the effects of drought were seen throughout the countryside. Poverty gripped the people of the land worse than ever. Crops failed; buildings deteriorated; gloom covered everything.

But, miraculously, this was not so with the members of that little church. Their crops flourished as though supernaturally watered. But more than that, the yields were extraordinary, bounteous, healthy, flavorful. Their fields were green, while those around were withering. Their livestock were sleek and strong. Relative abundance replaced abject poverty.

They even had an overflow of crops and goods that could be sold, and before long their tithes included money. They were able to build a much-needed new meeting house.

Despite his misgivings, the missionary and his people had learned that no matter how desperate the situation, no matter how deep the impoverishment, the principles of the kingdom can turn deprivation into abundance.

—Pat Robertson

The Test Of Endurance

When I think of physical struggles I remember a brave young man who came to one of our crusades in a wheelchair. He was suffering the last cruel stages of terminal cancer and was angry and bitter about it. He had read too many books promising health to the believer. Too many well-meaning Christians had promised him a miraculous healing from his disease. When he wasn't healed instantly, he grew more and more uncertain.

His loving parents carried him from one faith healer to another, and each one prayed for dramatic healing, but to no avail. The boy had prayed and fasted, and he sincerely believed, but still no miracle cure had taken place. Instead, he was dying. Our crusade was to be the last meeting that young man would ever attend.

The night he came, our Youth Night speaker was Joni Eareckson Tada. Most people know that Joni had been crippled several years earlier in a diving accident. She, too, had prayed for healing. And she, too, remained confined to a wheelchair as a quadriplegic. When she wheeled herself to the microphone that night, she did not oversell the Good News. She confessed her own early anger at remaining crippled after praying and believing in a miracle. Then she told how God met her in her pain and gave her life a new meaning and a new direction in spite of her suffering and disappointment.

Joni dared to tell it like it is. Her honesty set that dying young man free. Letting go of his bitterness and anger, he suddenly stopped seeing himself as a failure, as one who did not have enough faith. Instead, he came to see Christ in and through his pain. Not long after that meeting the young man died, but his parents were able to rejoice that he had not died angry and bitter. He simply gave his life back to his loving Father by giving himself completely to Jesus Christ. Then he went to be with the risen Lord where he would find freedom forever from his suffering.

—**Billy Graham**

Two Accident Reports

The early morning Los Angeles bound traffic was typical stop and go along the I-5 freeway. I was caught in its' midst. The sudden stops and starts triggered adrenaline into my still sleep-filled bloodstream. Suddenly, a car swerved into the lane next to me, and the driver began edging into my lane. The adrenaline now surged into my veins like an ocean surf being sucked into a sun-parched sandy beach.

Stifling my aggressive nature to hold ground and risk a side-swipe, I moved over a bit. The new pick-up I was driving was not mine. It was a delivery for a dealer. The lane intruder immediately sensed my caution and squeezed in a little closer. Behind me, the driver slowed as he watched our maneuvering. I nudged the gas pedal to further open the gap behind and looked ahead to check the car in front just in time to see his stop lights disappear below my hood. C R A S H ! The lane jumper spurted past into the now opened lane ahead and vanished.

A patrolman soon arrived and as I explained the collision circumstances to him, he began filling out an accident report. The driver I hit agreed with me: the accident was caused by the lane intruder, the one that sped away. "Not so," explained the officer. "The other vehicle was merely a distraction. You shouldn't have concentrated on him, but continued to look where you were going."

I felt defeated. That made my employer liable for damages to both vehicles, as well as any injuries to the other driver. Fortunately, neither he nor I were hurt.

For the rest of the day, I attempted to rationalize my actions. But that evening, I reluctantly came to the conclusion that the trooper's comment about distraction was right on target. I had been overly concerned with the distraction and failed to look ahead.

As I tried to sense what God might want to teach me, I quickly jotted down a number of verses with the words look, looked, and looking in them, and began reading the verses. Philippians 2:4 caught my attention: . . . *do not merely look out for your own personal interests, but also for the interests of others.* (NASB) An uneasy feeling crept over me. Yes, it was true. With the distraction, my thoughts and actions had centered on my own interests, endangering those around me. Though I had not been ticketed by the officer, I felt ticketed and convicted in the eyes of God. I made a new commitment to pay attention to the important things and not those things which are unimportant—but distracting.

—Carl Westling

3

Family

*And, ye fathers, provoke not your children to wrath:
but bring them up in the nurture and admonition of the Lord.*

Ephesians 6:4

Broken Promise

Recently, a 40-year-old man we counseled told us about a Saturday morning 28 years before that nearly stopped his heart—and is still affecting him today!

"I was just 12 when my Boy Scout troop planned a father-son camp out," he said. "I was thrilled and could hardly wait to rush home and give my father all the information. I wanted so much to show him all I'd learned in scouting, and I was so proud when he said he'd go with me.

"The Friday of the camp out finally came, and I had all my gear out on the porch, ready to stuff it in his car the moment he arrived. We were to meet at the local school at 5:00 p.m. and carpool to the campground. But Dad didn't get home until 7:00 p.m.

"I was frantic, but he explained how things had gone wrong at work and told me not to worry. We could still get up first thing in the morning and join the others. After all, we had a map. I was disappointed, of course, but decided to make the best of it.

"First thing in the morning, I was up and had everything in his car while it was still getting light, all ready for us to catch up with my friends and fathers at the campground. Dad had said we'd leave around 7:00 a.m., and I was ready a half hour before that. But he never got up until 9:30.

"When he saw me standing out front with the camping gear, he explained that he had a bad back and couldn't sleep on the ground. He hoped I'd understand and that I'd be a 'big boy' about it . . . but could I please get my things out of his car, because he had several 'commitments' he had to keep.

"Just about the hardest thing I've ever done was to go to the car and take out my sleeping bag, cooking stove, pup tent, and supplies. And then, while I was putting my stuff away and he thought I was out of sight, I watched my father walk out to the garage, sling his golf clubs over his shoulder, throw them into the trunk, and drive away to keep his 'commitment.' That's when I realized my dad never meant to go with me to the camp out. He just didn't have the guts to tell me."

How do you recalibrate a boy's heart after it has been damaged by a dad's broken promise?

How do you restore the capacity to trust after trust has been shattered?

How do you bring back a boy's joy and the sparkle in his eyes after they've been carelessly quellched?

That "boy" is now a man in counseling. His father is dead, but memories of a hurtful past have affected him and his own family for years. Is that not incredible power?

With God's help, a man can draw from the unfathomable depths of a child's heart the capacities to love, trust, serve, share, give, and create.

—Gary Smalley and John Trent

A Sunday school class of first-graders was asked to draw a picture of God. When the pastor stopped by to inspect their work, they were happy to show him their work. One child had depicted God in the form of a brightly-colored rainbow. Another had drawn the face of an old man coming out of some billowing clouds. And there was one rendition which looked like Superman. But, best of all, there was the one proudly displayed by a little girl who said, "I didn't know what God looked like, so I just drew a picture of my Daddy."

—The Preacher's Illustration Service

Understanding Love

Labor had lasted over thirty hours and many things had gone wrong. There was so much I didn't understand. I had never witnessed childbirth before. This was my first experience and my first-born child.

My soul cried for this to be over—my wife alternated between unconsciousness and a delirious haze. I was scared, tired, and sleepy, and feeling alone. I didn't understand why physicians, whom I hadn't met, began coming into the room.

"*Specialists*" I was told.

But nobody said why.

I was an "older" first-time father. Though I knew a great deal about parenting and counseling children, I knew nothing about childbirth. There were continuous, but unsolicited, assurances that everything would be fine. In my mind that could only mean something was wrong. For a long time I had wanted a son. I would name him after my father. I thought it would be an appropriate memorial to a man who died before my tenth birthday.

During my wife's pregnancy, I'd become quite anxious. For some reason I was scared things might not be right. Were my fears becoming real?

After consulting with four high-risk pregnancy specialists, I convinced my wife to agree to cesarean delivery.

Finally, my son was born! He was blue and the umbilical cord was wrapped where I knew it shouldn't be. His head seemed dented and he didn't breathe at first. But I was assured he was alive!

I was allowed to hold my son before he was taken away to the neonatal intensive care unit. He would "probably be okay," I was told. My wife was still somewhat delirious when I reached down and whispered, "He's got a dimple on his chin—just like you wanted. He's going to be okay."

She smiled and squeezed my hand.

As they took her away, I rushed down the hall to find the

neonatal intensive care and accidentally found my mother who had arrived from out of town. I didn't know she was coming and never felt more grateful to see her. We hugged each other and finally, I could *relax*. She let me settle down before saying a word.

"Dr. Haren says they'll be okay," she reassured me.

"I know. I believe him. I'm just tired. I've never felt like this before. I want that little boy to live so badly, I would give him anything I had. I would give it up without hesitation, without question. I've never felt like this before. I mean, I love you, Mom. But this is so different." I paused as my eyes began to fill with tears.

"I know, Son," my mother responded. "I know. I'm glad you understand. Now maybe you know how I feel about you. But more importantly, now maybe you know how much God loved us. He gave up his Son and watched him die for us. That's real love."

I paused and as my eyes cleared, I understood. "I understand that now, Mom." And for once in my life, I finally comprehended my mother's strength. I finally understood a few other things. I wanted my son to live far more than anything I had ever experienced. To give up my life for him was easy. To sacrifice him for someone else seemed impossible. God's love for me, however, is that powerful.

Later, I checked on my new son and wife and gave thanks for all of our lives. Then I rested. I began to understand love.

—**John Q. Baucom**

A Lasting Legacy

Last year saw the death of my father by cardiac arrest. I am only beginning to realize the full impact of that loss now, even though grief has been near every day since.

I don't know how you sum up a man's life in a few words. My father always carried himself with great dignity, from the way he marveled at the blue birds on his window sill to how he reveled in his latest plans for a trek to Egypt, Africa or somewhere else hot and sticky. He was my best source of counsel and encouragement. Frequently, I find myself repeating his pet expressions—"All of life is unfair," "Work before pleasure," "The truth will win out," and "Leave them smiling"—to my kids. I found in him a steady and sure friend.

He always seemed to know just what was needed—whether it was the quick fix of a dripping faucet, the three Littleton rules for negotiating a car deal or how to have a happy ministry—and I revered him for it. He was in all ways a gentleman. I knew I could go to him at any time with the secrets of my heart and be sure those secrets would not be divulged to anyone else, not even my mother (which surprised me and sometimes embarrassed her). He never scoffed at my dreams or belittled my latest obsession. In fact, he applauded them—forcefully, happily, rousingly and with that little twinkle in his eye that so thrilled me.

My father was my biggest fan when it came to my work in the ministry, public speaking, and writing. He read all my books, and would seek me out to give me his own very personal, usually encouraging critique (on my book on time-management—"I only read half of it; you saved me so much time, I didn't need to read the other half"). He walked with me through every major crisis of my life, and many minor ones.

He relished his frequent visits from his five granddaughters and was always quick to produce some coveted trinket he'd filched from an airplane jaunt, assuring each child he'd "saved it especially for them."

I loved him in all the ways only a son can, and I miss him deeply. Only a few men have had an impact close to that of my Dad in my life. Occasionally, I hear stories from friends or others about their fathers—stories about alcoholism, theft, divorce, abuse. I cringe when I hear such stories, wishing it could have been for them as it had been for me.

I think a good, strong Christian father has the power to mold young men in ways we can't even begin to imagine. I guess the thing I'm left with are the words of my father, each night as we went to bed. "See you in the morning."

Yes, I will, Dad, on that great gettin' up morning when we rise and shine for Him forever. I look forward to the day when I see you stand before Jesus. Undoubtedly, you will hear the words. "Well done, thou good and faithful servant," and I'll be there cheering, and clapping along with the rest of God's creation.

—Mark R. Littleton

A Poem

As I reviewed my son's papers from school one night last week, I came across one paper with a failing grade. I almost came up out of my chair. I started to yell his name when I suddenly remembered he was in bed asleep. It didn't matter that this was only his second year of school. At that moment I saw his academic career in ruins. I was angry.

But I put the paper aside and turned to the next one. It had some pencil scribblings and at the top of the page was written, "My Dad." It was a poem about me.

His poem included the time I had to leave work to take him to the doctor because he had broken his finger. I had forgotten about that. He talked about how I wrestled with him in the evenings. And he talked about a few other things he likes that I do.

That paper with the failing grade was suddenly not nearly as important as it had been just a few minutes earlier. I don't know if he planted the poem next to the failing grade in order to soften the blow, but it worked. Instead of a severe lecture, I talked to him about the poem as well as the failed assignment.

It began to make sense to me that I could include praise along with constructive criticism. I got the idea from a poem I read.

—**Paul Budd**

Anguish In The Night

When Raymond was awakened by the phone after midnight one Saturday morning, his wife didn't stir. As he made his way to the living room, his thoughts raced to his two married sons and a daughter in college.

He hoped for a wrong number. Phone calls in the night rarely bring good news. He offered a sleepy, muffled, octave-lower-than-usual, "Hello?"

All he heard was sobbing. He prayed silently, "Father, give me strength for whatever is wrong."

"Daddy?" the female voice managed.

"Yes," Raymond answered, his voice thick from sleep. His daughter sobbed. Raymond whispered so as not to disturb his wife, "Honey, what is it?"

"Oh, Daddy!" she said, fighting for control. He waited. "Daddy, I'm sorry."

Raymond hoped it was only a failed test, a failed class, a failed semester. She cried and cried. "Daddy?" she said.

"I'm here," he said.

"Daddy, I'm pregnant."

Raymond's heart sank. How could it be? He and his wife had raised their children in love, in the church, from the Bible. Each member of the family had a personal relationship with Christ, and each had an unusual ability to interact with the others. The kids had always been open about their struggles and temptations.

Yet Raymond didn't even know that his daughter had a boyfriend. Was the father a new love? Had she been forced? Was it someone he knew? With the phone pressed to his ear, his free hand covering his eyes, he prayed silently for strength, for the right words, the right response. He was broken-hearted.

Raymond had always feared he might explode in anger and embarrassment over such news. Yet now he found himself overcome with sympathy, pity, protectiveness for his precious child, still in the bloom of youth.

His daughter—clearly distressed, broken, repentant—begged for forgiveness. Raymond didn't ask for details. "We love you," he said through his tears. "We forgive you."

He was on the phone more than a half-hour, then sat crying until dawn when his wife padded out to hear the news. They went through the day in their pajamas, hardly eating, working on a letter. It assured their daughter that they would always be there for her and the baby, and that they would be available to counsel her or to support her decision on what to do about the father.

The post office promised the letter would be delivered early Monday morning. The waiting was torture.

Raymond prayed all weekend that God would somehow erase history, would put things back the way they had been just a few hours before.

On Monday morning a pale, bleary-eyed Raymond went to work. Midmorning he took a call from his daughter. "Daddy," she said, laughing, "what in the world is this letter all about?"

It had not been a joke. Not a crank call. It had been a wrong number—a tragic mistake in the middle of the night—two people in turmoil thinking they knew to whom they were talking. Raymond spent the rest of the day vainly trying to help the phone company determine *where* the call could have originated. He didn't want a girl racing home to a father she thought had forgiven her, only to find that he knew nothing about her situation.

Raymond, an old acquaintance, is a saint. He admits it was the most traumatic experience he's ever had, but he is grateful that it has made him sensitive to parents who do receive such unbearable news. "For forty-eight hours, my wife and I ached."

In a way, though, God answered Raymond's prayer. With the Monday call, everything had been put back the way it had been. Everything except Raymond. He will never be the same.

—Jerry B. Jenkins

A Prayer For Clayton Todd

Before you were born,
while your mother, my daughter, carried you,
I prayed for you.

And every day I continue to speak your name
to the Father of life.

Then as I have the joy of holding you,
I pray that you may become a mighty man of God.

I pray that your mind would be filled
with His thoughts, that your eyes
would learn to focus on His direction,
your ears would listen carefully to His instruction
and that your mouth would proclaim praises to His name!

I ask God to give you shoulders
to help bear the burdens of others,
arms that reach out in comfort,
hands that work hard
to build the message of Christ in the lives of many.

My plea with your Creator-God is for strong legs that
will walk the path of righteousness and for
feet that will avoid the Adversary's way.

I pray that you will grow
spiritually, mentally, emotionally and physically.

Most of all
I pray that you will grow up in Him
and that you will know Him
who gives you the very breath you breathe.

No matter what you choose as an occupation
may you worship Him
with all your heart, soul and mind.
May you find all joy and contentment in Him.

—**Grampa Brown** (Charles Brown)

The Midnight Roamer

I sat in my favorite chair relaxing when my son, Jonathan, called out, "Dad, I'm ready to pray and read the Bible." My son was tucked in bed when I reached his room. As I looked into the handsome face of his 17 years, my mind recalled when we started reading the Bible and praying together. We started when he and his brother and sister were all young. However, for Jonathan it had special meaning.

I remember the horror of the day when as a three-year-old he chased after a soccer ball into the street in front of our house. An oncoming car was able to stop just in time and barely avoided hitting him. Shortly after that, he started roaming the house after everyone else had gone to bed. He seemed to have trouble drifting off to sleep after his frightening narrow miss.

"Dad, I'm ready," my son interrupted my thoughts. After we had read the Bible and prayed together, my mind returned to that time and I remembered what had begun to help him drift off to sleep and calm his fears. Each night, as my "midnight roamer" started his travels around our house, I would rock him while reading him Bible stories and singing praise songs. He liked to listen to Bible stories being told on tape as well. At times he woke up again after falling asleep, and I felt frustrated. It seemed like he would never learn to stop his midnight roaming. But I would start the rocking again with another story and song.

"Goodnight, Dad, I love you." Jon interrupted my musings again as he closed his eyes.

I answered, "I love you too, son."

I stepped out of his room overwhelmed with gratitude for our night-time tradition which had so contributed to our great relationship. "Father, thank you," I whispered, "for Jon's midnight roaming, for if it hadn't been for that, we might not be praying and reading together now."

—Clay Ellis

The Myth About Work

One day my son, John, was scheduled to play basketball in a nearby city at 4:00 p.m. Since I can arrange my own schedule, I decided to drive to the game with Patsy, my wife.

I left work at about 3:00 p.m., jumped into jeans, and we headed off for the game. On the way there we passed the father of one of the other boys, who I assumed was also on his way to the game. We rolled down the window and exchanged a forty-mile-per-hour greeting.

It turned out that he was not going to the game after all, but he asked us to wish his son good luck. A couple of miles later we came to a traffic light. We turned toward our son's game, but the boy's father turned the other way. I wondered why.

When we arrived at the game, I was surprised to see only one other father. He had apparently come directly from the office because he still had on his tie. We sat down next to him, and I said something benign like, "Isn't it great to be able to watch our sons play basketball?"

"It sure is," he said, then added, "*I really wanted to come but I know I shouldn't be here*" (emphasis added).

"Bombs" began bursting in my mind, and before I could catch myself I blurted out, "Oh, yeah? According to whose value system?"

Actually, instead of taking my remark as an insult, this off-the-cuff comment led to a lengthy and healthy discussion about values and priorities. The man explained that he felt a sense of guilt and failure—that he was somehow letting his fellow workers down.

We agreed that this false sense of guilt drives many men to neglect their families. We also agreed that many men were addicted to their work—they would rather work than watch the game.

We also realized that the deceptive desire for an ever-increasing prosperity drives many men to create so many debts and duties that they operate too close to the edge. Their worlds are wired so tight that two hours off might topple their kingdom. Come on! *Get a life!*

Solomon wrote:

Better One Handful With Tranquillity
Than Two Handfuls With Toil
And Chasing After The Wind (Ecclesiastes 4:6).

I know work can be intoxicating. I know there are deadlines. I know the pleasure of feeling needed at the office. But as I sat in the bleachers at the basketball game that day, I could not help wondering, *How many men are not here today because they have both hands full?*

Obviously, many men have jobs that won't allow them to take time off for a late afternoon game. But where were the men who could take off? A missed game is gone forever. We don't get a second chance.

—**Patrick M. Morley**

"He's Not Too Fat!"

One day I was watching a video tape of the NBA all-star weekend with two of my sons. Included were the highlights of the slam dunk competition that had all of us on the edge of our seats, whooping and hollering with each fabulous display of athletic skill. There was a special sense of awe when the highlights featured 5'7" Spud Webb. Men who are 5'7" are not supposed to be able to slam dunk, but the film was proof positive. We all gave each other high fives and celebrated what we recognized as a remarkable feat.

The real lesson came later in the day when I was driving around town with my ten-year-old son, Brock, and my eight-year-old son, Zachery. We were running errands but our minds were still focused on the slam dunk contest we had just seen. We were verbally reliving antics we could only do in our dreams when Zachery spoke up from the back seat.

"Dad, how tall is that little guy who slam dunked?"

"You mean Spud Webb?" I asked not knowing exactly where this conversation was leading.

"Yeah, how tall is Spud Webb?" Zachery asked with an air of confidence in his voice.

"He's five-feet-seven inches tall," I said.

"Well, how tall are you, dad?" he asked as he masterfully took control of the conversation.

"I am five-feet-eleven inches tall," I responded with the eerie feeling that I was about to get slam dunked by my eight-year-old son.

Sure enough, Zachery did not disappoint my expectations as he inquired, "Dad, how come you can't slam dunk? Are you too fat?"

I wasn't sure how I was going to handle this. I had just been defeated by an eight-year-old. Part of me wanted to give him a stern lecture about how rude he had been. Part of me wanted to pull off to the side of the road, then get out of the car and give my son a standing ovation. As I was busy planning my response to having been outplayed, Brock came to my rescue.

"He's not too fat, Zachery. He weighs the same as Michael Jordan."

Words cannot describe the pride I felt at my oldest son's magnificent wisdom. He had just compared me to one of the greatest athletes who has ever played the game of basketball. I was wallowing in the victory Brock had just given me when reality hit.

Brock continued his explanation to his younger brother, "Dad's not too fat, Zachery, he's just too old!"

At this time I figured I had better keep my mouth quiet and remind myself that humility is as much a part of life as success and wisdom.

—**Bill Farrel**

Our three-year-old grandson, Daniel, stayed with us while his parents went on a weekend trip. As usual, we bowed our heads as my husband prayed out loud before all our meals. Daniel watched curiously each time his grandpa prayed.

On the day his parents came to pick him up, we all sat down at the table to have lunch. Just as his daddy started to pick up his sandwich, Daniel shouted, "Wait, daddy, we can't eat 'til Grandpa reads his plate!"

—**D. L. James**

My Soul Buddy

As a nurse, my wife, Margaret, knew it was dangerous to contract German Measles early in pregnancy. And since Margaret was near 40, her pregnancy was further endangered. When she sobbed that our child might be deformed, fear settled over me like a cloud. I worried I was not as close to God as I should be; that this was His punishment. Margaret and I had married late in life. We were both loners, I in particular, but that would change.

When Lynett was born, Dr. North was kind but frank. "This will be like hitting you with a sledgehammer, but your daughter is a Down's Syndrome child." Even though we'd wondered about that possibility, the shock still caught us off guard.

Lynett's problems started quickly, and as a result, Margaret fought depression. The baby didn't want to nurse and had a large hole between the two chambers of her heart. When Lynett began responding to our love, we felt it best that Margaret go back to teaching public health part-time at the University. She had to get her mind off of her disappointment, even though we had worlds of support and prayer from our church family. We never suffered what we feared most—rejection.

Babysitters came and went. Fortunately, I had a business of my own. When babysitters couldn't come, I took Lynett to the shop with me. She loved it and seldom gave me any trouble.

As she grew older, I took her for rides in my Karmann Ghia® to give Margaret a break. I was on a low-fat diet, but I would sneak Lynett into a restaurant for pie. One day, as we drove by that restaurant, Lynett pointed and said, "Pie Daddy."

My diet monitor wasn't dumb. "Do you come in here for pie?" Margaret asked sternly. I confessed.

We could see Lynett's growth, but at a private school for the retarded a psychologist pronounced her non-educable. It was true, she didn't understand a lot. But she did obey us after being shown what "No" meant.

I made her a stove with non-hot burners and knobs to turn like Mother's. She kept her little pans and dishes in the bottom cabinet. Once in a while she would cook Daddy a meal and set out dishes for two. Little cups and everything right. With her limited vocabulary, when she had it all on the little table, she would come to me and say, "Daddy." I always had time for these non-food feasts. I would go through the motions of eating with her on the other side. She would beam with delight.

Lynett would follow me around endlessly. Only once did I grow weary and send her away. As she went upstairs, her look cut me to the quick. But soon she came back down and I held her to make up. I played with her and her toys on the carpet. Invariably, when I came home she would be standing at the window waiting.

When Lynett was about five, I took her for a walk one warm day. She stopped frequently to sit on the curb. I waited, and then urged her on, concluding she needed the exercise. About 25 feet later she turned blue and fell. I thought I had killed her. In panic, I gathered up her limp form and rushed home. On the way to the hospital she recovered. The doctor blamed her heart, and I never pushed her again.

Later her adenoids expanded, so she often gasped for air. But due to the hole in her heart, the doctors wouldn't operate. I had to make a plywood sheet form with a padded hole so she could lie face down and breathe. This went on for endless nights. I had to sleep with her to adjust her body. It tore my heart in two to hear her gasping for air. The crisis passed, but Lynett came in more often at night saying, "Daddy, it hurts."

One day, when Lynett was six, there was snow on the ground. Margaret was in the car holding the door open. "Come on, Lynett," she said as my buddy hesitated at the snow. She obeyed, as always, but passed out in the car. Margaret rushed her to the hospital. A nurse phoned me at the shop and said, "Your wife and Lynett are here. You had better come." I suspected the worst. My buddy had gone to be with Jesus.

At her funeral, the newly-finished big church was jam-packed so full that people were standing in the hall. Lynett had done something I could never do by knocking on doors a hundred years. All these people were souls she had touched and influenced in her short life. And she had brought me out of my loner's shell.

I expect to see my darling girl again, standing and looking through a window of heaven, waiting for Daddy to come home.

—Laurence A. Davis

A little five-year-old boy ran to answer the telephone when it rang. His mother was busy taking care of his baby brother so the little boy decided he would answer while she was busy. The voice on the other end said that it was Mr. Jones calling. "I'm sorry, the little boy said, but there is no one here right now. May I take a message?" Mr. Jones heard the phone drop, and then the little voice said, "o.k., I'm ready now." "Who did you say is calling?"

"Mr. Jones."

"How do you spell Jones?"

"J-O-N-E-S."

After a long pause the little boy asked,

"How do you make a J?"

—The Preacher's Illustration Service

A Perfect Parent?

Over the years I've done literally hundreds of parenting seminars in churches around the world. I have found errors to be made in one of two directions. One occurs when parents don't take enough responsibility. However, the other occurs when parents assume too much. On one occasion, for two evenings I'd spoken at a church on the subject of parenting. Both times this one particular lady waited at the periphery of the group. The first night she disappeared before I had a chance to answer her question. The second night I noticed her coming back after my presentation.

The lady waited for over an hour, hovering on the edge of our group, never coming close enough to speak. She was a short woman whose brown hair was pulled behind her head in a large bun. Her leathered hands gripped a large, worn Bible which she held tightly against her body.

Finally, the others were gone and she could address me.

"Dr. Baucom, I'm Mrs. Smith. Thank you for your program. It was very good." Her head lowered as she cleared her throat. "I have a seventeen-year-old son. I've had to raise him by myself. My husband left fifteen years ago."

I could have predicted the rest of the story. Her son had been arrested several times. Currently, he was in a juvenile rehabilitation center. Mrs. Smith was struggling with guilt and self-criticism. She felt her son's predicament was her fault and wondered what she had done wrong.

"I don't want to do the same thing to his brother." By now she was crying aloud, no longer hiding her tears. I allowed her to continue.

"I know it's my fault. If I had been a better mother, this would have never happened. Maybe if I'd been more involved in church, or prayed more . . . ."

"You believe in God," I commented as a fact more than a question. My pause indicated to her I was awaiting a response.

"Yes." She seemed startled. "Yes, I do."

"Then do you believe God is perfect?" By now she was studying me with a curious frown on her brow.

"Well, yes. God is perfect." She nodded her head several times. The tears quickly dried from her eyes.

"Well, if God is perfect, then wouldn't He be a perfect parent?" I wondered aloud.

"Yes," she nodded again, "Yes. He certainly would be."

"And according to the Bible how did Adam and Eve behave?"

She hesitated for a moment and then began to speak, "I see where you're going, but . . ."

"No," I interrupted gently. "Wait. If any children ever had a chance to be good kids, it was Adam and Eve, right? They had one-on-one contact with God. Their relationship was intense and intimate. If anyone could raise obedient children, wouldn't it be God?"

She hesitated, as if weighing the evidence. "Yes, I guess so." She looked at me with the hint of a smile.

"Okay," I continued. "So if God is perfect and He raises imperfect children, how can you, who are imperfect, raise perfect children? You could do every conceivable thing right, and your kids would still be imperfect. At some point they make their own choices, just like Adam and Eve. They might make unfortunate choices. There's no way you can be a perfect parent. I don't think your guilt is going to help you or your children."

We paused and stared at each other for a moment. She thanked me and left. I haven't seen or heard from her since that moment. Yes, we do need to be involved and take responsibility for our children. However, regardless of how involved we become, our children still have free will. They can make the same choices that were made by our first parents many years ago.

—John Q. Baucom

Building Our Kids

One day an acquaintance cornered me and said with an angry edge to his voice, "I tried to call you the other night, but you have an unlisted phone number."

"Yes," I said.

"Well, I had important ministry business that I wanted to discuss with you. I can't believe you have an unlisted phone number! How can you be a Christian and have an unlisted phone number?"

"It's real easy, actually. All you do is call the phone company, tell them what you want, and they take care of everything!" I said.

Perhaps I was a bit too sarcastic because at that point he really let me have it. "I can't believe someone would make himself inaccessible on purpose. Jesus wouldn't have an unlisted number! Yak, yak, yak . . . Yip, yip, yap . . . Etc., etc." he droned on.

Finally I said, "Look, I'm willing to die for you until 6:00 p.m. But after six o'clock I only die for my family."

The only way to know for sure that we will have time for our families is to put it on the schedule like any other appointment. If not, we will find ourselves running right out of their lives.

I would rather be a nobody in the world but be somebody to my kids.

—**Patrick M. Morley**

Wake Up Call

Michael Ovitz, a well-known and highly-successful agent in the entertainment industry, was recently mentioned in the "Intelligencer" column of *New York* magazine. The columnist was passing on the gossip that Ovitz was now working from his Brentwood Park, California, home rather than his Beverly Hills office. For whatever reason, the item referred to this decision as "more evidence that everyone is getting into the spend-quality-time-with-the-family trend."

To everyone's surprise, the following letter soon arrived at *New York* magazine, signed by Ovitz's three kids:

We are avid readers of New York magazine, and so we were most interested in the December 12 edition of your "Intelligencer" column ("Ovitz In; Shapiro Out") revealing the newly-acquired nesting habits of our father, Michael Ovitz.

As it has been years since we have seen him at home on a weekday, we would be most grateful if you could reveal to us the exact vantage point from which our neighbors achieved these reported sightings. Indeed, catching a look at Dad in daylight, at home, on the odd Tuesday or Wednesday, would be well worth the few hours of surveillance necessary to record this historic event.

We thank you very much for consideration of our request and again please know how much we are looking forward to reading about Dad's comings and goings in your fine publication.

Do you need a wake-up call like that? As men, we tend to get so focused on our various pursuits that we develop tunnel vision. We can become experts in our vocations and avocations but ignorant about ourselves—especially our weaknesses.

—**Howard Hendricks**

Time Stood Still

The other evening, when our son yelled at me from his room that he couldn't sleep, I was reminded of the story of Joshua from the Old Testament when time stood still. There was a battle going on and they needed more time to finish the fight. So Joshua appealed to God, and the sun stood still while they concluded their military campaign.

Since I wasn't sure what my son expected me to do, I said something stupid: "You shouldn't have taken that long nap this afternoon."

I could tell right away that I didn't have to say that. I heard muffled noise from his pillow, telling me things he couldn't say.

So I went to his room. He let me lay down with him, sort of. Something he doesn't invite me to do so much anymore. It has to do with growing up. After a while he draped an arm over my neck. Kind of a half-hug.

We lay like that for some time. I don't know how long. No talking. No moving. Just the sound of breathing. And *time stood still*.

Then I thanked God that time can stand still. Because in a short while, one of us won't let something like this happen again. But for the moment, *time stood still*.

—**Paul Budd**

My Mother's Prayers

The frigate gently rolled, barely visible on the ocean, with the early morning clouds just lifting over its stacks. From the deck, my shipmates and I could see the destroyers and cruisers we supported looming large in the distance. With the lifting fog, we could make out tiny moving specks which were the Navy crewmen on deck.

Suddenly, Japanese bombers screamed through the clearing sky and began to drop their payloads. The sailors swung into action, bombarding the air with rounds of ammunition. The bombers circled and returned. Out of their ranks came the kamikaze attackers, diving headlong to sink our ships by suicidally destroying their planes.

I stood awestruck, stunned, on the deck of the frigate. My shipmates and I had been at sea for an entire year doing convoy and escort duty without ever touching land, but this was the fiercest and closest action we'd seen. We only had a three-inch and some 40mm and 20mm guns with which to defend ourselves, and all guns were firing.

We watched spellbound as the battle unfolded. The smell of burning oil, exploding ammunition, and stench from the beach putrefied the salty air. The sounds of screaming planes, booming guns, and exploding bombs overpowered our ears until all we could hear were rumbling noises. I looked up after a few minutes, which felt like hours, and saw a Japanese plane heading straight for our deck.

If I had been stunned before, now I was frozen. I had not lived for God in years, but I called on Him like He was my best friend. I promised I'd serve Him if He got me out this. I stared in disbelief at what was surely to be the last thing I would see on this earth.

Suddenly, the kamikaze plane dove into the ocean, just missing us, and exploded. Through the smoke, I could barely see the pieces floating on the water. It was gone. Vanished. My attention fell back to the ships where the battle was ending.

The calm of the ocean returned. The men on the destroyers started cleaning up, taking care of the wounded, putting out fires, beginning the rebuilding process to prepare for the next battle.

Months later, when I was finally home, peace was eminent. I knew I wouldn't be back at sea again because the war was ending. When I went home to discuss my plans with my mother, she asked me about the battle I had experienced. It was etched in my mind, and I'd had months to relive it. I told her about it in vivid detail. When I described the kamikaze plane exploding, she shrieked, "That was it!"

She had been lying in bed that same day when suddenly she sat upright and cried, "My son!" She didn't know what awakened her, but she prayed fervently, beseeching God's protection in my behalf, interceding with Him to rescue me, believing for a miracle. God heard my mother's prayers.

—Edwin Louis Cole

Adversity neither strengthens nor weakens, but rather brings out whatever strength or weakness was already in you.

A Prayer For Dad

In the morning give him strength
To meet the trials of the day.
When he worries, give him peace
Lord help him learn to trust your way.
In his quiet times expose him
To the room he has to grow.
In his travels, give him safety
Lord, protect him as he goes.
At his office Father guide him
Give him insight to stand tall.
And remind him that they watch him
And they notice when he falls.
In his friendships, help him reach out
For the Christ in every soul.
In his stress, Lord, give him peace
And the cool to gain control.
In his marriage, help him listen
To the feelings of his wife.
With his kids, Lord, give him time
To laugh, and lead them all through life.
With his health, Lord, keep him happy
Even in his times of stress.
With his money, may he give
Of that with which he has been blessed.
In the evenings, give him quiet time
To think back on the day.
And as he sleeps, renew him Lord
In each and every way.

—Darren Prince

"He Ain't Heavy, He's My Brother"

I have a physical and spiritual brother named Eric. He is my friend. We live in different cities separated by miles. We pursue different professional fields, and we don't see one another as often as we would like. But we are brothers. And we both know there is no limit to our commitment to each other. I would do anything for him. He would do anything for me. That's what brothers are for!

Sometime back when my oldest son was a senior in high school and his younger brother a sophomore, an incident took place that was to mark their friendship. Blake, the younger of the two, was adjusting to high school. Still somewhat naive of "acceptable" sophomore deportment, he had unwittingly drawn the ire of an older student in some way that to this day he can't figure out.

On the day in question, he was bent over reaching into the lower level of his locker. Without warning and with force enough to rip his shirt, an older, bigger, and stronger kid grabbed him at the chest, stood him up, and ripped him around to face-off. The kid squared off, mouthed some angry expletives, and prepared to beat the daylights out of the smaller Blake. A crowd gathered and tension shot down the hallway like an electric current. The spectacle was about to begin.

Later Blake told me, "Dad, I didn't know what to do. Run? Duck? Swing first? Stand and take it?" He went on to say, "But in the split second that I was trying to decide, something from the side caught my eye. It was big. And it was coming *fast!*"

It turned out that the something big and fast was Kent, Blake's six-foot-five older brother. Blake described Kent picking the other kid up, hauling him out of the hallway and into the school's courtyard, shoving him back against the wall, and announcing, "Don't you *ever* fight that kid in there. He's my brother. I don't even care if he starts it. Don't fight him. Because he's my brother and *I'll finish it for him.*"

Years later at Blake's wedding, he asked that Kent and Ryan (his younger brother), and his Dad all serve as his "best man." The four of us walked down the aisle together. I felt like a platoon leader again for the first time in years. As the four of us good friends stood there, the words Blake had written to Kent in the wedding program came back to me: "Kent, you are my older brother, and to those who have one—that says it all. You have shown me what the word 'loyalty' means and have been my example of unconditional love. Since the day you fought old 'so and so' off my back, I have held you on a shelf all its own. Thanks for always watching out for me and seeing to it that your younger brothers prosper. I love you, bro! . . . my oldest brother and friend, thanks for being a model I could follow. Your protection and love will always be deep in my heart." Brothers are born for adversity.

—Stu Weber

Dad Took The Beating

My father and mother were always involved on the platform on Sunday mornings at church. Dad would sing in the choir and mom was the church organist. My brother and I were given a lot of latitude during services. Most often we sat alone. Week after week, my brother and I carried on as we sat on the front right side of the sanctuary. At times, after the choir was dismissed from the platform, my father took one of us out for a paddling, which proved to be an embarrassment for both parents and child.

One Sunday is particularly vivid in my memory. It was a typical Sunday with mom and dad on the platform. This was a particularly fully-attended service and so the choir stayed up on the platform during the entire service. My brother and I couldn't contain ourselves. As the momentum of the service escalated, so did our abhorrent behavior: laughing, jumping up and down, scooting up and down the pew or the unforgivable, crawling under the pew.

When we got home dad said he wanted to talk to both of us. We knew it was going to be bad by the heaviness in dad's voice. But we figured it would be like any other Sunday. I would blame my brother for inciting me and he would take the beating. He was tough. He would just lay there on dad's lap and take it full bore, never letting out a whimper. Sometimes he even smiled.

On this Sunday, though, dad asked us to come down to the living room. Now we knew it was serious. He even had the yard stick out and ready. But this Sunday he did something different. Instead of asking us why we misbehaved and giving us a lecture as to how bad we were, he paused and said, "I feel like a failure as a father."

He held out the yard stick and continued, "I want you to hit me across the back of the hands because I need to be punished for being such a poor father and not teaching you to behave."

Both my brother and I thought he was joking and began to laugh. He wasn't laughing. Then we realized he was dead serious.

I had rarely seen my brother cry, but I will never forget my father having to shout at him to get him to pick up the yardstick. Then, as my brother began to smack our father across the hands, his emotion built inside until he seemed to explode with anguish. He couldn't continue. When it came to my turn, my arms went limp.

I will never forget the impression that left on me as a child. My father was willing to take the punishment that was due me. His Christ-like attitude spoke deeply to me and today, it encourages me as a father to sacrifice for my children. Needless to say our behavior changed. We never wanted to go through that ordeal again. Not that we became angelic-like, but we strove to never have our punishment taken by our father.

—David Hahn

A Red Rose For Rachel

About six months ago, I blew up at Rachel just before bedtime. Actually, I blew up about forty-five minutes after she was supposed to be in bed. It had been a long day, and I was extremely tired. For some reason, it seemed she kept lingering and hovering around the house. I wanted peace and quiet. Finally, Mount St. Helens blew. I'm sure the neighbors wondered what had so angered me. I told Rachel that she had fifteen seconds to be in bed—I repeat, *in* her bed.

She went to bed crying as the hot lava of my wrath pursued her up the stairs. After I came back down, Mary told me there were several good reasons she had been up. Some special event was to take place at school the next morning, and Rachel was getting ready for it. She wasn't lingering, she was preparing.

If I had bothered to ask Rachel what was going on, I could have discovered that for myself. But I didn't. I just vented on her. I made my way back up the stairs (careful not to step in the remaining pools of lava) and asked her forgiveness. I felt like a real jerk. We prayed together, and I tucked her in and decided the safest place for me was in bed as well. I told Mary I was turning in.

But I couldn't drop off to sleep. My explosion had unsettled me, too. I kept thinking of the enormous damage I could inflict on my exquisite ten-year-old daughter without even realizing it. The last thing I wanted to do was to crush her delicate spirit. Although we had patched it up and she had forgiven me, I couldn't get her off my mind.

After an hour or so, I got up, got in the car, and drove down to the twenty-four-hour supermarket. I found a red rose in a nice little vase, a card with a man peering out of a doghouse, and headed home. I wrote Rachel a note telling her that I really did love her and that I really was wrong. Then I placed the rose and the card on the kitchen table. It was the first thing she saw when she walked into the kitchen.

I figured after ruining her evening, the least I could do would be to make her day. It was worth the late-night trip. Instead of going off to school with memories of the red hot lava, she could think of her red, serene rose . . . and a dad who was genuinely sorry.

—Steve Farrar

A Dad Of Humility

I could never seem to get out of the sermons what my father did. But the hardest thing to take when I was growing up was when my father would respond to the invitation. How embarrassing. He would just get up and go forward, and then we would hear him at times crying or telling people how he was such a sinner. I wanted to run and hide. How could he confess his sins to other people that were just as sinful as he was? It seemed so humbling to me.

But it also told me that something was happening in that service that I missed. My father was the toughest guy I knew. He could be loud and angry. He worked long hours and was often exhausted when he got home. But in a service where God was speaking, he wouldn't hesitate to go forward.

I often wondered what it was that he received from God there at the altar. He always seemed more gentle, more sensitive to our needs after he met God there. More than ever it taught me, *Humble yourselves, therefore, under the mighty hand of God, that He may exalt you at the proper time, casting all your anxiety upon Him, because He cares for you* (I Peter 5:6–7 NNAS).

—**David Hahn**

Joy In The Midst Of Trials

Recently, our home Bible study group was studying the book of Philippians and our group leader asked some pretty tough questions. "In a group this size, many of us are bound to endure some serious challenges. Do you think you can experience His joy in the middle of your most feared circumstances?"

It was a tough question and most agreed we probably were not close to Paul's level of spiritual maturity. A few weeks later, Don was challenged in such an area. On a business trip, Don and Jerry, an associate, had a rather heated discussion.

"Wow, I can't believe you'd say that, Don! How could you possibly expect a teenager to go through with nine months of pregnancy and then give up the child? It would ruin her life. Wouldn't it be better to just terminate it in the beginning?" Jerry sighed with exasperation.

"Jerry, I'm not saying it would be easy for the girl. Making the problem just go away seems like the perfect solution. But that's because we often forget the real victim . . . the baby! Who's going to protect its rights, its very life?"

"Ah, come on, you don't think a six week fetus is a viable human do you?" Jerry countered.

Don answered slowly, his eyes fixed directly into Jerry's. "That's exactly what I think. It's what I know. God's Word says that He knows us even before we are formed in our mother's womb."

"Well, whatever, Don. I won't question your religious belief. Just think about what you'd really want *your* daughter to do if it happened to her! Hey, I gotta go. See ya next trip, buddy."

"Uh huh, next time Jer," Don mumbled back. He could not shake the image Jerry had suggested, that of having to face this issue personally. He'd just been talking to his wife, Sharon, about their sixteen-year-old, Sarah, this past weekend. Sarah had been a great student and a happy kid until she rebelled at thirteen with low grades and trying out drugs. Now she had continued a relationship with an older student for a year. Don and Sharon maintained tight boundaries and Sarah often complained.

Still, Don wondered, *is she crossing the line sexually?*

At the sound of his beeper Don snapped back to the present. "Hmm, it's Sharon, guess I better call her before the meeting," he thought.

When he reached her, she whispered, "Oh, Don. I don't know how to start. God's peace is carrying me through, but . . . Sarah's pregnant."

Don sighed deeply into the phone and took a few deep breaths. He felt the weight of the world on his shoulders. Feelings of anger toward her boyfriend, fear and anxiety all welled up in him at once. Then, a gentle tugging at his heart. He could almost hear Jesus saying, "Give it to me, let it go, Don. It's too big for you."

"Sharon, tell Sarah I love her," his voice cracked. "Tell her not to be afraid."

"Don, I think she was in shock that I didn't yell or scream. She thought she was going to ruin our lives!" Sharon's voice was wavering as she swallowed back the tears. "You know the greatest blessing? She never once mentioned an abortion."

"What did you tell her?" Don asked, the reality beginning to hit.

"I told her that God will show us what's right for her and the baby, and we have time to make these decisions together."

"Wow! You won't believe the conversation I had less than two hours ago!"

"What conversation?" Sharon asked.

"I'll tell you later." Don stood there thinking, *I guess Jer will really see what it means to live my faith.*

"And, Don, she said she'd been praying that we wouldn't hate her and not throw her boyfriend in jail!" Sharon said and she began to cry. "She said that God had already answered her prayer. She could hardly believe how calm I was when she told me. All I could say was that I loved her and we would be here for her. You know, this is our chance to show her that God's unconditional love has no limits."

A few weeks later, Don shared his heart with our fellowship group.

"When we started studying Philippians, I couldn't imagine feeling joy in a trial like my family is in right now. I wanted to be there, but I thought I'd really have to work hard to see things from Paul's perspective. That's where I was totally wrong. It's not working or doing that brings the joy. When Sharon told me Sarah was pregnant, I just felt the Lord telling me to give this incredible burden to Him. And in that moment, in obedience, I did."

"And the Lord flooded us with incredible peace," Sharon added. "We don't know how this journey will end. Sarah wants to keep the baby. We have so many things to think about. But, God is so faithful. We know that this little life is not an accident. We're trusting Him right now to show us what He would have us do. We're claiming His promise that we can do everything through Him who gives us strength."

—Lewis Boore

On His Shoulders

I was seventeen and off to college. Excited. Scared! Dad and I stood on the platform of the little brick railway station in Paducah, Kentucky, waiting for the 2:37 a.m. train. We were all alone. It was one of those quiet, still black nights, fog engulfing the station. The lights down the line looked like fuzzy glow-worms. The only sound was the rid-idit-tit of the telegraph key. We looked through the station window and saw the operator with his green eye shade and the green shaded lamp.

Then, almost as if on cue, we heard the train whistling over the river trestle and coming up through the glade some mile and a half down the track. It was then that Dad turned toward me and took my hand. He looked deeply into my eyes.

"You know, son, the years pass quickly," he said. "Yesterday you were a baby and today you are a young man. There seems to be so many things we need to talk about, and now there isn't any time left. Life is full of so much pain and suffering. I wish I could live that part for you. But that would cheat you, deny your quest for yourself."

I knew all this was difficult for him. It was difficult for me too. We had always been close, but I wouldn't say that either of us had been expressive of, or in touch with our feelings. We were just deeply fond of one another.

"Son," he said, as he continued to hold my hand, "this is a very special time for you. You're going to college, something I was never able to do, but always wanted for you. Stand tall, son, stand on my shoulders. Stand and reach for the stars. Reach for all those things I couldn't reach for."

At that moment the train glided into the station, engulfing us in a cloud of steam, and when it cleared we still stood there hand in hand, clinging to one another as best we could. Hugs between men were a bit foreign in those days.

"Bye Dad. Thanks for everything," my voice cracked with emotion. I squeezed his hand a little harder. Then I boarded the train.

I found a window seat and looked down at that lone, solitary figure on the platform, neither of us knowing what more to say. It wasn't just glass that separated us. I think both of us knew that if there were any more words I'd burst out crying. I was leaving my first, best friend behind, going off without him, doing things he had only dreamed of . . . and dreamed of for me.

And I knew that inside Dad there was a tearing and a crying out. But he'd learned long ago to hold himself, his life being full of pain and great sorrow after the loss of his own father at the age of twelve.

Suddenly we were moving and I waved, and so did he, and the distance between us grew until finally no matter how hard I pressed my face against the window, I could no longer see him. Then my tears finally came.

And now a half century later they come again as I write of that time. Those words . . . . "Son, stand tall, stand on my shoulders, stand and reach for the stars, reach for the things I couldn't reach for," have gone before me as a guidepost, as a beacon. My father's love, integrity and commitment are what I stand on, what my foundation is built of. And on many a dark night in my life I have leaned on all that I saw in him, and wanted to find in me.

Last year Dad went to his Heavenly Father. I grieve his absence. But I celebrate his life. Today I still stand on his shoulders. I still reach for the stars.

—**Charles R. Flowers**

Quality Time

My father died when I was ten years old. As a result, I don't have many memories of him, but those I have are very intense ones. One of these memorable experiences happened in the mid-1950's. My dad had a flattop haircut, as did nearly everyone else back then. We were riding in a 1955 Buick with the windows open. It was a beautiful spring afternoon as we drove through the countryside. The warm air rushed against my face as I stood in the back seat, my arms wrapped around his neck. He drove with his left hand and reached his right hand behind him hugging my neck. He was wearing Old Spice after-shave that I can still smell. I heard him say, "I love you, Son." And I replied, "I love you too, Daddy."

The entire exchange probably took less than ten seconds. But it was very intense. Its' impact will last my entire life. Soon after that interaction my father died. If he were still alive, he probably wouldn't even recall the incident. It may have meant very little to him. But it was an eternal gift to a young boy who mourned his father's death a year later.

Years later I understood why this moment with my father was etched so deeply in my memory. As I recall the incident, I can feel the wind in my face, smell his cologne, see the flowers and greenery of that spring day, and hear the love in his voice. It epitomized what is commonly called today, "quality time." Quality time can be brief and intense. But its primary characteristic is that it involves all the senses. These intense moments can be life-changing.

When one of my sons was only two years old, we first shared the splendor of focused time together while snow skiing. I was delighted to discover that tiny boots and skis were made for children his age. I fitted him with a set and off we went. Skiing, though fun, is work for me. To him it seemed to be no work at all. I spread my skis and inverted them into a snowplow. Placing him and his skis between mine, I leaned over, grasped his shoulders, and we swooped down the slope.

By the end of the day we had skied most of the beginner and intermediate slopes. My back, thighs, and arms all throbbed. But the profound joy we shared during that experience far outweighed the pain. Our intensity was composed of several key factors—physical contact, shared experience, cold air, speed, wind against our skin, conversation, and high emotion.

The experience was made more memorable by an event that could have resulted in a serious accident. Toward the end of our time on the slopes, we became rather confident skiing this way. At one point, we went down a slope where we probably should not have been. However, there were other novice skiers playing around in this general area. As we were going down the run, I noticed a narrow area we had to pass through. A beginning skier snowplowed slowly back and forth through the pass. I gave the customary advance warning, and called, "Passing on your right . . . passing on your right . . ." In response, the beginner mistakenly turned to the right in our direction. I was cautiously observant and noticed him heading toward us. In response, I protectively prepared a forearm lift that only a former linebacker could manage. I was going to protect my child at all costs. I swung as we collided, and he went soaring through the air and landed in a ditch. My son and I fell safely to the snow. We were unhurt but covered from head to toe with snow.

I was nervous that my son may have been injured, but to my relief he was laughing gleefully. He suggested, "Let's do it again, Daddy!" We took off our skis and walked back toward the unfortunate recipient of our cannon-ball express. As we neared, I overheard an argument near the collision point. As I got closer I realized that what I heard was his wife berating him.

"Didn't you hear him say he was passing on the right?" she shouted. "He had a baby with him, you idiot!"

I intervened on the poor man's behalf and explained that I was probably going too fast for the conditions. She didn't seem to be interested in my explanation. After a few minutes, I suggested

I'd be glad to work with them as a marriage counselor, then laughingly left.

That experience happened over a dozen years ago, yet it never fails. Each year, as Fall begins to evolve into winter, my son will come and ask me if we're going skiing this year. And then he'll ask me if I remember those incidents that happened when he was only two. He remembers it today as intensely as I remember the brief quality time with my father. That is the power of intensity. It is the gift of quality time.

—John Q. Baucom

Years ago, when my friend Louise would visit, my husband would sometimes entertain her three-year-old son, Kerry. Roger explained the game Hide and go Seek to Kerry. But as soon as Roger called "Here I come," Kerry would jump out from behind the couch. "Here I am!" Kerry would shout as he leaped into view, his arms flung exuberantly overhead.

At first Roger tried to explain to Kerry that he must stay hidden until found. But finally, and wisely, Roger concluded that Kerry had grasped the true objective of the game. The joy is not in hiding but in finding and in being found.

I see the Lord standing there, like Kerry, with his outstretched arms: "Here I am. There is joy in finding me and my joy is in being found." As far as I can tell, everywhere, God is jumping out from behind couches in self-revelation.

—J. Fleming

Fatherhood Emotions

One of my favorite memories of my father's care for me is an incident from the summer of 1983 when I was 19. The previous February, I had been in a serious car accident, in a coma for several months, and in the hospital for six months. I had recently come home to continue therapy as an out-patient. I detested the changes in my life that resulted from being injured so severely. I could no longer walk without a severe limp, my right arm was weak and I spoke in a gruff monotone.

On a hot August day, some neighbors down the street invited us to swim in their pool. My mother, sister, and I eagerly accepted and walked over to join them. I had not been swimming since the accident, so I was particularly careful. I felt so cool and free in the water! It provided just the right resistance and support to enable me to move almost normally. I confidently held my breath to swim underwater . . . but I had "forgotten" how to hold my breath. I had no control of my breathing. When my face submerged, I panicked and inhaled. Water filled my nose, and I jumped up, sputtering and coughing.

I was disappointed, but laughed and tried to respond graciously to friend's and family's efforts to make me forget it. But it was yet another area of my life that, I thought, had changed forever.

We soon went home, and were almost in the door when it hit me: a sickening feeling below my stomach, like someone was twisting my intestines. I hurried in the door and rushed to the bathroom, but didn't quite make it, and my bowels let loose before I hit the toilet. What a mess—the stuff was everywhere. Frustrated and embarrassed, I cleaned myself up, went into the living room, and sat down on the couch and wept. I felt discouraged as I realized again how the accident had made me different.

My father had been in the next room, but now came and sat next to me. "What happened?" he asked.

Was he blind? He couldn't help but see what had happened. Had he lost his sense of smell?

"Oh . . . nothing . . . I didn't think this *stupid* accident would *completely* ruin my life," I said indignantly between sobs, hoping for a little sympathy.

What I didn't say, but I muttered to myself, *You don't know what it's like, so don't even try to make me feel better. Besides, what do you care? It didn't happen to you!*

I glanced up at him, expecting him to show that he was angry about the accident, too. But there were tears in his eyes. He was crying with me.

I had seen Dad angry, laughing, frustrated, happy, disappointed—but I had never seen him cry, and I doubt he's cried since.

I know there were other times, when I was comatose or when the doctors delivered discouraging news, that he undoubtedly felt like crying, but checked himself for the sake of the rest of the family. But after the swimming incident, he felt free to identify with my pain through tears.

It takes wisdom to know when and how to control one's emotions. That's one of the reasons I admire my Dad.

—**Bob Treash**

Dad's Dress Address

My 14-year-old daughter, Karis, called me at work one day. "Daddy! I just got back from the mall! I found the perfect dress for the Valentine's party at school. It's marked down to $30! I have $15, and I'll make the rest of the money I need at my baby-sitting job Saturday night. I just need a loan until Saturday night."

My first thought was, *Since when did Karis start buying her clothes?* Then I recalled that my wife, Darcy, had told her that if she didn't want to wear one of the many ideal outfits that were already hanging in her closet, she could get something else. But she would have to buy it with her own money. My second thought was, *Since when can you get a party dress for $30?* When I asked Karis, she said it was a clearance sale.

I told her I would "spot" her the money and she could pay me back the following weekend. She thanked me and hung up.

The next day Karis arrived home from the mall at the same time I was getting home from the office.

"I got it, Daddy!"

"Great! What did you get?"

"My Valentine's dress."

Once inside the house she said, "I'll go upstairs and try it on so you can see it."

"Great."

But as she ran up the stairs to her room I noticed the bag she was carrying was small enough to fit through the stamped-letter slot at the post office. Not the big box or the long, flowing dress in a hanger under plastic that I'd expected. I got worried.

Darcy was at the stove stirring something in a pan. I was reading the mail at the counter when Karis entered the kitchen. She beamed with pride as her eyes searched my face for approval.

I looked at the dress, then back at her face. I glanced at my wife. Darcy rolled her eyes; she was thinking the same thing I was.

I turned to Karis again, "I can see why you wanted that dress. You look fantastic in it. It's cute, and so are you."

She told me she had hunted through a lot of stores and fell in love with the dress as soon as she saw it. But I didn't hear much of what she was saying. A war was going on in my head. The dress *did* look great on her, but it wasn't much of a dress—literally.

Karis is built just like her mom—tall and statuesque. The junior-high boys at the party would have enough problems with their eyes and their hormones without "stoking the fire."

I didn't want to break my daughter's heart. I understood her wanting a dress like that. It was the kind other girls her age were wearing. I remembered picking her up at the Christmas dance and noticing many of her friends in dresses that were next to nothing—skimpy, tight-fitting outfits. I also remembered the thought that crossed my mind when I saw their dresses: *Where in the world are those girls' fathers? Are they sleepwalking through the teenage years?*

"Karis, honey, your dress is cute. But I have one problem with it. You see, dresses are supposed to be high at the top and low at the bottom. Somehow yours got turned upside down." I went on to explain a little about how junior-high boys, even conscientious ones, are "wired."

I could see her countenance fall. She had already pictured herself wearing that dress at the party, and now her "old-fossil dad" was about to ruin her plans. She defended why she thought it was OK, and I let her voice her views. Then I suggested that we think about it for 24 hours. I wanted to make sure that I was being reasonable and that Karis would have time to consider my concerns. My wife told me later that she was glad I hadn't pushed the decision to finality in the heat of the moment.

The next afternoon I called my daughter from the office. "Karis, did you get a chance to think anymore about the dress?"

Her response nearly knocked me out of my chair. "Dad, I really like the dress, and I'd really like to keep it, but I decided to do whatever you want me to do and not complain about it." The secretaries had to jump-start my heart. I couldn't believe what I was hearing, but I was grateful nonetheless. My daughter is as capable of giving me a verbal run-for-my-money as yours might be, so I was surprised and delighted.

I told her how much I appreciated her great attitude and that it would help a lot in the position I felt compelled to take. In spite of how much she liked the dress, I wanted her to take it back. "But," I said, "I'll go with you to the mall and help you find the perfect dress for the occasion. If it costs more, I'll make up the difference."

As it turned out, Darcy took her to the mall. They found a gorgeous dress for the party. We nicknamed it "Plan B." It came all the way up to her neck and all the way down to the floor. Personally, I think it would make a great school uniform!

When you have to make an unpopular decision, you're in good company. If Jesus had caved in to popular opinion, none of us would be saved today.

—Tim Kimmel

Psychiatrists tell us that discipline does not break a child's spirit half as often as the lack of it breaks a parent's heart.

Availability Versus Structure

Availability is more important than structure. In other words, doing anything with your kids is more important than trying to devise a structured teaching moment. Let the activity provide the teaching opportunity.

My son wanted to help change a flat tire on my car. He couldn't loosen the lug nuts. He ran out of energy to unscrew them all. He couldn't lift the old tire off nor put the new one on. Once the new tire was on, he tried to get away with only putting on every other lug nut. It took twice as long with his help.

While he couldn't help me as much as he thought he could, he went away thinking he had helped me more than he did. The experience made a large spiritual impression on him. His self-esteem grew by a mile, and now he understands the concepts of diligence and excellence in a deeper way. Those are Biblical values, and I impressed them upon my son in a way that was natural, not contrived. I wasn't teaching him how to change a flat tire; I was teaching him how to be a man of God.

—**Patrick M. Morley**

4

Godliness

He must increase, but I must decrease.

John 3:30

"He Was A Saint"

I love to tell the story, of two brothers, known all about town for being crooked in their business dealings. They progressed from wealth to greater wealth until suddenly one of the brothers died. The surviving brother found himself in search of a minister who would be willing to put the finishing touches to the funeral. He finally made an offer to a minister that was hard for him to refuse. "I will pay you a great sum," he said, "if you will just do me one favor. In eulogizing my brother, I want you to call him a 'saint,' and if you do, I will give you a handsome reward." The minister, a shrewd pragmatist, agreed to comply. Why not? The money could help put a new roof on the church.

When the funeral service began, the sanctuary was filled by all the important business associates who had been swindled through the years by these two brothers. They were expecting to be vindicated by the public exposure of the man's character.

At last the much-awaited moment arrived, and the minister spoke. "The man you see in the coffin was a vile and debauched individual. He was a liar, a thief, a deceiver, a manipulator, a reprobate, and a hedonist. He destroyed the fortunes, careers, and lives of countless people in this city, some of whom are here today. But compared to his brother here, *he was a saint*."

I first told this story at a conference held in Amsterdam that was attended by ten thousand delegates from all over the world. When I later watched the response of the audience on video, every face was in uproarious laughter. It was understood by every person present because, no matter what part of the world we come from or what strata of society we represent, we must all admit our own shortcoming—that we only feel exonerated when we gauge our level of saintliness in comparison to someone else of lesser esteem.

—Ravi Zacharias

Kill That Tree!

The ficus tree in our front yard was a big selling point for us. Planted by the previous owner, it had grown higher than the roof line, provided a shady oasis in our yard, and gave the kids something to climb. It was an incredible tree—lush, green and healthy.

Six months after moving in, our sewer backed up. When we opened the front door for the plumber, his first words were, "ficus tree." When I asked for an explanation, he said, "You have a ficus tree. That's why your sewer is clogged."

"How do you know?" I asked. "You haven't even been in the house!"

"Because it's a ficus tree," came the reply. "It's the worst tree there is for sewers. I've been called to a house where there wasn't a tree for one hundred yards. But a football field away there was a ficus tree—and it clogged the drains."

"You're kidding!"

"Nope," he responded. "Those little roots find the little cracks in a sidewalk, swell up and destroy the concrete. I've seen it split a foundation. Are your toilets getting loose?"

"How did you know?" Both of our bathroom fixtures had lost their secure hold on the floor.

"Those little roots get into the sewer and work their way up the pipes. Sometimes they actually invade the wax ring that seals the toilet to the floor, and loosen its' grip."

By now I was worried. I pictured my house changing zip codes when I wasn't looking. I asked the obvious: "What should I do?"

He responded with the obvious: "Get rid of the tree."

"Just cut it down?" I said.

"Nope—if you do that, the roots will keep going. First, you have to kill the tree."

"So how do you kill a ficus tree?" I asked.

"With copper. Pound some copper spikes into the trunk and

wait about six weeks. The copper will poison the tree. Then when it withers, you can cut it down."

It worked. We cut the tree down, and haven't had any plumbing problems for the past three years.

Some sins are like ficus trees. They're comfortable, I enjoy the way they look, and they have great "curb appeal." I've heard they can cause damage, but I don't really believe it'll happen. Occasionally, I drop in some spiritual Drano to handle some uncomfortable result in my life—but the roots are still doing their damage. Finally, the Master Plumber comes along and says, "kill the tree and cut it down, or it will destroy your life."

It sure would be simpler if I planted the right tree in the first place.

—**Michael Bechtle**

Controlling Your Wait

We sat on the edge of the bed holding hands and staring toward the bathroom. I kept glancing at my watch as five minutes ticked slowly away.

Negative . . . no pink dot . . . and my wife and I continue our long vigil.

I remember well the day we had another negative pregnancy test and the phone call we received that evening from my younger sister.

"Guess what?" she exclaimed. "You're going to be an uncle again."

After several minutes of sharing her happiness, I hung up the phone and choked back the too-familiar emotions of a wanna-be-daddy.

"Why God? Why can't Susan and I have a baby? We'd be terrific parents. You know how wonderful we are with everyone else's children!"

My angry outburst, born out of years of infertility frustration, presented no new information to our ever-patient Heavenly Father. But it did help me realize something. Many times, enduring the waiting process has drained my strength and energy when God intended for me to rest while He worked out His plan.

Waiting is not a new phenomenon for most of us. My first lengthy experience came when I was a young adult in my mid-twenties. After a series of medical tests, the diagnosis was a chronic illness called ankylosing spondylitis, a form of arthritis that caused inflammation and pain in several of my joints, particularly my left hip. Even though I was young for a hip replacement, my health quickly deteriorated to the point that an artificial joint was the only logical form of treatment. The surgery was successful and dramatically improved the quality of my life. However, by the age of thirty-six the prospects of marriage and a family became more and more remote in my mind. But God had His own plan.

"Prepare yourself for marriage by learning what it takes to be a good husband," advised a pastor friend of mine.

He was also the one who asked me to teach a singles' Sunday school class at his church. On the fourth Sunday of teaching, I had only one student—an attractive single woman in her early thirties. Fourteen months later, that same woman became my wife.

Although it was our dream to have several children during the next few years, it was not to become a reality. In desperation I argued, pleaded, hinted, suggested, reminded, and bargained with God concerning our childless situation.

God, you know how virtuous we are, and we're talented with children. We'll teach four-year-olds in Sunday school, lead vacation Bible school, work with the first grade boys' camping program, and serve in the church nursery—if you bless us with our own kids. Lord, you don't want Your omnipotent status jeopardized by an oversight concerning our fertility, do you?

For all of my prayers, it didn't seem to move the hands of God to resolve our fertility problems. Now, in our eighth year of barren marriage, the best we can hope for is the dubious honor of becoming the Abraham and Sarah of the '90s.

Fortunately, I cannot control the duration or circumstances of life's waiting periods. I can only control the perspective with which I view this important period of time. My days of waiting are not over, but God is helping me to develop an attitude of excitement about what He will teach me as I wait. And that makes the waiting period just a little bit easier.

—Ed Horton

"Did What Again?"

Some time ago I was touched by what a brother shared with me. After having failed at a point of sin often besetting him, he had prayed, saying, "Lord, I don't even feel I deserve to come to You today about this . . . I've failed this way so many times. I'm here today because I did it again." Then, he said, "The Holy Spirit whispered the words of the Father to me, and said, 'Did what again?' "

"Did what again?" Can you hear it? It was only in that moment that my friend said he truly understood how fully Father God means, "Their sins I will remember no more." After we have confessed our sins, not only have they been removed completely from the books of heaven, but by His power God has chosen to remove them *forever* from His mind!

—Jack Hayford

After Sunday School one morning, a mother asked her little girl what she had learned. The daughter responded, "I learned how Moses built his pontoon bridge across the Red Sea, and how all these people were transported across, the bridge was blown up just as the Egyptians were coming across, and they were all drowned in the Red Sea."

The mother was astonished and asked if that is what the teacher had told her. "Oh no," the little girl replied, "but you would never believe what she really said."

That little girl is like a lot of people. They think that faith is believing what is not true. And for others, faith is little more than wishful thinking.

A Lesson On Forgiveness

In August of 1992, after much soul-searching, we announced our decision to move to Athens, Georgia, and assume the helm of Christian Campus Fellowship (CCF) at the University of Georgia.

The day before our departure, I rented the biggest moving van available and soon it was fully loaded with everything we possessed. Prayers and good-byes accompanied us as we started off on an exciting new adventure. My wife, Sheila, drove the car. I maneuvered the moving van. After several hours of driving and crying, we stopped for the night in Corbin, Kentucky, and celebrated our 14th wedding anniversary.

The next morning we all awoke early, ready to continue our adventure. As Sheila and our two daughters, Missy and JJ, got ready, I decided to check on things. After searching the parking lot, I returned to the room and announced, "I can't find the truck."

Sheila teased, "What do you mean you can't find the truck? How could you lose a moving van?" When I didn't tease back, they knew I was serious. The van was gone.

Empty words hung frozen in the air and all the color drained out of our lives. Missy began to cry. JJ sat staring at both of us. The seriousness of the moment began to sink in.

Over the next several hours we were caught in a blur of questions, police reports, calls to the moving company and trying to list everything in the moving van—all of our personal items accumulated over 14 years. All the while the giant cold fist of fear grew larger and larger. Reality loomed. We bravely hid the worst from our children. We refused to let fear reign, but what would we do? How could we survive? We had no savings, so how could we replace anything?

Our better judgment told us to pray. While none of us felt like praying, we agreed it seemed to be the right thing to do. Only a few months earlier, our family had experienced a preliminary lesson in forgiveness when a farm venture collapsed. That was the most serious thing we had ever had to forgive—that is, until now! The Scripture in Hebrews 12:1-2 spoke to us: *Wherefore seeing we also are encompassed about with so great a cloud of witnesses, let us lay aside every weight, and the sin which doth so easily beset us, and let us run with patience the race that is set before us. Looking unto Jesus the author and finisher of our faith; who for the joy that was set before Him endured the cross, despising the shame, and sat down at the right hand of the throne of God.*

Witnesses were looking on. Jesus was in charge. The weight of worldly goods was stripped away. God was going to use this experience in our lives.

The four of us knelt beside the bed, touching fingertips, and praying. I led as best I could, "Please, Father, help us to forgive those who stole our things. Don't let a root of bitterness grow up in us."

Sheila followed in a voice raspy from crying, "Thank you, Lord, for protecting us," and continued to cry softly.

JJ softly whispered, "Please catch the ones who did this and if you could, would you get my bike back?"

Missy silently nodded and added her few words, "Dear God, please help Mommy and Daddy get our stuff back."

In abject humility and simplicity, we prayed, not prayers of eloquence, but plain and simple heartfelt requests. In that few minutes of prayer, God granted us true forgiveness. His love carried us through the rock bottom hardness of that hour and through the next few months of rebuilding our lives. Neither of our daughters complained or whined about their losses.

When the police recovered our moving van, it contained my desk and a few cartons of books. God gave us exactly what we needed to get started at CCF. He would provide more later. A package of private love letters we exchanged while on a missions trip to Africa were strewn all over the truck bed. Picking them up and fathoming the invasion of privacy broke our calm countenance. Our tears flowed freely. The children helped gather the letters and retie them with a ribbon found on the van's floor.

Every year when our wedding anniversary rolls around, Sheila and I recount the theft. We thank God for His forgiveness and for enabling us to forgive. We continue to thank Him for His provision through His people. Our memory banks forever hold the image of going to the mailbox and receiving, over $16,000 in cash given over a period of two months. Along with this, we also received household goods, appliances, furniture, food and clothes. Many of these gifts are from people we've never met. Our family never suffered or lacked for anything.

We were able to say to our children, "That's what the church really is." Our family learned a valuable lesson in forgiveness. It cost us all that we possessed.

—**Timothy L. Hudson**

Good News And Bad News

One day, two elderly men were talking about their favorite sport—baseball. Discussing the "American Pastime" added purpose to their lives. Their dialogue, although often philosophical in nature, always alluded to baseball.

"Do you think there'll be baseball in Heaven?" Joe asked.

"Of course there will be," Mickey responded, "otherwise it wouldn't be heaven."

That evening Joe passed away. Then, one night while Mickey was sound asleep, Joe appeared in all his glory. He emerged as a bright light which emanated from the sky to the foot of Mickey's bed. As the light awoke Mickey, his face was flushed with fear and apprehension.

"Calm down, Mickey," Joe assured his friend. "Everything is going to be fine. I just returned to bring some good news and some bad news."

"What's the good news?" Mickey asked.

"The good news is that there is baseball in heaven."

"That's great," Mickey responded. "So, what's the bad news?"

"Well, Mickey, the bad news is, you're pitching this Sunday."

—**Eric Scott Kaplan**

No Instant Maturity

Waiting for God's timing is tough. You will struggle with it, and at other times you will fight it. But that's OK. It's part of the process as you learn to accept the control of the One whose thoughts are not your thoughts.

A young boy carried the cocoon of a moth into his house to watch the moth emerge. When the moth finally started to break out of his cocoon, the boy noticed how hard the moth had to struggle. The process was slow, exceedingly slow. In an effort to help, the boy reached down and widened the opening of the cocoon. Soon the moth was out of its prison.

But as the boy watched, the wings remained shriveled. Something was wrong. What the boy had not realized was that the struggle to get out of the cocoon was essential for the development of the moth's muscle system. In a misguided effort to relieve the struggle, the boy had doomed the moth.

God never allows the cocoon to open until the time is right. You may be feeling you will be plateaued forever. You may be discouraged because you have been stuck between floors longer than you thought possible. Don't lose heart! God is overseeing your struggle between floors. Remain open and teachable and at the right moment, He will do for you what He has done for so many others. He will provide a way of escape. And you will not only be free of your cocoon, but you will be fully developed and ready to fly.

Leonard Ravenhill tells about a group of tourists visiting a picturesque village. As they walked by an old man sitting beside a fence, one tourist asked in a patronizing way, "Were any great men born in this village?"

The old man replied, "Nope, only babies."

There is no such thing as instant greatness or instant maturity.

—Steve Farrar

"Are You God?"

Shortly after World War II came to a close, Europe began picking up the pieces. Much of the Old Country had been ravaged by war and was in ruins. Perhaps the saddest sight of all was that of little orphaned children starving in the streets of those war-torn cities.

Early one chilly morning, an American soldier was making his way back to the barracks in London. As he turned the corner in his jeep, he spotted a little lad with his nose pressed to the window of a pastry shop. Inside, the cook was kneading dough for a fresh batch of doughnuts. The hungry boy stared in silence, watching every move. The soldier pulled his jeep to the curb, stopped, got out, and walked quietly over to where the little fellow was standing. Through the steamed-up window he could see the mouth-watering morsels as they were being pulled from the oven, piping hot. The boy salivated and released a slight groan as he watched the cook place them onto the glass enclosed counter ever so carefully.

The soldier's heart went out to the nameless orphan as he stood beside him.

"Son . . . would you like some of those?"

The boy was startled.

"Oh, yeah . . . I would!"

The American stepped inside and bought a dozen, put them in a bag, and walked back to where the lad was standing in the foggy cold of the London morning. He smiled, held out the bag, and said simply: "Here you are."

As he turned to walk away, he felt a tug on his coat. He looked back and heard the child ask quietly: "Mister . . . *are you God?*"

We are never more like God than when we give.

God so loved the world that He gave . . . .

—Charles R. Swindoll

The Old You

Who you were before you got saved was nailed to the cross. Now this raises a question. If your old you was nailed to the cross, how come your old you is still kicking?

The reason is that the old you is so contaminated by the principle of sin that still pervades your body that the old you reacts almost like a reflex. Even though it's been crucified, your old self still reacts to sin as though it's alive.

Any mortician will tell you that cadavers can do very interesting things. For example, a dead person's hair and nails continue to grow for a period of time. One mortician friend told me that the cadaver sometimes quivers on the table, which explains why I will never be a mortician.

Another mortician told me that on one occasion, the cadaver had a muscular nerve reaction and actually catapulted itself off the table—which means that if I were there, there would have been two dead people in the room.

But it never bothers my mortician friend, because he says, "Even though there may be the quivering, jumping, nail-and hair-growing actions of life, I know and act on something the average person doesn't understand, and that is that dead is dead even when it acts alive."

So it is with you and me who are crucified with Christ. Even though sin still rears its ugly head because the sin principle is still around, you've got to know that it's your old cadaver wanting to act like it's alive. But you must recognize that it's dead because it was crucified.

—Tony Evans

Greatness Of Life

Jack King is a field representative for Christian Men's Network. We work, pray, travel, and serve together all over the world. He came to the ministry with a remarkable testimony.

"Execution Style Murder" screamed the newspaper headlines when Jack's father was found murdered by gun shots to the face. For years Jack carried a gun and spent most of his time planning to bring to justice the man who murdered his dad. A former U.S. Army Drill Sergeant, Jack had a rugged toughness that translated into a keen sense of hatred for the killer and a thirst for revenge. Worst of all, he believed he knew who the killer was—a business associate of his father's.

Then Jack was converted and Jesus Christ transformed his life, instantly releasing him from his intense hatred. But even as a recreated man, that hurt of his dad's murder lingered in his heart. One evening, during a church service, Jack heard God's Word that if he didn't forgive, God wouldn't forgive him. At that moment he prayed and asked God to forgive him for the hatred and murderous attitude he once had. He believed God heard and answered his prayer, but he was unprepared for the immediate test God gave.

A few evenings later his wife asked him to go to the meat market for some ground beef. As he drove through the darkness, he saw a commotion from a fire on the next street. As Jack drew closer, he recognized the location as the warehouse where he had found his murdered father, now owned by the man Jack had believed responsible for the execution.

Thinking to himself, "It serves him right," Jack continued onto the store. However, a "small voice" told him he needed to go find that man and ask his forgiveness. When he left the store and started home he found he could not silence that inner voice and spontaneously turned down the other street to see if he could find his former enemy.

Getting out of his car at the spot where his father had died, Jack walked up the darkened alley to examine the chaos and see if he could find the business associate. In the flashing lights of the fire trucks, Jack saw another man standing in the darkness with him. Peering through the dark and smoke, Jack saw it was the very man he was after. Summoning every fiber of strength, he took a step toward him and asked, "Do you know me?"

"You look familiar," was the clipped reply.

"I'm Jack King."

Despite the darkness, Jack could see the man blanch with fear. Later, Jack learned that the man thought he had set the fire and now wanted to complete his revenge.

"God has changed my life," Jack told him, "and I've come to ask you to forgive me for accusing you of my dad's murder. I'm trying to make the things right that I did wrong before my conversion. One of the things I need to do is ask you to forgive me for my hatred and for haunting you these past few years. And for trying to ruin your life, your family, and your career."

"Yeah, well—" was the reply.

"I want you to forgive me for all the harm I've done to you," Jack pressed. "Please forgive me."

"No problem. You're forgiven," the man said quickly, apparently wanting the conversation to end.

"No," Jack persisted, growing stronger with every word, "I mean really forgive me, not just in saying it, but in living it. I never want to offend you or hold ill-will against you again. I want you to know that."

There was a long pause. Finally, the man let out a deep sigh and affirmed his forgiveness. Jack held out his hand and they shook on it.

With the awkwardness now over, Jack spent the next half hour telling his former enemy of how Christ had changed his life and what it meant to his family. The conversation ended with Jack praying the prayer of salvation with the man. Then Jack impulsively threw an arm around the man and the two wept on each other's shoulders as the years of hurt, hatred, and fear melted away.

On the way home, Jack's tears were almost a hazard to his driving. The emotion-packed encounter had brought such release. Jack had the joy of knowing he had acted like a "real man." To this day Jack King is a new man. After all his "tough guy" days in football, the Army, and his career, Jack learned that accepting responsibility for his actions and making restitution gave him a sense of manhood not found anywhere else.

God never asked Jack to take on the responsibility of his father's murder. God is taking care of that. *Vengeance is Mine, I will repay*, says the Lord (Romans 12:19). Jack's responsibility was to have a pure heart, full of forgiveness toward others, so God would forgive him.

Individually or corporately, being responsible determines greatness of life.

—**Edwin Louis Cole**

5

Grief

Surely he hath borne our griefs, and carried our sorrows . . . .

Isaiah 53:4

Take Time For The Moment

In the past year, two men in our Friday morning Bible study have lost children. One died from a gunshot wound, the other in a motorcycle accident. One of them was David Baker.

A quiet teenager, David loved reading books and watching "Dr. Who." Countless volumes of science fiction passed before his eyes. Birds of prey especially intrigued David, and he earned a college scholarship for his volunteer work repairing the broken wings of eagles. He loved Christ.

Here are some excerpts from a letter I received from his dad:

One evening when I came home I was greeted by a tall, blonde teenaged girl whom I had never met. David had struck up a conversation with her in the grocery store and invited her to stay in our home. Her name was Debbie. Her parents had beaten her and kicked her out of their home. She was battered, physically and emotionally. She lived with us for five weeks, recovered, and now lives with an aunt. Debbie is now a Christian. David took time for the moment, and it made a difference.

I scolded David several times for not being home on time in the late afternoons. He said nothing in his defense for this repeated behavior. Only much later did I find out where he had been and what he was doing. One of his friends had an eye disease and was going blind. He was reading books to her. He took time for the moment.

One Friday afternoon about 3:45 p.m. I called my wife from work to tell her I loved her and see how her day was going. She told me that David had stopped by after work for a visit. I remember that day when I spoke with David, and he and I talked for a few minutes, arranging a shopping trip to buy his mother's Christmas present. We agreed to meet at 6:00 p.m. I told him I loved him and heard the reply, "I love you, too, Dad. Good-bye." David died in an accident fourteen minutes later.

How precious that brief moment on the telephone has become. How many fathers never hear those words? How many of us are too busy to take time for the moment. We are not really in a position to judge if we have time because we do not know what a difference that moment can make in someone's life.

That moment has caused me to care more, look deeper, search harder, pray longer, and seek understanding.

David left the legacy of taking time for the moment. He defanged much of the sting of his death. He left a treasure trove of memorable moments that helped anesthetize the awful anguish of his family. David learned to take time for the moment and left a heritage for his family. The lesson of David's life can be a heritage for us, too.

—Patrick M. Morley

An Encounter With Death

After working for years in the mental health field, I abruptly found myself unemployed. I took the first job offered—as a social worker in a hospice program. I had no prior experience with death and dying and was more than a bit nervous in this new endeavor. But I felt a "nudge." There was a purpose for me in this job.

One day I was visiting the home of a family new to our hospice program. The patient's wife, Norma, was unhappy with the way our phone service had worked over the weekend. I was there to reassure her. A family friend was in the back bedroom talking to the patient, Jack, while I spoke with Norma. Suddenly the friend called us back to Jack's room. His breathing was becoming more and more irregular. Jack was dying, and there was nothing anyone could do to stop it. Norma held Jack, the friend held Norma, and I tried to hold all three of them. Then Jack stopped breathing altogether, and we all knew he was dead. I was amazed at how peacefully it happened. Norma was crying, of course. One can never be fully-prepared for something like this. But the whole experience was . . . perfectly natural.

Not being a nurse, I really had nothing more to do at the home. Norma had moved out to the kitchen and was sitting silently in shock. Without knowing why, I moved behind her and placed my hands on her shoulders. I felt extremely awkward and out of place, but I didn't know how to disengage myself from the situation. So I just stood there. I knew any words would have been totally inadequate. I should have just quietly said good-bye and left, but I didn't. I just stood there, my hands on Norma's shoulders. I probably looked as foolish as I felt.

Norma called me a few days later. She was so grateful for my presence that fateful day. Me? What had I done? "You will never know what strength I felt pouring into me from your hands. I have thanked God so many times for your being there!"

I had felt myself almost an intruder, an inadequate and uninvited stranger in the middle of an intensely painful and private experience. I really shouldn't have even been there, right? Wrong! I had been led there. God needed me for His work. *My inadequacies were totally irrelevant.* What an exhilarating, yet humbling experience. I will never forget it. And I will keep obeying those "nudges," so I can be a conduit for the power of the Holy Spirit.

—Alan Willcox

Trained Up By My Child!

On Wednesday, November 25, 1987, the day before we were to give thanks for God's blessings, a gentle breeze of memories exploded, like a high mountain storm, into a howling wind of grief.

"Be thankful in all things? How is it possible, Lord? My daughter, Chris, died yesterday. For thirty-four years, You've loved me through her, and let me love her back. I miss her. I prayed for her healing. It didn't happen. How come?"

Two days before, my receptionist entered the dental operatory. "Doctor, your son-in-law, Jerry, is on the phone. He sounds urgent."

I took the phone. "Hi, Jerry, what's up?"

His reply was a jolt. "Chris is seriously ill."

Tiny needles stroked my neck. "What's wrong?"

"We're not sure. She's surrounded by specialists in the Intensive Care Unit here at St. Luke's Hospital. I thought you'd want to be here."

"Of course, Jerry, we'll be there as soon as possible."

"How could this be?" I thought. "I had stayed overnight with Chris and her family only five days before. Everyone was healthy and excited about our Thanksgiving celebration the next week."

I completed the patient's work while I prayed my throat would relax. Finally I could tell my staff, "cancel tomorrow's patients. I'll call later about any changes. Chris is very ill. Please, pray for her and her family."

At home my wife, Dot, sensed my anxiety. "What's the matter, Dick?"

My voice was octaves above its normal pitch. "Jerry just called. Chris is very sick. I'll tell you about it on the way."

Our moods matched the gray sagebrush flashing past as we raced for Boise, Idaho. When I told Dot Jerry's story, she asked, "How could she become so sick in such a short time?" I couldn't answer her. We prayed for strength for Chris and Jerry and our eight and ten-year-old granddaughters, Amy and Erica.

A distraught Jerry met us at the Intensive Care Unit. "It's been a hard fight. Earlier we thought we'd lost her. She's fighting back now. You can see her. She won't respond—but she'll know you came."

My daughter was a smiling, vivacious, blond extrovert who enjoyed life and people. Now I saw before me an unconscious Chris full of tubes, wired to blipping and flashing monitors, and struggling for every breath. Tears filled my eyes.

I leaned close to an ear I'd washed so many times and prayed, "Let her hear, Lord." Then I spoke, "Hi, Chris, it's Dad here beside you. Get well. I'll see you in the morning."

I stepped back. Dot moved close and touched her arm. "Hi, Honey, it's Mom. We're praying for you."

I wanted to hold my little girl and rock her back to health as I had so many times, but I had to step aside. This life and death battle required special nurses.

In the secluded waiting room Jerry said, "I want to tell my girls what's happening. They're staying with a neighbor."

After he left, I sat in the waiting room and wondered, *They've diagnosed a virulent pneumonia and are loading Chris with antibiotics. Is she reacting to the drugs? What else can they do to help her?*

When Jerry returned, he suggested Dot and I go to his house for some sleep. "It'll be a while before we know anymore," he said, "I'll call if anything develops."

He called at 5 a.m. Tuesday morning. "You'd better come over, things are going badly!"

This time a hospital chaplain waited with Jerry.

"She's doing poorly," Jerry said, "I want to be with her. Will you wait?"

Again, my mind labored: "Dear Lord, I don't understand. Children aren't supposed to die before their parents. Chris has so much to teach her youngsters yet. She loves you, Lord. She wants the world to love you. It can't be time for her to leave yet."

Jerry stepped into the room. His eyes were wet and his jaw

quivered. He managed a moment of stoicism. "It was a hard battle . . . Chris fought magnificently . . . but she lost."

We embraced and tears wet shaking shoulders. The hope to share Chris' love and inspiration in years ahead was gone.

As I journey through my grief process, soft breeze memories re-awaken howling winds of grief: sharing rides at Disneyland, shoe-skiing on a Norton Lake glacier, the agony of saying "No" to a peer-pressured teenager. But, as lichens cling to mountain rocks and withstand storms, I cling to God's promises and withstand the winds of grief because Chris taught me to read the Bible each day, and one day I read: *Brothers we do not want you to be ignorant about those who fall asleep, or to grieve like the rest of men, who have no hope. For the Lord himself will come down from heaven, with a loud command, with the voice of the Archangel and with the trumpet call of God, and the dead in Christ will rise first. After that, we who are still alive and are left will be caught up together with them in the clouds to meet the Lord in the air. And so we will be with the Lord forever* (I Thessalonians: 4:13, 16-18 NIV).

It was then I knew I had been trained up by my child. When I chat with Chris in God's Holy Kingdom, I will give her a special hug and say, "Thanks."

—**Dick Hagerman**

Measuring The Value Of Life

The value of life grows in magnitude when we stare death in the eye.

Death is no stranger to my household. I have hosted its' unwelcome visit too many times. The two visits I recall most vividly are the times the black angel came for my parents.

I remember my father's final words—how can I forget them? But what haunts me are my last words to him.

Death often leaves a burden of guilt to the survivors who are plagued by memories of things left unsaid or undone or of hurts imposed on the deceased. My guilt resides in the insensitive, nay, the stupid words I said to my father. I said the wrong thing, the juvenile thing for which death gave me no opportunity to say, "I'm sorry."

I long for the chance to replay the scene, but it is too late. I must trust the power of heaven to heal the wound. What is done can be forgiven—it can be augmented, diminished and, in some cases, repaired. But it cannot be undone.

Certain things cannot be recalled: the speeding bullet from the gun, the arrow released from the bow, the word that escapes our lips. We can pray that the bullet misses or that the arrow falls harmlessly to the ground, but we cannot command them to return in mid-flight.

What did I say that makes me curse my tongue? They were not words of rebellion or shouts of temper; they were words of denial—a refusal to accept my father's final statement. I simply said, "Don't say that, Dad."

In his final moments my father tried to leave me with a legacy to live by. He sought to overcome his own agony by encouraging me. He was heroic; I shrank from his words in cowardice. I could not face what he had to face.

I pled ignorance as I only understood enough of his words to recoil from them. He said, "Son, I have fought the good fight, I have finished the race, I have kept the faith."

He was quoting the apostle Paul's closing words to his beloved disciple Timothy (2 Timothy 4:7 RSV). But I failed to recognize that fact. I had never read the Bible—I had no faith to keep, no race to finish.

My father was speaking from a posture of victory. He knew who he was and where he was going. But all I could hear in those words was that he was going to die.

What impertinence for me to reply, "Don't say that." I rebuked my father in the most valiant moment of his life. I tramped on his soul with my own unbelief.

Nothing more was said between us—ever. I put his paralyzed arms around my neck, hoisting his useless body partially off the ground, supporting him on my back and shoulders, and dragged him to his bed. I left his room and shifted my thought to my homework assignments.

An hour later my studies were interrupted by the sound of a crash from a distant part of the house. I hastened to investigate the sound. I found my father sprawled in a heap on the floor with blood trickling from his ear and nose.

He lingered a day and a half in a coma before the rattle of death signaled the end. When his labored breathing stopped I leaned over and kissed his forehead.

I did not cry. I played the man, being outwardly calm through the following days of funeral home visitations and burial in the grave. But inside, I was devastated.

How much value did my father have to me then? I would have done anything I could, given everything I had, to bring him back. I had never tasted defeat so final or lost anything so precious. That was 34 years ago, but it does not require a psychiatrist to recognize that I am not over it yet.

—R. C. Sproul

Real Tears

We live by a cemetery. Which means we have quiet neighbors. It also means we have to face our mortality on a daily basis. However, most of the time we choose to admire the beautiful trees, because the colorful leaves divert our attention from the reality of the burial grounds.

Last Saturday, there was a burial in the early afternoon. As we drove by I didn't say anything. But my young son took it all in. (People my age look straight ahead as they go by funerals.)

A few moments later, my son said, "I just saw a man crying." As I wondered why that might be a strange thing for a funeral, he added, "I've never seen a man cry . . . except on television, where it isn't real." I wanted to tell him about the times I had cried but that suddenly seemed too defensive.

I decided it was good enough that our son is beginning to know the difference between what is and isn't real. Maybe I should take him by the cemetery more often and not look at the road or the sky or the trees, but to look into our feelings. And share them. Because God gave us those expressions of joy, grief and sadness. Sometimes it's all right to cry. Even if we are men.

—**Paul Budd**

Final Words, Final Acts

In a recent trip to my hometown I took some time to go see a tree. "A live oak tree," my dad had called it (with the accent on "live"). It was nothing more than a sapling, so thin I could wrap my hand around it and touch my middle finger to my thumb. The West Texas wind scattered the Fall leaves and caused me to zip up my coat. There is nothing colder than a prairie wind, especially in a cemetery.

"A special tree," I said to myself, "with a special job." I looked around. The cemetery was lined with elms but no oaks. The ground was dotted with tombstones but no trees. Just this one. A special tree for a special man.

About three years ago Daddy began noticing a steady weakening of his muscles. It began in his hands. He then felt it in his calves. Next his arms thinned a bit.

He mentioned his condition to my brother-in-law, who is a physician. My brother-in-law, alarmed, sent him to a specialist. The specialist conducted a lengthy battery of tests—blood, neurological, and muscular—and he reached his conclusion. Lou Gehrig's disease. A devastating crippler. No one knows the cause or the cure. The only sure thing about it is its' cruelty and accuracy.

I looked down at the plot of ground that would someday entomb my father. Daddy always wanted to be buried under an oak tree so he bought this one. "Special order from the valley," he had boasted. "Had to get special permission from the city council to put it here." (That wasn't hard in this dusty oil field town where everybody knows everybody.)

The lump got tighter in my throat. A lesser man might have been angry. Another man might have given up. But Daddy didn't. He knew that his days were numbered so he began to get his house in order.

The tree was only one of the preparations he made. He

improved the house for Mom by installing a sprinkler system and a garage door opener and by painting the trim. He got the will updated. He verified the insurance and retirement policies. He bought some stock to go toward his grandchildren's education. He planned his funeral. He bought cemetery plots for himself and Mom. He prepared his kids through words of assurance and letters of love. And last of all, he bought the tree. A live oak tree. (Pronounced with an accent on "live.")

Final acts. Final hours. Final words.

They reflect a life well-lived. So do the last words of our Master. When on the edge of death, Jesus, too, got his house in order:

A final prayer of forgiveness.
A plea honored.
A request of love.
A question of suffering.
A confession of humanity.
A call of deliverance.
A cry of completion.

Words of chance muttered by a desperate martyr? No. Words of intent, painted by the Divine Deliverer on the canvas of sacrifice.

Final words. Final acts. Each one is a window through which the cross can be better understood. Each one opens a treasury of promises. "So that is where you learned it," I said aloud as though speaking to my father. I smiled to myself and thought, "It's much easier to die like Jesus if you have lived like Him for a lifetime."

The final hours are passing now. The gentle flame on his candle grows weaker and weaker. He lies in peace. His body dying, his spirit living. No longer can he get out of bed. He has chosen to live his last days at home. It won't be long. Death's windy draft will soon exhaust the flickering candle and it will be over.

I looked one last time at the slender oak. I touched it as if it had been hearing my thoughts. "Grow," I whispered. "Grow strong. Stand tall. Yours is a valued treasure."

As I drove home through the ragged oil field patchwork, I kept thinking about that tree. Though feeble, the decades will find it strong. Though slender, the years will add thickness and strength. Its' last years will be its best. Just like my father's. Just like my Master's. "It is much easier to die like Jesus if you have lived like him for a lifetime."

"Grow, young tree." My eyes were misting. "Stand strong. Yours is a valued treasure."

He was awake when I got home. I leaned over his bed. "I checked on the tree," I told him. "It's growing."

He smiled.

—Max Lucado

The Journey

It was well-known author and pastor Charles Allen who first told the story of a little lad named John Todd, born in Rutland, Vermont, in the autumn of 1800. Shortly after the boy's birth, the Todd family moved to the little village of Killingsworth. It was there, when John was only six, that both his parents died. All the children had to be parceled out among relatives. A kind-hearted aunt who lived ten miles away agreed to take John, to love and care for him, and give him a home.

The boy lived there for some fifteen years and finally left as he went on to school to study for the ministry. Time passed gently as he began and later excelled in his work as a pastor. While he was in middle life, his elderly aunt fell desperately ill. Realizing death was not far off, in great distress she wrote her nephew. The pitiful letter included some of the same questions all of us must one day ask: "What will death be like? Will it mean the end of everything?" Fear and uncertainty were easily traced in the quivering lines of her letter.

Moved with compassion and swamped with the memories of yesteryear, he wrote her these words of reassurance:

> It is now thirty-five years since I, a little boy of six, was left quite alone in the world. You sent me word you would give me a home and be a kind mother to me. I have never forgotten the day when I made the long journey of ten miles to your house in North Killingsworth. I can still recall my disappointment when, instead of coming for me yourself, you sent your colored man, Caesar, to fetch me. I well remember my tears and my anxiety as, perched high on your horse and clinging tight to Caesar, I rode off to my new home. Night fell before we finished the journey, and as it grew dark, I became lonely and afraid.
>
> "Do you think she'll go to bed before I get there?" I asked Caesar anxiously. "O no," he said reassuringly. "She'll sure

stay up FOR YOU. When we get out of these here woods you'll see her candle shining in the window." Presently we did ride out in the clearing and there, sure enough, was your candle. I remember you were waiting at the door. You put your arms close about me as you lifted this tired and bewildered boy down from the horse. You had a big fire burning on the hearth and a hot supper waiting on the stove. After supper, you took me to my new room. Then, you heard my prayers and sat beside me until I fell asleep.

You probably realize why I am recalling all this to your memory. Some day soon, God will send for you, to take you to a new home. Don't fear the summons—the strange journey—or the dark messenger of death. God can be trusted to do as much for you as you were kind enough to do for me so many years ago. At the end of the road you will find love and a welcome waiting, and you will be safe in God's care. I shall watch you and pray for you until you are out of sight. Then I'll wait for the day when I, too, shall make the journey and find you waiting at the end of the road to greet me.

I can hardly read those words without choking back the tears. Not only is it a beautiful, true story, it is the hope of all who serve. It is the way it will be. It is the *Well done, good and faithful servant* we shall hear. As the letter indicates, we are expected. He is waiting to welcome us. To those who serve, to those who stand where Jesus Christ once stood many years ago, He promises a reward. And we can be sure He will keep his promise.

—**Charles R. Swindoll**

Be Ready

I'll never forget one evening when the phone rang and my wife, Pat, answered it. She hurriedly walked into the living room with the cordless receiver held to her ear.

Over the clinking sounds of plates and bowls, I heard a few sniffles and her voice crack. But she quickly regained her composure. From the single side of the conversation I could hear, I thought one of her grade school students might be seriously ill or hurt. Pat's voice faltered again as she said, "Thanks for calling, pastor."

I toweled my hands dry and went into the living room. "What's wrong?" I asked. The theater in my mind pictured a student lying in a hospital bed surrounded by balloons and flowers.

"Jan Boyd just died," she managed to say.

"No! Not Jan—it can't be!" I uttered the words in disbelief and rushed to my wife's side as I thought of our friend. Our children joined us as we wept and sobbed from the shocking news.

Jan was only 39 years old and had been in perfect health. She had been a loving wife to Rod for 20 years and they were raising their four children.

The Boyds and our family had spent a great deal of time together before my work moved us from Illinois to Arizona ten years ago. Although many years and a thousand miles separated us, Rod and Jan remained our best friends. Just a few weeks earlier, Rod traveled out to fly-fish with me in the mountains. Pat had planned on mailing a letter to Jan the next day.

We learned that on the previous Sunday afternoon, Jan awoke from a nap with a terrible headache. When her breathing became irregular, Rod dialed 9-1-1. It was too late. She never recovered from a brain aneurysm.

She can't be dead. My mind tried to trick me into thinking it was not really true, but I knew, deep in my heart, that Jan was forever gone from this world. And it hurt.

My thoughts flashed back to the sermon in church that very morning. Our pastor had read Jesus' words from Luke 12:40 (NIV):

You must be ready, because the son of man will come at an hour when you do not expect him.

Clearly, the message was regarding Christ's Second Coming, but the words burned into my heart. I realized the urgency of preparing daily to meet my Lord face-to-face—either at the rapture or through death.

Of all the people I have ever known, Jan was one of the most ready to see her Savior. She was not afraid of death and talked about it openly. My wife found a letter Jan wrote less than six months before she died. She penned these words:

"A little sad that another Christmas has passed. What if this is our last year on earth? I want to dwell on knowing God better this year. To improve in my spiritual life!"

Our friend could not have known at the time she would not live to see another Christmas on earth. But her attitude was one of constant readiness.

As my family endeavored to accept the finality of Jan's death, I thought again of the succinct words from the morning's sermon: "Be ready!"

—**Dave Getz**

6

Marriage

Husbands, love your wives, even as Christ also loved the church, and gave himself for it.

Ephesians 5:25

"Shoooooppping"

After a tearful session with my wife, I decided to commit myself wholeheartedly to understanding and relating to her. But I didn't know where to start.

Suddenly, I had an idea that I knew would get me nominated for Husband of the Year. I could do something adventurous with Norma—like going shopping! Of course! My wife loves to shop. Since I had never volunteered to go with her before, this would demonstrate how much I really cared. I could arrange for a baby-sitter and then take her to one of her favorite places in the world: the mall!

I'm not sure what emotional and physiological changes ignite inside my wife upon hearing the words "the mall," but when I told her my idea, it was obvious something dramatic was happening. Her eyes lit up like a Christmas tree, and she trembled with excitement—the same reaction I'd had when someone gave me two tickets to an NFL play-off game.

That next Saturday afternoon, when Norma and I went shopping together, I ran face first into a major barrier that bars many men and women from meaningful communication. What I discovered blew open the door to understanding and relating to Norma, and steered me toward emotional word pictures for help. Here's what happened:

As we drove up to the mall, Norma told me she needed to look for a new blouse. So after we parked the car and walked into the nearest clothing store, she held up a blouse and asked, "What do you think?"

"Great," I said. "Let's get it." But really, I was thinking, *Great! If she hurries up and gets this blouse, we will be back home in plenty of time to watch the college game on TV.*

Then she picked up another blouse and said, "What do you think about this one?"

"It's great, too!" I said. "Get either one. No, get both!"

But after looking at a number of blouses on the rack, we walked out of the store empty-handed. Then we went into another store, and she did the same thing. And then into another store. And another. And another!

As we went in and out of all the shops, I became increasingly anxious. The thought even struck me, *not only will I miss the half-time highlights, but I will also miss the entire game!*

After looking at what seemed like hundreds of blouses, I could tell I was beginning to lose it. At the rate we were going, I would miss the entire season! And that's when it happened.

Instead of picking up a blouse at the next store we entered, she held up a dress that was our daughter's size. "What do you think about this for Kari?" she asked.

Taxed beyond any mortal's limits, my willpower cracked, and I blurted out, "What do you mean, 'What do I think about a dress for Kari?' We're here shopping for blouses for you, not dresses for Kari!"

As if that wasn't bad enough, we left that store without buying anything, and then she asked if we could stop and have coffee! We'd already been at the mall for sixty-seven entire minutes, which beat my previous endurance record by *half an hour.* I couldn't *believe* it—she actually had the nerve to want to sit around and discuss the kids' lives!

That night, I began to understand a common difference between men and women. I wasn't shopping for blouses . . . I was *hunting* for blouses! I wanted to conquer the blouse, bag it, and then get back home where important things were, like my Saturday-afternoon football game!

My wife, however, looked at shopping from opposite extremes. For her, it meant more than simply buying a blouse. It was a way to spend time talking together as we enjoyed several hours away from the children—and Saturday afternoon football.

Like most men, I thought a trip to the mall meant going shopping. But to my wife it meant *shooooopppping!*

—**Gary Smalley**

The Angel And The Teddy Bear

A few years ago my wife and I attended a retreat for married couples. We were having some serious marital difficulties, mostly because of my outbursts of anger and rage that I could not explain nor at times control. We attended the retreat as a last resort to save our marriage. One afternoon we met with a small group of people who were assigned to listen to some of our problems and pray for us. I hesitantly shared about my anger and frustration, and my inability to get to the root of it.

One of the couples present at that meeting approached us later on that same day with a large brown paper bag and a card. When I opened the bag I was amazed to find a big cuddly brown teddy bear inside. I never mentioned anything about toys from my childhood during that prayer session. I asked them how they knew to buy a teddy bear for me, and they explained that during the prayer session one of them saw a brown fuzzy teddy bear in her mind and knew it was meaningful for me! They knew they had to go out and find one to give to me that weekend.

Upon receiving my new bear I began to cry and shared that my father was a very strict and sometimes cruel disciplinarian when I was a child. When I was six years old, I disobeyed my father. As my punishment he took my favorite brown teddy bear outside to the backyard incinerator and burned it. I never got over that loss, and developed a lot of anger and unforgiveness towards my father, which I could see had lasted for years.

I was so awed and deeply touched that this couple would give me back something that meant so much to me as a child. It also seemed to be directly connected to the years of unexplained anger that affected my marriage and family life. I was so profoundly affected by receiving the teddy bear that I got up on stage the last morning of the retreat to share what had happened to me that weekend. Without any embarrassment I held up my new brown teddy bear for everyone to see, with tears in my eyes and my wife standing by my side. That incident was the beginning of a long-awaited emotional healing for me as a man, and has transformed my unhappy marriage. I will never forget that weekend, the prayers of others who cared, and the couple who gave me back a missing link to my childhood.

—Mike Hayes

"When I said 'Tonight's the night,' George, what I meant was to take out the garbage!"

Born To Be Mild

When I was in high school, I owned a motorcycle. I've always enjoyed motorcycles, and hoped to one day own another. But with a wife and two daughters depending on me, I was reminded more than once that "motorcycles are too dangerous."

And so throughout our marriage, whenever it was my birthday, or if someone would ask what I'd like for a Christmas present, my standard answer was "a motorcycle." For twenty-four years this continued, but I could never justify the expense or get past my wife's reasoning that "it's too dangerous."

In the Fall of 1994, my desire for a motorcycle was strong again. I decided to appeal my case one more time, explaining logically that I have no expensive hobbies—power tools, golf clubs, fishing or hunting gear, etc. Having a motorcycle is something I would enjoy. It would be "my thing." I would really enjoy cruising the Wisconsin back roads on a sunny Saturday afternoon. This would be my recreation.

The arguments seemed to work. Joyce said. "Okay, if you can find the money, go ahead." And I did. A friend at church sold me his 1983 Honda Goldwing at a super price. On October 31, 1994, I drove it from Middleton to my home in Verona. When I pulled it into the garage I was surprised at my own reaction. I thought I would feel: "Wow! Here it is. I finally have a motorcycle!"

But my true feeling was more like: "So, now I've got it. Big deal." I re-learned a lesson at that moment that I knew was true all along. And it's this: Only one thing matters, and that's relationships.

Nothing is as satisfying as good relationships, first with my Lord, and secondly, good loving relationships with my family and friends. The motorcycle was really nice, but it didn't make me a happier person.

I put the cycle away for the winter. In the spring it was shined-up and ready to conquer the road. Alison, our adventurous 17-year-old, wanted a ride, and I was glad to accommodate her. I fired-up the cycle, let it warm up, and Alison climbed on the back seat. With helmet in place, I kicked the kick stand, and we promptly fell over.

Hmmm. Must be more to this than I thought. My neighbor rushed over to help me pick up the 700 pound machine. Then he suggested I may want to invest in training wheels.

I took it out for a few more rides, and I did okay. But every time I put Alison on the back, we would fall over. When we stopped, the trick was to get both feet planted firmly on the ground. But Alison was a good sport and didn't make too much fun of her dad. And she was getting good at helping me pick it up from the street!

That spring, my business forecast showed that it was going to be a rough year financially. My debts were mounting, income was down. I couldn't justify keeping an expensive toy while our debts mounted so I sold the cycle. I wasn't happy about it but I wasn't crushed either.

Two lessons stick with me today: First, channel my energy into good relationships because toys won't make me happy. Secondly, keep both feet planted firmly on the ground.

—Don Tofel

A Woman's Desire For Security

After speaking with thousands of women over the years, I am still amazed at how consistently the concept of security comes up on their lists of "most desirable traits" in a husband. Your wife needs to know that nothing on earth will separate you from her. That you took your marriage vows seriously on your wedding day. That you're committed to formulating a clear plan for growth for the entire family and then taking the lead in accomplishing it, no matter what the cost!

This desire for security isn't unique to American culture. As I have ministered from Romania to Africa, I've heard women express this same deep-seated need.

At one conference in Ghana, Africa, I saw men become so convicted about the need to provide security and honor to their wives that they'd stand up in the meeting and say, "My wife is a queen, and from now on, I'm going to treat her like that." Joyful smiles broke out on wives' faces throughout the packed auditorium!

But honor isn't just a matter of expressing it to our wives in public. It's perhaps even more powerful when it comes in private.

Recently, we've been honored to have as a co-sponsor of our seminars the wonderful people at DaySpring Greeting Cards. Why link up with them? Because women tell us that receiving a special card from their husbands is one of the primary ways they feel most honored.

Children get a sense of security and love from such cards, too—in honor of a good grade, a sports achievement, a nice art project, any all-out effort regardless of the outcome, or for no particular reason at all. Words of love and encouragement are always appreciated, and especially so when we've gone to the time and trouble to say them in writing.

Recently, at a gathering of almost 400 men, all leaders in their churches across the country, I was struck by a thought about honor that came to me right when I was speaking. I was saying that most men get really excited about symbols of accomplishment: golf trophies, tennis medals, diplomas, or mounted fish or game.

Spontaneously, I mentioned that I had recently caught a 27-inch Dolly Varden trout on a trip to Alaska and had just mounted it on my wall. And then I said, to their laughter, "I don't have a big picture of Norma at either my home or work office. But I've got trout I've caught mounted in both places!"

As the laughter poured in, my words suddenly caught in my throat. I had to stop and admit how amazing it was that I had never thought about that contrast before. Norma is of much higher value to me than any of the things I might accomplish, catch, or mount. Yet those "things" were more prominently displayed on my walls.

Rest assured that by the time you read this, two beautifully framed pictures of Norma will be hanging in prominent places both at home and at work.

—Gary Smalley

© 1997, Larry Thomas

"So as you embark on the sea of life . . ."

Passion

For a week or two, it was to be a sexual paradise. That's the way we had it pictured. Florida, the hot sun, the beach, and, best of all, the bedroom. Pure ecstasy. After a victorious and difficult struggle to remain sexually pure before our marriage, Lynne and I were finally going to get what we deserved. Sex. And plenty of it. That was before some cosmic sense of humor kicked in. Our honeymoon was a disaster. We could easily write a book of memoirs, *We Flopped in Florida.*

First came the sunburns. Severe ones. The kind that bring nausea; then blistering and peeling. Our cries of "I want you, I have to have you!" turned into "Don't you dare touch me!" While we were recovering from our sunburns, Lynne developed a cold sore. Not just an average cold sore, mind you: it stretched from her lip to the middle of her neck. I am exaggerating a little, but not much. I laughed about it. Lynne, not surprisingly, accused me of being insensitive. She didn't exactly feel like Cindy Crawford. That was our sexual debut.

The early years of our marriage didn't exactly scorch the planet either. Due to our ignorance and circumstances, we did just about everything possible to eliminate sexual fulfillment. I was a full-time youth minister and a full-time college student. We had two boarders and their dogs living with us in a two-bedroom, cracker-box house. Lynne had two full-term pregnancies, during which she was sick four to five times a day for nine months, and two pregnancies that ended in miscarriages, during which she was just as sick. Add to that the all-too-common inability to communicate about sex, and you get the idea. When we were hot, it was often in anger, not passion. We lived like this for years.

On our eighth wedding anniversary, I wanted to make up everything to Lynne. We would finally get to be the sexual dynamos we knew we really were. With the help of a friend, who was the manager of a hotel, I planned an elaborate anniversary celebration. A veritable sexual feast.

At first, everything went according to plan. We had a romantic dinner together, and then, after checking into our hotel, we were awestruck with our room; it was the mother of all honeymoon suites: mirrors everywhere, a huge Jacuzzi and sauna, and, in the center of it all, a bed on a platform. For the next few hours, we enjoyed all the accouterments. We watched a movie, lit the candles, and enjoyed the evening. And we were both confident that the best was yet to come. But time was slipping away; the midnight hour was approaching.

I decided to whisper something incredibly sensuous into my wife's ear, to plant a tender seed that would sprout into wild romance: "Honey, let's hit the sack," I blurted out. We blew out the candles, climbed into bed, and looked up at the mirrors. Just as I wrapped her in my arms, I heard her whisper, "The curtains aren't closed tightly enough."

It didn't matter to her that we were on the twenty-fifth floor. She said she wanted to sleep in, and the morning light would wake her. She got up. "Should I turn the light on?" I asked. "No," she said, and then I heard a strange noise, followed by a soft "Oh-oh." I turned the lights on. Lynne had walked into one of the four-cornered mirrors around the bedpost.

It took seven stitches to repair the damage to her forehead. Our passion was spent, not in a honeymoon suite but in the emergency room of a hospital.

—Bill Hybels

Making The Difference

"How would I tell my wife?" I thought as I sat numb and listless on the steps of our back porch. The weight from the day lay heavy on my shoulders. Seeing my wife pull into our driveway, I forced a smile.

"Craig, what's the matter?" asked Debbie, opening the car door. "Why are you home so early?"

Without a word, I walked over to her and gave her a long strong embrace. I looked into her eyes and said. "They let me go. Today was my last day at work."

"What!" my wife exclaimed. "How can that be?"

"Why don't we go inside and I'll tell you all about it?" I said putting my arm around her shoulder.

This was the third time in our five year marriage that I had lost my job. Each time my faith in God and in my ability to provide for my family was stretched to almost the breaking point. How much farther would God stretch me?

As we sat at the kitchen table, I told her how my boss at the recovery mission had let me go. I had spoken the truth to a probation officer about one of the men I counseled at the mission. The man in question was not working the program but was very popular, especially with my boss. My disclosure to the probation officer had cost me my job.

"Officially, they told me I was not a team player," I said. "I know and God knows that I did everything possible to work as part of the team. Up until today all my evaluations have been excellent." I shook my head in disbelief.

Silent moments passed as I remembered the shame of rejection as my boss walked me out to my car earlier that day.

"Craig," my wife said. "Are you OK?"

I reached out and held her hand. Catching her gaze, I said. "I'm sorry, Debbie."

"It's not your fault. God will provide another job." As the

words came out of her mouth, I noticed a small brown bag from the grocery store she had brought in from the car.

"What's that?" I asked.

Debbie sighed. "Well. I think I may be pregnant. So on my way home from work, I picked up a pregnancy test."

I smiled. "Deb, how many tests have you bought? I've lost count. Do you really think you're pregnant?"

"Well, there's only one way to find out," she answered.

Five minutes later my wife was yelling from the bathroom, "Craig!"

"What is it?" I said running to the room.

"Look," she whispered pointing to the plus sign. "I'm pregnant. I'm pregnant!"

We hugged and cried and laughed all at the same time. For two-and-a-half years since my wife's miscarriage, we had been trying without success to get pregnant.

"God has a sense of humor, doesn't He?" I laughed, holding my wife in my arms.

"He sure does," Debbie replied. "Well, His timing is always perfect so we need to trust that He'll provide all we need."

In the days and months that followed, my wife and I witnessed God's provision for us in the most incredible ways. For the entire nine months of Debbie's pregnancy, I was unemployed. Every day I sent out resumes or went on interviews. During those nine months, I collected unemployment (compensation) and Debbie continued to work part-time, yet we still lacked $300 each month.

Each month, without fail, God made up the difference. Sometimes it came through a check in the mail, through free groceries or an unexpected rebate. For the last few months of Debbie's pregnancy, an elderly friend who was receiving treatment for cancer, stayed in our home. She paid us $300 each month for a room. My wife's medical bills were paid in full through a medical continuation plan from my prior employment.

Our daughter Sophia was born on July 2, 1993. Two weeks later, God provided a full-time position for me as a social worker at a convalescent hospital. I viewed my work as a ministry and felt

God had called me there. As we had decided years before Sophia's birth, my wife stayed home full-time with our daughter. Each month we still lacked $300 for our bills, but each month God continued to provide for our financial needs. Living by faith was not easy but it had become a way of life for us. We waited in anticipation to see how God our Father would provide each month.

Recently, God opened up a new door of employment for me. My new job provides a larger salary which meets all our needs and more.

If it were up to me to decide how we had paid for our needs in the past, I would not change a thing. The peace and security God has given us over the years cannot be bought or taken away. He truly is our Provider, our "Jehovah-jireh." Without fail, God has made up the difference in our finances and in our everyday lives.

—Craig A. Nell

Meeting Needs

I was sitting in a marriage seminar when some curtained portion of my mind was suddenly jerked open. The speaker had been talking about how a husband and wife need to respond to one another's physical and emotional needs. In one chilling instant, I realized that 100 percent of my sexual energies had been devoted to figuring out ways for my wife to stimulate, please, and satisfy me, my ego.

It had never occurred to me that she might have sexual needs and desires, too. I just assumed she must need the same things I did. I had never thought to ask her about it or to look for reasons why she didn't feel sexually responsive to me at times.

Instead, if she frustrated my desires at all, I would become instantly angry. I would jerk myself over to my side of the bed and lay there with my back toward her, alone and brooding. I didn't even want her feet to touch mine. And when she would reach out to me in the darkness and say, "Gary, don't you want to talk?" I would pull away and tell her to leave me alone.

It had been like that since our honeymoon. Either she performed according to my expectations or I would slam the door on any communication at all.

I don't know how much of the seminar I heard the rest of that day. I guess I'd heard more than enough. My mind was blown open to the fact that most of my life had been centered on myself. For the first time (but not the last), I realized just how self-centered a man I am. I remember getting alone by the couch that night after Norma went to bed and falling on my knees. I confessed to God that I was the most self-centered person I knew, but that with His help I wanted to spend the rest of my life finding out how to meet my wife's emotional and physical needs.

I determined to back off trying to satisfy my own desires for a while, and wait on God to reveal Himself and His ways to me.

In the meantime, I did everything I could to focus on Norma's needs and wants.

Several weeks later, she grabbed my arm and looked me right in the eyes. "You haven't mentioned sex in three weeks," she said, "and I need to know what's wrong. Don't I appeal to you anymore? Have I done something to offend you?"

"No," I said with a smile. "I just want to concentrate on meeting your needs . . . for a change."

As Norma realized I was serious, an amazing thing began to happen in our bedroom. The more I focused on trying to please and satisfy her, the more I found my own needs fulfilled. We were both experiencing more joy and satisfaction in our sexual relationship than we ever had before.

I was reminded of the Lord's words that "whoever wants to save his life will lose it, but whoever loses his life for me will find it." If you give up your life—or part of it—for the sake of Christ, He always finds ways to give it back to you. You lose what you try to grab for and hold on to. You get back what you give up. It was a pleasant surprise for me as a young man to discover that the Lord's faithfulness to this principle held true even in my sex life.

—**Gary Smalley**

7

Integrity

Lord, who shall abide in thy tabernacle? who shall dwell in thy holy hill?
He that walketh uprightly, and worketh righteousness, and speaketh the truth in his heart.

Psalm 15:1–2

Patience

For several years two dozen men, (half were black and half were white) met each month on a Saturday morning. A racial disturbance in our city had prompted both groups of us to ask the same questions, "Who are these people, and how can we know them?" So we started meeting to find some answers. Our purpose was not to change the city, but to change ourselves, to learn how to love one another.

One day at lunch three of us were discussing an issue. The confident, radiant demeanor of one of the men, a black pastor, commanded respect. During our conversation, however, he made a radical statement about remaining patient that seemed out of character. Immediately, the two of us jumped on him like a dog on a bone.

He slowly turned his eyes to explore each of our faces; then he began to speak, deliberate and restrained. In the next few minutes he revealed an astonishing addition to my understanding of who he was.

"When I arrived at my first church," he began, "weeds had taken the place over. The building was in shambles. Five pastors had come and gone in three years. No one in the community had any confidence that I would be any different, so no one came to worship.

"My wife and I patched and painted and replaced the broken windows. Over time we restored the church building to a functional state. I made calls around the community, but still no one seemed the least bit interested.

"So, not knowing exactly what to do, I decided to prepare and preach my sermons as if the place were full. Every Sunday morning I stepped into the pulpit and preached my best sermons to empty pews—completely empty pews except for my wife. Every Sunday for three years I preached as though the place was packed, but in reality it was still empty."

"Finally, after three strained years, God gave us one family. He became my Sunday School superintendent—his kids were the only ones we had in Sunday School. Slowly, over the next few months, however, God began to bless. He rewarded my faithfulness all those years. My preaching to an empty church may not have been smart, but it was faithful; I was patient, and I persevered."

By now my friend and I had melted into an embarrassed puddle of humbled awe. We had questioned his radical statement about patience. The real lesson for the day was about jumping to conclusions, about not taking time to know the true identity of one we called our friend.

—**Patrick M. Morley**

Those of us who fish know that when you throw a lure toward the shore and reel it back in quickly, it skims across the surface of the water. The slower you reel the lure toward the boat, the deeper it goes. I find myself longing for a slower, more focused, deepening experience, not only with life, but with my Lord.

Pass The Hot Dog

During lunch at the Indianapolis Promise Keepers conference in 1994, we were all playing yet another game of "hall cramming." All movement had stopped as we waited next to the concession stand. The brother I was with decided to have a hot dog while waiting for lunch and bought one from the woman manning the stand.

Realizing that all the condiments were on the opposite side of the hallway (with probably forty guys in-between), he handed the hot dog to the stranger next to him and said, "Catsup and mustard, please."

The woman at the counter snickered, "You'll never see that again!"

Several minutes later when the hot dog returned, she just shook her head and said, "You guys must be Christians."

—Philip Wiese

The Test

Six minutes to six, said the clock over the information booth in New York's Grand Central Station. The tall young Army officer lifted his sunburned face and narrowed his eyes to note the exact time. His heart was pounding with a beat that choked him. In six minutes he would see the woman who had filled such a special place in his life for the past 18 months, the woman he had never seen yet whose words had sustained him unfailingly.

Lt. Blandford remembered one day in particular, the worst of the fighting, when his plane had been caught in the midst of a pack of enemy planes. In one of those letters, he had confessed to her that often he felt fear, and only a few days before this battle, he had received her answer: "of course you fear . . . all brave men do. Next time you doubt yourself, I want you to hear my voice reciting to you: 'Yea, though I walk through the valley of death, I shall fear no evil, for thou art with me.' " . . . He had remembered that and it renewed his strength.

He was going to hear her voice now. Four minutes to six.

A girl passed close to him and Lt. Blandford stared. She was wearing a flower but it was not the little red rose they had agreed upon. Besides, this girl was only about eighteen and Hollis Maynel had told him she was 30. "What of it?" he had answered, "I'm 32." He was 29.

His mind went back to that book he had read in the training camp. "Of Human Bondage" it was; and throughout the book were notes in a woman's handwriting. He had never believed that a woman could see into a man's heart so tenderly, so understandingly. Her name was on the bookplate: Hollis Maynel. He got a hold of a New York City telephone book and found her address. He had written, she had answered. Next day he had been shipped out, but they had gone on writing. For thirteen months she had faithfully replied. When his letters did not arrive, she wrote anyway, and now he believed he loved her, and she loved him.

But she had refused all his pleas to send him her photograph. She had explained: "If your feelings for me had no reality, what I look like won't matter. Suppose I am beautiful. I'd always be haunted that you had been taking a chance on just that, and that kind of love would disgust me. Suppose that I'm plain, (and you must admit that this is more likely), then I'd always fear that you were only going on writing because you were lonely and had no one else. No, don't ask for my picture. When you come to New York, you shall see me and then you shall make your own decision."

One minute to six . . . he flipped the pages of the book he held. Then Lt. Blandford's heart leapt. A young woman was coming toward him. Her figure was long and slim; her long blond hair lay back in curls from delicate ears. Her eyes were blue as flowers, her lips and chin had a gentle firmness. In her pale-green suit, she was like springtime come alive.

He started toward her, forgetting to notice that she was wearing no rose, and as he moved, a small provocative smile curved her lips. "Going my way, Soldier?" she murmured. He made one step closer to her. Then he saw Hollis Maynel. She was standing almost directly behind the girl, a woman well past 40, her graying hair tucked under a worn hat. She was more than plump. Her thick-ankled feet were thrust into low-heeled shoes. But she wore a red rose on her rumpled coat. The girl in the green suit was walking quickly away.

Blandford felt as though he were being split in two, so keen was his desire to follow the girl, yet so deep was his longing for the woman whose spirit had truly companioned and upheld his own, and there she stood. He could see her pale face was gentle and sensible; her gray eyes had a warm twinkle.

Lt. Blandford did not hesitate. His fingers gripped the worn copy of "Of Human Bondage" which was to identify him to her. This would not be love, but it would be something special, a friendship for which he had been and must be ever grateful. He squared his shoulders, saluted, and held the book out toward the woman, although even when he spoke he felt the bitterness for his disappointment.

"I'm Lt. Blandford, and you're Miss Maynel. I'm so glad you could meet me. May—may I take you to dinner?"

The woman's face broadened in a tolerant smile. "I don't know what this is all about, son," she answered. "That young lady in the green suit, she begged me to wear this rose on my coat. And she said that if you asked me to go out with you, I should tell you she's waiting for you in that restaurant across the street. She said it was some kind of test."

—S. I. Kishor

A Plan

Years ago as a rookie pastor in my first church, I met with a group of guys every Tuesday night. After the meeting, I went with one of them to a local coffee shop. It was the coldest night of the year, and I was "freezing," so I did something I never do. I ordered a cup of hot coffee. I never drink coffee. In a year's time I may drink three or four cups max. No kidding. I just don't like the stuff. But on that particular night, as we sat there and talked I was so cold that I had at least five cups of cream and sugar with my coffee.

I got home about 10:30 p.m., watched the late sports on the news, and went to bed. I couldn't go to sleep; I was wide awake. After about an hour, I went downstairs and turned on Carson. When Carson was over, I went back to bed, but no luck. I was so wired on caffeine, I couldn't blink my eyes, let alone close them. So I got up and read the new *Sports Illustrated* that came in the mail that afternoon. Now it was around 2 a.m., and I went upstairs to give it another try. At three o'clock, I got up to see if there was an old movie on the tube. There wasn't.

I was getting a little ticked by this time. I had read everything in the house, and there was nothing on TV. Then I got an idea. My subscription to *Time* had recently run out, and I decided to visit the local twenty-four hour convenience store to see if they had the new one. So off I went at 3:30 a.m. to find a *Time* magazine.

As I was looking for *Time*, I picked up *Newsweek* and flipped through it, then *US News and World Report,* and before I realized it I had picked up *Playboy* and was rapidly turning its pages. Suddenly, I came to my senses and thought, *what in the world am I doing? What if my wife were to see me doing this, or someone in my congregation? What kind of pastor would do something like this? I'm standing here like some kind of adolescent trying to get some jollies.* I felt utterly ashamed as I put down that magazine. I looked around and saw no one else in the store but the clerk. I assure you that I had not planned to pick up that magazine when I went into that store. But I did it. I'd been picked off in a weak moment.

As I was preaching the next Sunday, one of my points dealt with integrity. I commented on how easy it is to teach the truth without applying it to your own life. My greatest fear is to fall into the trap of teaching the very thing I am disobeying. So I did something extreme. I told the congregation what had happened to me on Tuesday night. I told them the whole story. I asked them to forgive me for being such a poor example. And that extreme decision helped me to decide that I never wanted to have that kind of humiliating experience again.

I learned a valuable lesson from that situation. From that point on, I developed a plan as to how I would handle pornographic material before ever entering any store or newsstand. I had to have a plan in place to defeat the sexual temptation that comes to me through my eyes. I learned that I must anticipate and determine how I will act before I ever get into a tempting situation.

—**Steve Farrar**

Humility

God is jealous. He hates pride. He has a way of putting us in our places. Sometimes He's kind enough to nudge us with something humorous. Like the time my eight-year-old was showing off my published works to the neighborhood kids and announced, "These are all the books my dad has read!"

They were impressed.

A flustered admirer, upon meeting her favorite author, gushed, "Once I put your book down, I couldn't pick it up again!"

"You write books, huh?" an unimpressed man once snickered to an author. "Must take you months. You could just buy one for about ten bucks."

A noted Christian pianist relates a true story that keeps him humble. He was practicing in an empty church sanctuary several hours before a concert when the custodian charged up the back stairway and burst through the door.

"Oh, it's you," he said. "I thought some kids were up here bangin' on the piano!"

—Jerry B. Jenkins

An Apology

Dale Galloway, my pastor, once did something that offended me. I went to see him about it. I told him I felt he was using me to accomplish his purposes. I said I wanted to help him, but I didn't want to be used or be seen as a means toward his goal.

I don't know what I expected. A denial, perhaps. Maybe an "I'm sorry if it looks that way to you, but that's not true at all." From a less-principled and more manipulative pastor, I might even have expected the approach: "You must be out of fellowship with God, or you wouldn't feel this way. How much time have you spent in prayer and Bible reading this week?"

Dale simply said, "I'm sorry. Please forgive me."

In that moment, he gained lasting respect from me. Was he guilty of using me, as I charged? I don't know. Somehow it doesn't seem to matter. I didn't want blood from him. I simply wanted an acknowledgment of my feelings and my worth as a human being and brother in Christ.

In asking my forgiveness, in acknowledging his imperfection, Dale did not grovel. He walked in the light, which made it possible for us to continue having fellowship with each other.

—Stanley Baldwin

Stop On A Dime

Allentown, Pennsylvania, has an efficient little airport that's as pleasant as any if you have to sit and wait. I was on my way home, and I missed my kids.

I often say it that way—that I miss my kids, without including the fact that I miss their mother, my wife, too. Dianna knows that missing her goes without saying. We're one. And when I am away and miss the kids, she feels for me, even though she might rather be with me and enjoy the chance to miss them a little.

One of the reasons I missed my boys was that I had just spent a couple of days in the home of Ron and Christine Wyrtzen. The popular Christian recording artist and her husband have an adopted daughter and son, and the very close and special relationship they all have can make you long for home.

Ron and Christine talk to their kids. They listen to them. They include them, care about them, treat them like equals. They don't pretend the kids don't need supervision, guidance, and discipline, but in the Wyrtzen home, children are people.

That environment stood in clear contrast to what happened at the Allentown airport on my way out of town. I sat near a mother and her four- or five-year-old daughter. Standing near us in the busy gate area was a middle-aged couple in animated conversation. As they chatted, the man pulled his hands from his pockets to gesture and a dime slipped out and bounced to the floor, rolling near his feet.

Neither the man nor his wife noticed. But the little girl and her mother did. The girl made a move for the dime, but the mother grabbed her arm. "I want that dime, Mommy," the girl whispered.

What an opportunity to teach a child ethics, fairness, politeness, courtesy!

"I know," her mother said, giggling. "Wait till they walk away."

"He doesn't see it!" the girl said.

"I know. Just wait." The girl fought against her mother's grip. "Just wait, honey," she said. "As soon as he leaves, you can have it."

The man and his wife looked toward the ticket counter. The mother and daughter tensed, smiling. When the couple began to move, I picked up the dime. "Excuse me, sir. You dropped this."

The man looked incredulous. "Hey, thanks a lot."

As I sat back down, I stole a glance at the mother and child. I wasn't trying to be self-righteous or smug. A dime might seem insignificant, but I grieved for that child and the values she was learning. I could only hope her saucer-eyed look indicated that she wished she had given the dime back to the man.

There was no question about the young mother's tight-lipped scowl. She wished I'd minded my own business. I wished her daughter was my business. And despite what I tried to say with a stern return of her gaze, I'm still kicking myself for not saying anything.

Like: "Great job of parenting, lady. I hope your daughter doesn't grow up to be a certified public accountant. Or a civic leader. Or a mother like you."

Mercy. It's better I kept my mouth shut.

—Jerry B. Jenkins

8

On The Job

And whatsoever ye do, do it heartily, as to the Lord, and not unto men.

Colossians 3:23

The Child Who Stumbles

Before we had to make the decision about amputating my arm, I started on oral antibiotics. That freed me up to resume my speaking responsibilities; but I found that traveling was harder on me than before. The sustained use of antibiotics was beginning to take its toll. And the continuing chaos around our house didn't help. My study was a mess. A landslide of mail covered my desk. Phone messages were scattered around like piles of leaves. And there were boxes of things people wanted me to sign—baseballs, baseball cards, pictures. There were speaking requests for motivational speeches and there were requests for me to be a spokesperson for certain political causes.

I was angry with myself for not being able to do it all. And I was angry for not being able to say no.

So much of my professional life had been concerned with pleasing other people—my manager, my teammates, the fans. When I became a Christian, God seemed like just another person to please.

Could it really be true, as C. S. Lewis suggested, that if only the will to walk is there God is pleased with our stumbles? Could He love me that way, the way a father loves his toddling child?

How could He? My prayer life "stank". I prayed out of desperation, not devotion. I felt I was drowning. I don't mean dangling my feet in the deep end of the pool. I mean I could feel myself going under. I called to the Lord the way Peter did when he walked on the water and started to sink: "Lord, save me!" I had so little time to pray, and when I did I felt guilty. After all, there were so many letters to answer, phone calls to return, baseball cards to sign.

So many urgent things.

A big reason why the requests were so hard on me is that I have a hard time doing something if I can't give it one hundred percent and do it right. I knew I wasn't equal to the task. Not only couldn't I do it all, but what I could do, I couldn't do very well. And that "ate my lunch."

A big part of the problem was me. I tried to do everything myself, to be a one-man team. I don't know why I felt that way, because even when I was on the mound, I had eight other guys backing me up. And there were plenty more in the dugout in case any of us needed relief.

Another one of my problems was that I kept trying to keep score with God, just as I did when I was a ballplayer. To a professional baseball player, everything is tied to performance. Your batting average. Runs batted in. Number of errors. For a pitcher your ERA was the main statistic everyone looked at. The letters stand for Earned Run Average. It means the average number of runs you allow to score in nine innings. So if your ERA is three, that means on an average you let the opposing team score three runs in the course of a game. The lower the pitcher's ERA, the better chance his team has of winning. If I went nine innings and gave up a minimal number of hits, no walks, and maybe one or two runs, my manager and teammates would give me a pat on the back and acknowledge my performance. But all of a sudden, there was no scoreboard, no manager to pat me on the back and let me know how I was doing.

But I knew I wasn't doing well. And I was so angry with myself.

But the person I took it out on was Jan. It all came to a head on Friday, April 19, 1991. I'll never forget that day. I was supposed to speak that night to the youth group at Youngstown Baptist Church, but I felt like such a hypocrite. Here I was getting ready to tell a bunch of teenagers how to make Christ the center of their life, when he wasn't the center of my life; he was buried somewhere under the mountain of mail.

We were in my study when my anger vented: "How can I share Christ with them when I don't have time to spend with Him myself?"

"Don't worry," Jan said, trying to ease my frustration. "You'll do fine."

"Don't worry," I snapped back. Then in a rage I swept all the letters off my desk. "I'm sick of this! I'm done! Finished! I can't do this anymore!"

I was sick and tired of it all. Tired of the pedestals people had put me on and tired of being in the spotlight and expected to inspire people every time I spoke.

I felt lousy that night. But I went. And I spoke. I felt so unworthy to be standing there in front of all those people that looked up to me. If they just knew what I was really like, what thoughts went through my head, what words came out my mouth, they'd get up and walk out the door.

But when I finished speaking, they didn't walk out. Instead one of the men in the church came forward. He was a thirty-four-year-old welder. He had been having an affair with another woman but was in the process of trying to put his marriage back together. He wanted Christ to come into his heart and change his life.

He went home that night a different person. In the weeks that followed, everyone around him noticed the change, people in the neighborhood, at work. No one noticed more than his wife.

Five weeks later that man went to get a tool from the toolbox on his flatbed truck when another truck backed into him, crushing his chest. He died instantly.

Later, when I was speaking on a nationally broadcast radio program, during the call-in segment of the show, his wife called in. She told me that those five weeks were the best days of their marriage. Choking back the tears, she thanked me.

Me, the hypocrite.

Me, the guy who was done, finished, who couldn't do this anymore.

Me . . . the child who stumbles.

—Dave Dravecky

Fame

Like other people, I have had my share of illusions. I spent many years wanting to be "great." I was never quite as driven as some. I just wanted to be widely known and recognized for the superior skills I believed I possessed.

There are two ways I could have become disillusioned. I could have realized I was never going to achieve the goals I thought would bring me happiness. (This is said to be an important element in the typical mid-life crisis.) Or I could have reached my goal, only to discover it was not nearly as fulfilling as I had anticipated.

In my own case, I achieved my goal. In 1970, I was summoned from a pastorate to the editor's desk of *Power* papers at Scripture Press. I had been an avid reader of *Power* from my teens. Even to write for *Power* was a great honor and achievement, in my mind. To become editor was close to the ultimate for me.

Still, who pays any attention to editors? Few readers of any publication can tell you who the editor is. It's a behind-the-scenes job. So, as much as I considered being the editor of *Power* an achievement, it did not satisfy my desire for wide recognition.

However, the *Power* position soon led to even better things. Scripture Press was beginning its book-publishing division at that time, and I was tapped to become the first editor of Victor Books.

This led in turn to my writing some of their early books—and to the recognition I had always wanted.

My new stature was epitomized when our marketing division put me on "Mt. Rushmore." What I called Mt. Rushmore was a brochure that Victor produced to promote its books and authors. The way the pictures of the authors were displayed was suggestive (unintentionally, I think) of the famous South Dakota mountain where the faces of four American presidents are carved in stone.

There I was, on evangelicalism's Mt. Rushmore, along with

such notables as Warren Wiersbe, Joyce Landorf, and Howard Hendricks. That was exhilarating. I had it made.

Over the next couple of years, however, it became apparent to me that recognition wasn't going to do all that much for me in terms of personal fulfillment. Yes, it was nice to have, but what good did it really do me? Even if millions of people came to know my name, I would never see them, never hear from them, certainly never know them, and really not know if they were blessed and helped by my writing. I realized that fame was a totally intangible thing that had little to do with the quality of my life.

Did you get that? Fame gives one no more inner resources than he has without it. One is not enriched by it, as a person.

The overflowing life is not dependent on externals such as fame, success, wealth, privilege, popularity, and power. In the last analysis, you will either have an *inner* spring of water that satisfies your deepest thirst and overflows to water others, or you will go unfulfilled.

—**Stanley Baldwin**

In The Belly Of The Whale

The problem with leading a moral life is that we can deceive ourselves into thinking that our good choices are also God's will. I learned the hard way that just because an idea is good and not evil does not necessarily mean it is "God." There is a huge difference between a *good* idea and a *God* idea.

I built a Tower of Babel and made a name for myself. One day in mid-1985 we assembled our management team to discuss how to secure equity financing for one of our buildings. Instead, the discussion focused on a growing, vague feeling that our industry was getting ready to take a fall. Overbuilding was rampant. Greed, not market studies, fueled business planning. Lenders showed up at the door with wheelbarrows full of money. It was a time to get skittish.

Nevertheless, you don't turn a freighter on a dime. The average building project takes five years from conception through leasing it up.

The next year, 1986, three months after I made the commitment—"I want to live the rest of my earthly life for the will of God"—my world came undone. The Tax Reform Act of 1986 was passed, and I was thrust into a season of crisis.

I woke up in the belly of a whale. Like Jonah, I had gone off in my own direction. Now God was going to turn me back, but not without a crisis.

It was like the water main had broken. The giant hand of government reached over and turned off the spigot. Prospective tenants went on holiday. Suddenly, investors stopped returning phone calls. Lending sources dried up. The flow of capital ceased. All this didn't work too well for a freighter fueled by a constant stream of new capital. Like a jet that ran out of fuel in midair, we went into a nosedive.

One day a couple of months later, our lead lender "suggested" that we trim staff and expenses. I had never had a layoff. In fact,

I had worked hard to create a family atmosphere in which we truly cared for one another. That all changed when I let the first seventeen people go.

At a meeting with the remaining headquarters staff I wept. I told them how I hoped this would be enough, but fortunately, I didn't make any promises. I told them I thought we had solved the problem. I was wrong.

Things became so dismal I didn't even know how to pray. I could not think of any specific meaningful prayer. The following Wednesday when I met with my weekly prayer partner, he asked how he should pray for me. I said, "Ken, all I can think of is to pray that God will grant me strength, courage, hope, grace, and mercy. If He grants me those five things, I can make it through"

In the meantime, we were scrambling to find a new source of capital. Finally, we found a company to help. We spent an entire year putting together a comprehensive equity package, only to be bounced by their chairman of the board minutes before we expected final approval.

At that point I felt doomed. I felt like someone had pushed me out of a perfectly good airplane at midnight on a black moonless night, blindfolded, without a parachute, not knowing how far I was from the ground. I was free-falling through the air, gaining speed, knowing I would splatter all over the ground any moment, but not knowing when. All in all, a pretty helpless state.

At the next layoff I invited the "cut" associates to attend the meeting at which I would explain what was happening to the remaining associates. I had just read an article that said when a limb, like an arm, is dismembered, the arm still feels pain, just like the body. So I knew that everyone was hurting, and I wanted to be as humane and therapeutic as possible. But it really hurt. My knees wobbled, and my stomach churned as I walked into that room.

Except for a period in 1987 when I thought everything would work out, I had to live each day with the specter of going bankrupt from May 1986 to October 1993—more than seven years. Ironically, the most productive years of my personal ministry were simultaneously taking place.

It would have been easy to throw in the towel and give up. Yet, somewhere deep within me I sensed God was calling me to fight for survival and not give up. Don't misunderstand. I can't say I ever felt like I knew He would deliver me, but I can say I always sensed I knew I should never give up.

Two years later we settled with the investor, and I was able to completely avoid bankruptcy. By God's grace I was spared. It took seven years, but I was able to work completely out of all personal debts. It's interesting. I spent seven years piling up debt, and it took seven years to get out of it. In the Bible, seven is considered the "perfect" number. Today I owe no man anything "except the continuing debt to love one another" (Romans 13:8). Praise be to God!

Even though God spared me from bankruptcy, I realize two things. First, if I had gone bankrupt, I would have deserved it. It was only the kindness of God's grace working in me to stay the course that resulted in deliverance. Second, there were no guarantees that I would be spared. Many wonderful men are forced into bankruptcy. There is no disgrace in declaring bankruptcy *if you have done everything humanly possible not to.*

—Patrick M. Morley

Successful leadership depends far more on the follower's perception of the leader than upon the leader's abilities. Leadership is in the eye of the follower.

—Kouzes & Posner

Take This Job And Love It!

Recently I have been trying to apply some of the principles I have learned about working around the house "to the glory of God." One day I spent several hours working on a lawn mower. I would rather have spent the time writing or working on something that seemed more "spiritual." But I concluded that if the apostle Paul could lay aside some spiritual responsibilities to make tents (Acts 18:3), I wasn't too important to fix a lawn mower. I thought I was doing OK on the mower—until I discovered that I'd installed a bearing retainer backward. Because it was rubbing against another part, I knew the mower could not be used that way. To correct the problem I would have to dismantle the machine entirely and start from scratch. I began to get upset.

Then something occurred to me: if I could insert a spacer next to the bearing retainer, the mower would work. I would have to custom-make the spacer, but it would save several hours. In a matter of minutes I had made and installed the spacer, and the mower was working fine.

Suddenly it dawned on me. Even the snag I had encountered helped me glorify God. The Lord had not made an unimaginative robot when he created me. He had made a creative and resourceful problem-solver. I glorified God by using my God-given talents.

The next morning, Marge and I negotiated about who would wash the outside of the windows in our second-story bedroom. I quickly lost the argument, being unable to convince even myself that she could place and climb a twenty-foot ladder as well as I could.

"To the glory of God," I reminded myself as I polished those window panes. When I finished I went inside to inspect my work. The tiny dust spatters from earlier rains were gone, along with all the unexplained smudges. The glass gleamed in the sunlight, like a work of art.

The beautiful result of my work made me reflect on God's

excellent works. Suddenly I began to see the glory of God all around me. How beautiful that wood grain was on the panels of our doors and cabinets! Like the windows and the lawn mower, our woodwork represented a joint effort of man with God. He made the trees with wood grain wrapped inside, but man milled the wood into panels and then applied a finish that highlighted the grain. When we do good work, we reflect God's excellence.

—**Stanley Baldwin**

The Saturday Evening Post ©1990

"Would you mind, Arthur? There's a spider near the sink?"

Wasteland Of Enlightenment

I was young, newly married, and unemployed. I had my ideals of what a husband should be. Chief among them was "provider," which I was not. I struggled with dead-end job prospects, torn between a need to work and the impossibly-low wages which were offered. I refused to apply for jobs which paid too little to support my wife and me. I even refused some potentially-profitable opportunities in the name of my principles—one store offered me a great salary to do work which I was absolutely qualified to do. But because they sold a tiny selection of pornographic magazines, I turned it down. It was a step of faith which, after several months later and still out of work, I questioned in spite of myself.

Finally, I was hired for an on-call position which paid well. I was so excited to be able to work that I never stopped to consider whether this was the job for me. Within a few months I was going crazy—the stress of not knowing whether I would work the next day, the terror of an environment which changed radically on a regular basis, and the alienation of a vocation which isolated me from my co-workers, accelerated a process which had been going on in my head since college. A lull in the job came over the summer, but when work started up again, I was even worse-off than before. I all but refused to get out of bed; I did refuse to go to work.

I had a breakdown—a crisis as much in spirit as in mental health. My mind was taxed to its limits with humiliation, anxiety, and false hopes; it had virtually shut down, leaving me unable to function socially. Even more, my faith was pushed as far as it would go. I could not understand why God would lead me to marriage, only to withhold from me the ability to provide for my wife. I could not explain why my steps of faith in marrying and turning down "immoral" job opportunities had only been met with failure and rejection by supposedly "moral" career options.

I felt rejected by the church and Christians as a bad husband who refused to work. I prayed day and night to be shown what great and terrible sin had made God withdraw His favor from my life. I was miserable and wretched, caught in a downward spiral of failure and self-criticism which nearly killed me.

Eventually, God gave me a two-part solution. First, He defined my problem; second, He gave me therapy to deal with it.

The definition was *clinical depression*. At that moment of identification, I understood that I was experiencing something real and identifiable. In a society of would-be victims trapped by mental and physical disorders, God gave me freedom by showing me that the problem was not my spirit. It was my body. It was not the weight of sin that burdened me day and night, but the under-production of certain important chemicals by my frantic, hopeless brain. While I could not shake the problem overnight, the power I felt from having my torment named, categorized, and determined treatable was tremendous.

Next was the therapy. "Therapy" too often conjures up images of lying on a couch and spilling one's guts to a bespectacled psychiatrist. I did speak with a psychologist from time to time, but that was not the therapy which God offered me. Instead, he gave me a low-paying retail job with long hours. It did not appear to be much, but it was a job I thoroughly enjoyed and one in which I took great pride. Occasionally, I felt embarrassed when asked by friends and peers what I did for a living. But more often, I enjoyed a sense of purpose and fulfillment which I had never felt so consistently in my adult life. I was not the sole provider for my family, but I was providing, and I was not committing spiritual immolation in order to do it. The Holy Spirit had launched a two-pronged attack against my despair, healing my soul just as He was healing my body.

Through these trials, God taught me much which I have held onto ever since. I learned that a true provider is not so much the main breadwinner as a loving husband and a joyful, God-fearing head of the home. I learned that there is honor in work so long as it is honest work, and that no man should be thought less of simply because of his occupation. Sadly, I learned how easily a man can deceive the world around him, even those closest to him, into thinking that he is healthy and happy when, in reality, he is dying inside.

Most importantly, I learned that God is faithful and loving in ways so far beyond our comprehension that we often sin by demanding mere human-level love—the "He would give me this if He loved me" attitude which caused me to seek trinkets from heaven as proof of God's affection. Actually, He offers divine love.

I believe I have gleaned something valuable from my time in the wasteland. God can use suffering to mold men's hearts. But it can never be an excuse for one to ignore the hurt of others. There is a world of pain hidden in the shadows of many men's souls. Pain which will devour them from within if the love of God does not reach them and heal them. God will triumph over our pain. He asks only that we believe him, sometimes despite what our eyes and hearts perceive. And he asks those of us who are stronger to lift up our brothers with arms of love.

—Todd Gordon

Leadership is the function that fosters and maintains a congregation's focus on divine purpose, promotes rational efforts to achieve it, and keeps counterproductive processes in abeyance.

—Joe Ellis

9

Mentoring & Friendship

Be ye followers of me, even as I also am of Christ.

I Corinthians 11:1

Surprised And Encouraged

I remember playing my heart out for a high school football coach who rarely (I actually thought never!) used his gold sword to encourage or praise. It was late in a game we were supposed to win, but we were losing. And while I thought I had played a good game, in the fourth quarter, I was pulled out after making a tackle.

"Here it comes!" I thought to myself as I jogged up to the coach. As the captain of the defense, I was going to get blasted for losing the game and benched. But that's not what happened.

"John," he told me, "I just wanted you to know that I wish I had ten more of you out on the field. I'm proud of how you played tonight. Now get back into the game."

It has been more than 20 years since I nearly fell down after hearing his words. I remember floating back onto the field and playing even harder than before. We lost the game, but I won something that never showed up on the scoreboard—encouragement.

—John Trent

The momentum of a team—a group of individuals joined together to achieve mutual outcomes in the pursuit of an inspired vision—creates an unstoppable force. When everyone has compelling reasons for action, peak performance is a natural result.

Focusing On His Abilities

They hadn't looked that big from shore. In fact, when my feet were on the sand, most of the waves looked pretty manageable. But now that the ocean surrounded me, the foamy curls in the distance seemed gigantic as they roared closer to me by the second. Now, I had no choice; the wave roared toward me, and we would meet. My teeth chattered, but not from the cold. I felt my heartbeat pulsing in my head.

"Paddle hard! You can do it!" my teacher yelled to me.

Partially out of fear, partially out of obedience, my arms worked furiously. Finally, the wave and I met. I felt the swell as I was lifted into the air. Tasting the salty spray, I slid softly down the backside of the wave.

"OK, get ready for the next one! This time, move up a little on your board," he called.

I had always been afraid of the tossing waves since the first time I went to the ocean. I remember being caught in a breaker, thrashing uselessly to get out. That fear never left—but neither did the desire to surf.

I was still scared that first day on a surfboard. But this time it was different, because my teacher, Michael, was with me. I knew my abilities were limited—but he had been surfing for sixteen years. I was confident that he wouldn't let anything happen to me. The more I focused on *my* ability, the greater my fear. But the more I focused on *Michael's* abilities, the greater my confidence.

When I look at my abilities in life, I get scared. But when I see that God is with me and I focus on *His* abilities, I gain confidence in making it through the scary parts of life. God said, *I will never leave you or forsake you.* I don't have to be afraid of the waves when I'm with the One who made them.

—**Tim Bechtle,** 14 years old

Compliments

The organization which employs me once engaged the professional services of a management consultant. His opening gambit was to raise the following question:

"What are the five most meaningful compliments you've ever received?"

The consultant handed me a pencil and a piece of paper and asked me to jot down in brief the five compliments that came to my mind, noting from whom I had received them and at what point in my life they had come. I filled out the paper as instructed and was surprised by the things I discovered about myself and my life.

One of the five memorable compliments I wrote on the paper came from my eighth-grade English teacher after completing a homework assignment. We had been instructed to write a descriptive paragraph, letting our imaginations roam freely as we made our virgin attempt at creative writing. When the papers were graded the teacher announced, "Before I return these papers, there is one I want to read aloud."

To my unmitigated shock, she exposed to the ears of everyone in the class the content of my descriptive paragraph and posted my paper on the bulletin board where everyone could see it. Few grasped the significance of that act for my dignity. The bulletin board was normally reserved for the display of the students' artwork. I was the poorest art student in the class and had the ignominious distinction of being the only student to never have had his artwork displayed on the bulletin board.

In one fell swoop, I made the big time as my English composition was considered a work of art. After class, I went to the front of the room to gaze at the impossible, to stare at my trophy which carried me to the heights of glory. There, emblazoned on the margin, beneath the grade, were the words of my teacher, "R.C., don't ever let anyone tell you that you can't write."

—R. C. Sproul

"Turning Away A Friend"

I understand feelings of inferiority. I grew up in a home where I was the youngest of four children. My mom, dad, and all my siblings were older, bigger, smarter, and more powerful than me. They reminded me of this every time they called me "Babe."

I dealt with self-doubt through withdrawal. I kept people at a distance. I figured what others didn't know about me and my business couldn't hurt me.

This attitude caused others to misunderstand me. I was seen as aloof, arrogant, or hostile, when I actually was unsure of myself. I wanted friends, I wanted people to like me, but at the same time, I practically shoved people away.

One particular experience symbolized my early life. It happened one winter during the austere early days of my Bible training. I was living with my little family in extremely humble quarters in a small town far from my ancestral home. We were very poor.

We couldn't afford garbage service. As wastes accumulated, I tried to bury them out in the yard. The ground was frozen rockhard, however, so I couldn't bury anything very deep.

I was out there one day, scratching at the frozen earth, when a town native passed by. He called a friendly greeting from the road and would have engaged me in conversation, but I was short with him. I didn't want him to know what I was doing.

As a result, I not only turned away a brother who wanted to be a friend, I also prevented myself from learning what he surely would have told me at once—that in their town, municipal garbage service was provided without charge to all residents.

—**Stanley Baldwin**

Being Called A Man

I had a college student who was a victim of cerebral palsy. He was able to walk, but with great difficulty as his legs and arms would fly in all directions, out of control of the motor impulses which make walking a normally simple task. His speech was slurred, slow and agonizing, demanding great concentration on the part of the listener to understand. There was nothing wrong with his mind, however, and his sparkling personality and spontaneous smile were an inspiration to his classmates and to all who encountered him.

One day he came to me vexed by a problem and asked me to pray for him. In the course of the prayer, I said something routine, with words like, "Oh, God, please help this man as he wrestles with his problem." When I opened my eyes the student was quietly weeping.

I asked him what was wrong and he stammered his reply, "You called me a man—no one has ever called me a man before."

—R. C. Sproul

"I Always Wanted To Read The Bible"

Entering the school library, the man in his early fifties hesitated, then stopped. He appeared reluctant, almost ready to flee. Hurriedly, I rose from my chair and walked toward him. With a smile on my face, I extended my hand and said, "Jeffrey? I'm Mr. Garten, your teacher."

He grabbed my hand, a hesitant smile spreading across his ruddy face, "Hi," he said. Clearly he was nervous—both about meeting me, and walking into a school setting.

I invited him to my office. He followed as I walked to my desk and indicated a chair for him. His gangly six-foot frame barely fit into the school-sized chair. Rigidly, Jeffrey faced me.

I smiled again, hoping he'd relax a bit. "I'm retired," I began, "and decided I needed to do something in my spare time. This Independent Study program in our school district includes adults. Right now, I'm teaching three adults who want to graduate from high school." I paused. "I guess you and I will try a reading program."

He nodded slowly.

"Well, in this reading program you go at your own pace."

That seemed to reassure him a bit. "I dropped out of school in tenth grade . . . and never did know how to read. The teachers just kept passing me along to get rid of me." He paused and twisted his hands. "Now I'm fifty . . . and I sure do want to learn to read before I die," admitted Jeffrey.

As we talked, I discovered he was a construction contractor. Obviously, he knew his numbers and letters, and perhaps more. I told him I had been in construction, which meant a time for reminiscing.

Then we talked about his reading. He had tried several reading programs—but was quite unsure of himself. Deep down, I had the feeling he could read more than he thought. But I kept it to myself as I explained the program and the contract he needed to sign.

"I sure do appreciate your telling me about this," Jeffrey said as he left. "I'll call you and let you know the date when I can start."

I waited for his call until I doubted he was sincere about this last reading attempt. Then the phone rang.

"You said we could meet at your house," Jeffrey said. "Would that be OK? I don't want anyone to know I can't read."

A deep secret that was years in the making: he knew how to bluff others and feared they'd discover his deception.

"Of course," I said. "How about tomorrow at 2 p.m.?"

Jeffrey arrived the next day. It was as I suspected. The reading program he brought along was one he had stopped years before—but did remember. As the weeks passed and I gave him encouragement, he blossomed, sounding out words and phrases and writing correct answers. His perseverance was astounding, as if he was guided by a power and encouragement far greater than himself.

One day Jeffrey's wife came with him. My wife often would join us at the lessons end, and as we talked the conversation drifted to our mutual faith in the Lord. Immediately, I knew Who had driven Jeffrey to succeed.

Suddenly, he said, "I sure wish I could read the Bible, but the print is so small."

At those words, my wife went to our office and brought back our large print Bible, which she handed to Jeffrey. "Here, take this," she said. "Maybe it will help."

We could see the tears in Jeffrey's eyes. "Are you sure? I could just borrow it."

"Take it," said my wife. "Now we know why we've had it on our shelf."

As Jeffrey's lessons continued, he steadily improved. I taught his wife procedures to use at home to increase his confidence. He blossomed and became eager to do two or three lessons at a time and even tried to read the newspaper. It was all so exciting for me that I felt truly blessed and fulfilled at his accomplishments.

When the semester drew to a close, I gathered his assignments and book for evaluation and submission to the Independent Study office. One more week loomed, but what could I give as an assignment?

Then I remembered Jeffrey's Bible. The assignment was clear: Luke 2:1-20 because it was the Christmas season.

The following week Jeffrey arrived by himself. We talked for a while and I returned his reading book and assignments. Then I instructed him, "Turn to Luke 2 in your Bible and read the passage to me ."

Obediently, he opened his Bible and began reading. *And it came to pass in those days that there went out a decree . . . .* He continued to read through the sixth verse.

Suddenly, Jeffrey turned to me, a brilliant smile on his face. "The reason I wanted to learn to read was so I could read the Bible."

"And that's what you're doing, isn't it?" I said. I knew my eyes were wet.

He nodded solemnly as he turned back to Luke. Then I understood a little more about God's plan for all of us.

—**Vernon Garten**

Being Fathers In Christ

Once a ten year old boy came to speak with me. I put my hand on his head. I did not give him any blessing, but I began to think. It is something solemn when a man who loves God and walks with God puts his hand on your head and says, "I believe God is going to use you." You never forget it.

When I first came to the USA, there was a man from California, a respectable elder in a local church, who took me aside one day. He said, "Luis, I believe that the Lord is going to use you to bring millions of people to Jesus Christ. I expect to live to see it happen." To me that was from the Lord. I have never forgotten it. And it has already taken place to a great measure. That word of blessing from a spiritual elder sealed something deep in my soul.

When Charles Spurgeon, the famous 19th century British preacher, was six years old, a preacher came to his grandfather's house. At breakfast one morning, this preacher took the little boy Charles, sat him on his knee and said, "I believe that this little boy will be used of God to preach the Gospel to all of England and win thousands upon thousands to Jesus Christ." He was only six, but he never forgot it. He started preaching at sixteen. At twenty, he was preaching to twenty-thousand people.

After that breakfast, the preacher took the little boy to a grove in the grandfather's garden. The preacher sat him down and for two hours gave him counsel. That is really something, isn't it? We tend to look at a six year old and say, "Go play, boy; get out of my way." But this preacher noticed Spurgeon and gave him counsel—Spurgeon became one of the greatest Bible preachers of all time.

—**Luis Palau**

She Believed In Me

By the fifth grade, I was bearing all the fruit of a kid who feels insecure, unloved, and pretty angry at life. In other words, I was tearing the place apart. However, my teacher Miss Simon apparently thought that I was blind to this problem, because she regularly reminded me, "Howard, you are the worst behaved child in this school!"

So tell me something I don't already know! I thought to myself, as I proceeded to live up (or down) to her opinion of me.

One time I got so out-of-hand that she physically grabbed me, shoved me into my desk, tied me to my seat with a rope, and wrapped tape around my mouth. "Now you will sit still and be quiet!" she announced triumphantly. So what else could I do?

Needless to say, the fifth grade was probably the worst year of my life. Finally I was graduated—for obvious reasons. But I left with Miss Simon's words ringing in my ears: "Howard, you are the worst behaved child in this school!"

You can imagine what my expectations were upon entering the sixth grade. The first day of class, my teacher, Miss Noe, went down the roll call, and it wasn't long before she came to my name. "Howard Hendricks," she called out, glancing from her list to where I was sitting with my arms folded, just waiting to go into action. She looked me over for a moment, and then said, "I've heard a lot about you." Then she smiled and added, "But I don't believe a word of it!"

I tell you, that moment was a fundamental turning point, not only in my education, but in my life. Suddenly, unexpectedly, someone believed in me. For the first time in my life, someone saw potential in me. Miss Noe put me on special assignments. She gave me little jobs to do. She invited me to come in after school to work on my reading and arithmetic. She challenged me with higher standards.

I had a hard time letting her down. In fact, one time I got so involved in one of her homework assignments that I stayed up until 1:30 in the morning working on it! Eventually my father came down the hall and said, "What's the matter son? Are you sick?"

"No, I'm doing my homework," I replied.

He kind of blinked and rubbed his eyes, not quite sure whether he was awake. He'd never heard me say anything like that before. Finally he shook his head and said, "You're sick!"

What made the difference between fifth grade and sixth? The fact that someone was willing to give me a chance. Someone was willing to believe in me while challenging me with higher expectations. That was risky, because there was no guarantee that I would honor Miss Noe's trust.

Everyone likes the end product of mentoring, especially when it yields a peak performer—the star athlete, the successful businessperson, the brilliant lawyer, the impressive communicator. But how many of us want to deal with the person at the front end of the process?

—Howard Hendricks

Ten Marks Of A Mentor

The ideal mentor is a person who . . .
   1. Seems to have what you personally need.
   2. Cultivates relationships.
   3. Is willing to take a chance on you.
   4. Is respected by other Christians.
   5. Has a network of resources.
   6. Is consulted by others.
   7. Both talks and listens.
   8. Is consistent in his lifestyle.
   9. Is able to diagnose your needs.
  10. Is concerned with your interests.

—Howard Hendricks

When Billy Sunday was America's leading evangelist, he made an interesting gesture prior to each engagement. Booked into a certain town, he would write the mayor in advance. Did the mayor know people in his community with special needs? Billy Sunday and his staff would like to be praying for them before they arrived. According to this account, the mayor of a great metropolis thought that request over and sent the evangelist their city telephone directory.

"I Knew You'd Come"

You've probably heard the powerful story coming out of World War I of the deep friendship of two soldiers in the trenches.

From time-to-time one side or the other would rise up out of the trenches, fling their bodies against the opposing line and slink back to lick their wounds, bury their dead, and wait to do it all over again. In the process, friendships were forged in the misery. Two soldiers became particularly close. Day after day, night after night, terror after terror, they talked of life, of families, of hopes, of what they would do when (and if) they returned from this horror.

On one more fruitless charge, "Jim" fell, severely wounded. His friend, Bill made it back to the relative safety of the trenches. Meanwhile Jim lay suffering beneath the night flares. Between the trenches. Alone.

The shelling continued. The danger was at its peak. Between the trenches was no place to be. Still, Bill wished to reach his friend, to comfort him, to offer what encouragement only friends can offer. The officer in charge refused to let Bill leave the trench. It was simply too dangerous. As he turned his back, however, Bill went over the top. Ignoring the smell of cordite in the air, the concussion of incoming rounds, and the pounding in his chest, Bill made it to Jim.

Sometime later he managed to get Jim back to the safety of the trenches. Too late. His friend was gone. The somewhat self-righteous officer, seeing Jim's body, cynically asked Bill if it had been "worth the risk." Bill's response was without hesitation.

"Yes, Sir, it was," he said. "My friend's last words made it more than worth it. He looked up at me and said, 'I knew you'd come.'"

—Stu Weber

I Got What I Needed

Two weeks before the beginning of my senior year, I moved to a new school and entered a new basketball program. At the beginning of the year I found that I was a bit of a novelty because I was new, but as the season wore on, I discovered that I didn't fit very well in the system run by this new coach. As a result, I spent more and more time sitting on the bench. The agony was driven into my heart as weekly I received the newspaper from the town where I was supposed to play my senior year. The team in that town was winning their league title while the team I was on was in the middle of the pack. The team I left behind would have had me as the starting point guard while the team I was on was enjoying my contribution in practice only.

In the midst of this struggle I became friends with Allen. Allen believed in my abilities and was seeking ways to encourage me because he knew I was playing below my ability. Halfway through the season he said, "I've got a deal for you. If you score in double figures in any game this season I will buy you a steak dinner."

That was the new motivation I needed to work hard again. I began to give it my all in practice, again thinking I would get another shot. But the opportunity was slow in developing. In the next six games I played a total of ten minutes. Allen sensed the dilemma I was in so he modified the deal.

"If you score in double figures for the rest of the season combined, I will buy you a steak dinner."

I took his challenge to heart with joy and anticipation. I knew we would not win a championship. I knew we would not even get to the playoffs. But with six games left in the season, I thought I would at least have a personal victory if I could score enough points. The next three games saw me with three-and-a-half minutes of playing time so my hope of meeting his challenge was dissipating. In one last desperate attempt to encourage me, Allen modified his offer one more time.

"Bill, if you score even one basket, I will buy you a steak dinner."

With three games left to play, I was a man on a mission. My dreams of a championship season were history but my desire to give Allen a chance to make good on his offer were very much alive. In the first game, I played 30 seconds. In the second game, I played 16 seconds. No points, no victory.

My opportunity came in the last game of the season. The coach put me in with one minute and 35 seconds left in the game. We were trailing by fifteen points with no hope of winning. I was frantically running around the court trying to steal the ball. Finally my chance came. With twelve seconds left in the game a teammate and I trapped a player at half court. I stole the ball with six seconds left on the clock and went the length of the court for a lay-up. With two seconds left in the game the ball fell through the net. We had just lost by thirteen points but I was running down the side of the court pointing to my friend who was sitting in the top row of the stands.

I was jumping up and down like we had just won the league championship shouting, "You owe me, Allen. You owe me."

Allen was on his feet, pointing back to me, shouting, "You did it, Bill. You did it!"

What I wanted was a championship season my senior year in high school that I could brag about for the rest of my life. What I needed was a friend like Allen who would let me know I was valuable because of who I am not just for what I do. I didn't get what I wanted, but I got what I needed—a true friend.

—**Bill Farrel**

Fellow Soldiering

A long time ago in what seems now like a galaxy far, far away, this nation was at war in the Republic of Vietnam. In the fall of 1967, freshly graduated from college, and at the heart of the season when the war was building to its peak, I found myself at Ft. Benning, Georgia. For junior officers bound for the Republic of Vietnam, Ft. Benning—home of the U.S. Army Infantry School—was a common stop. In those days virtually every young Regular Army lieutenant had orders to the U.S. Army Ranger School there.

I was no exception. With my head shaved, my body fit, and my mind alert, I stood in formation with 287 other men equally tense, proud, brave, and fearful all at the same time. A grizzled old Ranger cadre noncom stepped boldly in front of us, ordered us to "Stand at ease and listen up!" and began to speak.

Actually, he was shouting.

His head moved back and forth across the formation. It seemed as though his eyes met each of ours in turn. He was formidable. The guy had been around the block. He'd been to "Nam and back." And he had something to say.

Other training situations had been just that. Training situations. Somehow this was different. The man who swept his flinty gaze across our ranks had a presence about him. Everything about him—his appearance, voice, eyes, experience—demanded attention. Besides that, we were men who knew something of our destiny: We were in the pipeline to Vietnam. Lyndon Johnson had opened the spigot, and the current was flowing. You could feel it. This was for real.

The old Ranger's speech was as lean and tough as his body. Every punctuated word of it seemed to come from his gut: "We are here to save your lives. To do so we are going to do two things with you over the course of the next nine weeks. First, we are going to see to it that you overcome all your natural fears—especially height and water. And second, we are going to show you how much incredible stress the human mind and body can endure. Many of you will not complete the nine weeks. It is simply too tough. But for those who do, when we are finished with you, you *will be* the U.S. Army's best. America's best. You *will* be confident. You *will* survive, even in combat. And you *will* accomplish your mission!"

After his remarks designed both to inspire and intimidate, the man gave us our first assignment. "Step one in your training is the assignment of your 'Ranger Buddy.' "

It was an amazing statement when you think about it. He had just told us that we faced an unbelievably daunting task. He had just told us it would prove to be too demanding for many of us. (He was right. Of the 287 candidates, less than half finished the nine weeks, and only ninety or so were awarded the coveted "Ranger tab" to be worn proudly on the soldier's left shoulder.) But he had also made a highly- insightful statement about the nature of a man's soul.

When you walk a rough road, it's best to walk beside a friend. Together is better!

By making step one the assignment of a Ranger Buddy, the intent of the old soldier's next words were burned into our minds:

"Difficult assignments require a friend. The two of you will stick together. You will never leave each other. You will walk together, run together, eat together, sleep together. You will help each other. You will encourage each other. And, as necessary, you will carry each other."

We got the point. It was the Army's way of saying, "Never go into the water alone. Never go into battle alone. Never, ever walk alone. Stay together, Rangers! Live together . . . and if necessary, die together."

It is a theme that rings strong and clear from the pages of the New Testament. Life is difficult on this broken, soon-to-be-judged world. Believers need one another. God's soldiers need fellow soldiers. God's man needs a Ranger Buddy.

—**Stu Weber**

Big John

It was graduation day and, believe it or not, there was John. He was the first one in his family ever to receive a high school diploma. Only months earlier no one in their wildest imagination would have ever dreamed this day would be a reality.

You might say that John was disadvantaged because his mother died when he was a small child, leaving his dad to raise four sons by himself. John and his three older brothers were the trouble-making terrors of every school they attended. John's brothers had all been expelled from high school and he was following in their footsteps. In fact, he was about a breath away from expulsion on the day he instigated a sit-in by the students who were demanding a lounge for smoking.

John definitely was a "bully" and had earned for himself the nickname "Big John." The students were either afraid of him and stayed their distance or they admired his macho style. In any case, he made no friends among the faculty of the high school, that is, until this new teacher, Mr. Price, came into his life.

John was leading a group of about 200 students in that sit-down strike on the lawn in front of the school. Their lobbying for smoking rights, of course, was doomed for failure. I approached and asked, "John, do you really think this is the way to get what you want?"

There was some dialogue between us for several minutes when it occurred to me that I could make an agreement with this young man that would be beneficial to everyone. I said, "John, if you help me keep our class in order (my classroom had the riffraff of the school), I'll make sure you graduate and get a good job. Have we got a deal?"

It didn't take long to learn that Big John liked my proposal. Within minutes after class started that day the typical noise erupted. Big John stood up and made his way to the front of the room and boomed out, "Shut up, you guys, Mr. Price is talking!"

From that day forward John made no allowances for disrespect from his classmates. He began to excel in his studies and was already hired for a great paying job which would begin the day following graduation.

When it became apparent that John was going to graduate, his father came to school to talk with me. He stated, "I don't know what you did, but it's something I could never have done and I want you to know that I sure appreciate it." Of course, I was deeply moved and grateful for those kind words.

The experience with Big John taught me the value of caring. As a teacher with a provisional teaching credential who was really "green" in the classroom, I discovered that I didn't need to have all the answers. A little caring truly did make a BIG difference. Out of this came the realization that *people don't care how much you know until they know how much you care!*

—**Harvey Price**

A Simple Comment

Some time ago, I took a friend into my confidence and told him of a problem that made me feel ashamed. I confessed to occasional bouts of irrational jealousy when another friend enjoyed applause that normally comes my way.

It had taken some time to work up the courage to share my struggle with my friend, and when I did, I expected him to be thoughtfully intrigued and to explore my problem with compassionate fascination. Instead, his brow furrowed in immediate concern as he replied, "Larry, jealousy is really ugly. I've seen it do terrible things to people." That was it. No follow-up, no question. He changed the subject.

His remark caught me off guard. It was not at all what I had anticipated or wanted. I felt unfairly rebuked, entirely unhelped, and more than a little annoyed. A better counselor, I told myself, would have helped me *understand* my jealousy so that I could better deal with it, not quickly judge me for it.

I now believe that his simple comment, one that broke most of the rules of accepted counseling procedure, had more potential to stimulate deep change than hours of insightful, non-judgmental exploration ever could have. On the other hand, had I merely accepted his comment as a scolding, confessed my jealousy as sinful, and tried hard to act in ways that did not reflect a jealous attitude, change would have been quickly aborted. In other words, had I heard his rebuke as an exhortation to moralistic living, I would not have been helped. Neither insight nor exhortation, by themselves, will ever change us from self-centered to other-centered people.

—**Larry Crabb**

10

Ministry

*Now we exhort you, brethren, warn them that are unruly,
comfort the feebleminded, support the weak, be patient toward
all men.*

I Thessalonians 5:14

Willing To Go To Jail In Russia

More than once I was asked, "Are you willing to go to jail for what you are doing?" I was about to leave for Russia with a tour group traveling under the umbrella of the American Express Company—except I was going with a box of Bibles in the Russian tongue. I was aware of the possibility that they could choose to detain me as they had many others of late. Some had gone to jail and others were expelled. But if God wanted the Bibles delivered to spiritually-starved Russians, He could make a way.

Urgently I called my church congregation to prayer. I publicly spread the Bibles on our church altar explaining that only the hand of God could hide so many Bibles from the enemy's searching eyes. Tearfully and sincerely the crowd extended their hands and lifted their voices in beseeching prayers. Not the least of which was my worried wife who was reluctantly staying home to mother our little nine-month-old daughter who was ill.

At last in Berlin, I confided to my unsuspecting tour group that I was on a special mission. "I have two suitcases: one is for my personal effects, the other is filled with Russian Bibles which I hope to share in the Soviet Union," I confessed. "One solution might be to discard the second bag and distribute the Bibles around in all of your bags." But there was not a single volunteer. God seemed to say to me, "It's your mission and no one else is to be jeopardized."

At last our plane rolled to a stop in Moscow and we were herded toward the customs building. As tour guide, I assisted everyone else while the probing inspectors tore into bag after bag and purse after purse. Nothing was overlooked. Some of the people in line were even physically frisked. Now it was my turn and all my friends were desperately praying and watching closely. It was the moment of truth. I could be arrested on the spot. I could be detained and expelled from the country. Or God could answer the prayers of a lot of people.

The tough old inspector ripped into my bag and didn't miss a thing, it seemed. Then he was suddenly distracted and, turning away, he became disoriented. When he turned back, he absent-mindedly stamped that bag and the second bag that he had not even opened. It was the only item of any size overlooked including purse, bag, and hand-carried packages. The one and only one not inspected was the bag filled with Bibles.

Grabbing all their luggage, and mine, the incredulous crowd rushed for our tour bus and a haven at the hotel. Suddenly, it seemed, each member felt a burning desire to distribute these God-protected good books. Everyone agreed that we were truly on a mission.

—D. Leroy Sanders

Closing The Open Door

It's no surprise that my spiritual lows come when I'm busy, preoccupied, focusing my attention on everything but God, and my spiritual highs come on "Sabbath" days of rest and relaxation. God instituted Sabbath not only because the human body needs physical rest, but more so because human activity frustrates intimacy with the Creator.

That means that at times I've had to take forceful steps to make this happen.

As a people-person and activist, I've prided myself on having an open-door policy. So for years people regularly interrupted my devotions, but it didn't bother me much. When I started my journey of knowing God, I knew something had to change; I had to find uninterrupted time with God. So I started coming to church earlier for my morning devotions.

Then people who wanted to see me learned a good time to catch me was early in the morning. Still, I kept my door open and kept coming in earlier and earlier to be alone.

One early morning as I was in my office praying, a drug addict named John, to whom I had been ministering for months, came to my door and said, "I don't have any money for the train. Can you give me a ride to work?"

"I'll give you some money," I said.

"I'll be late for work. I need you to give me a ride."

He pressed his plea, and so finally I drove him. When I returned to the office, I never was able to resume my devotions.

I woke early the next morning looking forward to my devotions. I settled into my chair at the office and began reading the Bible. Minutes later John showed up again at my door. Same request. Again I refused. He begged me, and once again I grudgingly interrupted my time with the Lord to drive him to work. Once again I couldn't resume my devotions later in the day.

The next morning, John reappeared at my open door. "I'm not driving you to work," I said firmly. "I have a commitment."

"Coach, you have to! I'll be fired if I don't get there on time."

"That's too bad. I have a commitment."

John pleaded and pleaded with me. Finally I said, "Okay, okay, I'll drive you to work, but if you come to my door tomorrow, I'm not driving you. You'll just have to lose your job."

The next morning I was not surprised when John stuck his head in my office (with that kind of persistence, how could he not succeed in life!). But this time I held firm. Angrily he rushed out to take the train, and he didn't lose his job.

That experience seven years ago was a turning point for me. Though contrary to my nature, I started saying no to people to guard my time with the Lord. I now close and lock my outer office door during devotions. When someone knocks, I don't answer, nor do I answer my phone. I have told the congregation, "If you come knocking on my door early in the morning, I'm not going to answer. I need to be alone with God. I don't want to know about God, I want to know God."

—Wayne Gordon

Knowing The Sheep Individually

The funeral service when my father died was not an event I looked forward to. In times of grief, our senses are numbed to what is going on around us and recollections tend to be fuzzy. But one aspect of this funeral service stands out vividly in my memory.

During the eulogy, the minister of our church made passing mention of my father's style of walking. He remarked that when my father came to the church, the minister knew it was my father approaching "by his footfall."

After the funeral I asked my mother about this remark which puzzled me. I was not aware of any distinctive characteristic to my father's gait, as he neither limped nor shuffled.

My mother's eyes, weary from tears of grief, began to sparkle as her face broke into a knowing smile. "Yes, your father did have a certain style of walking that was just a part of him. I knew exactly what the minister was referring to, and I was surprised that he was aware of it."

My mother was deeply moved by the mention of a subtle trait that was part of her intimate knowledge of her husband. I was impressed, because the minister had a congregation of over 2,000 members, and that he would know their idiosyncrasies was more than I could imagine. In this moment of family grief, he touched a tender nerve because he took the time to get to know his people.

—R. C. Sproul

Significant Words

In 1988 I began pastoring a small church in San Diego County, California. At that time I was 29 years old and full of anticipation. I thought that this church would welcome all my new ideas with open arms; then line up and follow me to the Promised Land. The only thing I lacked was maturity and confidence. After two years of leading this ministry I was out of "tricks." I had done everything I knew as a pastor. I was either going to have to get help or move on to another ministry.

I started looking for a mentor who could give me guidance in my professional and personal life. I made a list of ten men whom I respected in ministry. I wasn't sure if any of them would want to take an interest in me; but I had to try. I took this list and prayed over it for 30 days. After that month, I prioritized the list in the order I wanted to approach them.

At the top of the list was Jim Conway. I met Jim when I was a student at Talbot Theological Seminary. His classes in Pastoral Counseling were invaluable in teaching me how to give people lasting help. But what really impressed me was the willingness of Jim and his wife, Sally, to put their relationship on display by teaching together and inviting students over to their home to get to know them. My wife, Pam, and I had maintained a casual friendship with Jim and Sally and I was pleased that Jim was willing to help with the installation service when I accepted the call to pastor this church. Now, two years later, it seemed appropriate that he would rise to the top of the list.

I called him one day and said, "Jim, I have been praying for a mentor. I would like you to consider meeting with me every four to six weeks and help me sort out my life. I will bring the agenda. It will include questions about how to be a more effective pastor, and questions about my relationship with Pam, my personal growth, and my responsibilities as a father."

I expected Jim to call me back and say that he was honored

to be asked but he was too busy to take on that type of commitment. I was amazed when Jim called back and said, "I would be honored to be a mentor to you. I need to be needed as much as you need a mentor."

I have been plagued with thoughts that ministry is a destination rather than a process. I have been guilty of thinking that I would be successful as soon as my church grew to over 1,000 attendees. Rather than rejoicing in each step of growth, I would become frustrated because the church had not jumped to 1,000. Rather than being glad that the church was growing, I complained that the church was growing slower than I had planned. Instead of recognizing the significant changes God had made in the lives of many of the people in our church, I was discouraged that we hadn't influenced more people.

I found that I was unable to enjoy the work God was doing because I was focused on the work God wasn't doing. I was trying to explain this to Jim one day, hoping that he would give me some magic answer that would catapult the church into instant success. I said to him, "I hope that Pam and I can build a significant church in the San Diego area that God can really use."

Jim leaned forward in his chair, looked me directly in the eyes and said, "Bill, you do have a significant church."

I was stunned. He didn't say the church had to be bigger. He didn't say the church needed to be more active. He didn't say I needed to attend more conferences. He simply said the church was already significant.

It was as if I woke up that day. My thoughts have changed radically since that conversation with Jim. I still hope the church I pastor continues to grow, but I no longer think significance is related to size.

—Bill Farrel

God Took Hold

Jeff was no longer a young man. His sons weren't even young anymore. In the days of his youth Jeff had done what he'd wanted; with little regard for the needs of others. He was in jail when he found Jesus. What a conversion! Jeff felt new and different. He shared his faith with the most important man in his life, his father, Ralph.

Ralph listened very intently. He saw and appreciated the changes in his son. But Ralph quietly said, "Son, it is fine for you, but don't ever mention your religion again."

Jeff's pain was real and deep. His prayers for his father were as real and deep. When the last years of Ralph's life began, he still had not come to know Jesus. Jeff's prayers continued strong. He was desperate to introduce his father on earth to his Father in heaven.

I was part of a Christian club at a school where Jeff worked and served as our advisor. He shared his concern for his father as a prayer request.

As we closed the meeting with each head bowed, a new kid led us in prayer. And God was in that room. After the prayer, the new kid said, "What if you aren't the one? Jeff, can you let go of being the one to lead your father to the Lord? Can you accept that you have planted the seed with your words and your life, but that someone else might be the one to bring in the harvest?"

Jeff looked at him in utter incomprehension. The thought had never occurred to him. It didn't set well with him now. "I only know I need to lead my father to the Lord and his time is running out," was all he could say.

Meanwhile, in a little town nearby, a man was waiting at the door for someone to answer. A woman responded to his knock.

"I'm the new pastor at the church down the street and I'm going around the neighborhood learning my way and just talking to people." Peg, the woman behind the screen, seemed weary. "I was wondering if I might trouble you for a drink of water," he added.

"Certainly," Peg answered, not knowing what else to say.

When she returned with the glass, he accepted it graciously and turned and sat on the top step of the porch. Again, she didn't know what else to do, so she sat beside him. He mused, the people seem nice and, though a little reluctant, they're friendly once they've gotten to know me. Have you been in the neighborhood long?"

Peg replied that she had been in the neighborhood for five years. She was full-time caregiver of Ralph, Jeff's father. It was Ralph's call to her that ended the conversation. The new pastor in the neighborhood apologized for keeping her and left.

Returning to the house, Peg glanced at the clock. She had been on the porch talking with the new pastor for nearly half an hour. She felt rested from the full-time care of an invalid. And the pastor hadn't mentioned the church or God.

Four days later, the pastor came by again. When he asked for a drink of water, Peg brought one for herself. The pastor asked about the man who had called to Peg.

It was easy for Peg to talk to the pastor. To tell him about Ralph, his illness and loneliness.

The following week the pastor came by again and during the talk on the porch, when Ralph called out, the pastor said, "I like football, like you said Ralph does. Why don't I talk with him while you finish whatever I interrupted?"

Every few days, when the pastor returned, both Peg and Ralph welcomed him. And the pastor never mentioned the church or God. He came and talked. It was Ralph who started the conversation. It was Ralph who asked Jesus into his heart.

At school, it was Jeff who found joy in his father's salvation, and Jeff who found it easier to accept his father's death a few days later. Jeff reminded the members of the club that the last shall be first and the first shall be last. When Jeff let go, God took hold.

—Sam Hinman

Pearl Of Wisdom

Many years ago while serving a church as youth director, a "seasoned" pastor, who was serving our church on Sundays as interim preacher, seemed eager to mentor me and share his wealth of experience. Several times this individual indicated his desire to get together for a seasoned-pastor-to-fledgling-pastor chat. The "seasoned" pastor's wife and four young children were usually with him on Sundays. Consequently, this precluded anything that resembled private conversation. Finally, after months of anticipation, the day arrived when he and I were able to have our much-awaited mentoring session. Given my prior experience with this fellow, I cynically expected a long-winded discourse, full of very pointed and personal advice.

My colleague and I spent several hours together at my home and, as imagined, during this time he did plenty of talking. But it soon became clear that, rather than needing to shower me with sage admonitions and stern warnings, what the poor guy *really* yearned for, almost desperately, was someone to listen to him and his story.

But what about the advice that had been dangled before me as bait? Not a word of it had passed between us. After all the weeks of build-up to this meeting, I was curious, not wanting my friend to get away without sharing the promised pearl of wisdom. As time was running out I was forced to ask, "Wasn't there something else you had to say to me?"

At first my guest paused, trying to remember. Then his face brightened. I was on the edge of my seat, waiting with mounting impatience.

He stared me in the eyes and said, "People are funny."

People are funny? After my friend's departure, I shared these words with my wife. We laughed and laughed at the surprising summary statement. This was the essence of pastoral wisdom?

Of course, people are funny! Even a twenty-something person had lived long enough to know that!

Several years ago, my wife had a paperweight engraved for me with that now infamous quote. While she gave the gift as a joke, as time goes on, it becomes less so. After many years in the ministry, how often have I summed up a situation, within or without the church, with those words! The early recognition that people are funny helps immeasurably in ministry and life situations. I glance regularly at the engraved reminder on my desk, in a personal effort to maintain some perspective and remain reasonably sane.

—Jeffry R. Zurheide

The Motive For Good Deeds

One of our men's ministry leaders hit me in the solar plexus with a devotional based on Matthew 6:1, which says, *Take heed that you do not do your charitable deeds before men, to be seen by them. Otherwise you have no reward from your Father in heaven* (NKJV).

He challenged us to consider why we wanted to serve as leaders; why we attended our weekly Bible study; and why we attended seminars and did our quiet times. It was very convicting, and during a time of prayer, I repented. To repent means "to change direction."

Unfortunately, sometimes we can't change direction until we know the direction in which we are already going.

The next day I learned that I was going to be asked to take a lesser role in a citywide rally in another city. The rally was part of an ongoing ten-year plan for which I had the original vision. The year before, I had been a keynote speaker. This year they wanted to demote me to emcee. There is a world of difference between acting as a master of ceremonies and delivering a keynote message!

When I heard the news, I went ballistic! *I've paid my dues! I spent years and years doing emcee work!* For forty-five minutes I ranted at the chairman of the mission. I even halfheartedly threatened to not attend at all, admittedly the height of immaturity, and an act that would have damaged the continuity of the program. Finally, he suggested we give it a rest and discuss it again the next day.

The following day I called him on the phone from an airport. "Tom, I would like to apologize for the way I acted yesterday and ask for your forgiveness."

"You don't need to apologize," he offered.

"Yes, I do. Yesterday I showed you what I was capable of doing in the flesh. Today I would like the opportunity to show you what I can do by the Spirit. First, let me say that I will definitely be there. You can count on me. I would like you to put in writing exactly what you and the Executive Committee would like me to do, and then I will respond."

What devastated me the most about this incident was how quickly I collapsed into such a despicable display of flesh. God was showing me where I needed to change direction.

The Bible says the flesh is deceitful. The Bible says the flesh is wicked. The Bible says the flesh is weak. However, the flesh is most deceitful, most wicked, and most weak, when disguised as piety. The only thing worse than flesh is pious flesh.

Through self-deceit, I had constructed a mirror that reflected what I wanted to see. It was a warped image. God smashed my mirror, and I was surprised to learn there was a mirror behind the mirror. This second mirror gave a true reflection of who I am, and I didn't like what I saw at all. Once the distorted mirror was shattered, I could see in the second mirror behind it how I had misjudged my motives, my pride, and my ambition.

If there is any one most important lesson I have learned lately, it is this: The sins of our piety far exceed the sins of our immorality. The problem is that we do our sins of immorality in our own name, but we do our sins of piety in the name of Jesus.

God used this regrettable incident to reveal that my motives were not pure. I was not acting as a servant—I was trying to be a star. I was not motivated by wanting to serve Christ—I was trying to make a name for myself. I had started out with the idea of wanting to be used. Instead, I was acting like I wanted to be something. I was guilty of wanting to be seen. I had to ask myself, "What is the motivation for my good deeds?"

We worked it all out. I did everything they requested. Lately, I've been more sensitive that maybe my motives for doing good deeds need watching after. I do know this: As far as is possible, I have given up working out of my own righteousness.

—**Patrick M. Morley**

Priorities

Years ago my wife worked at a large laboratory to help us make ends meet on my pastoral salary. We were getting along well, but the emotional distance between us began to grow. Not intense arguments, but petty little picky things, unsettling and unnerving. Like barbs under the skin, they were poison to our attitude.

One Monday morning I was sitting in the church office with my staff seated around me. Nancy was on her way to work. The staff and I were going over yesterday's blessings during Sunday's service and activities, talking about tomorrow's plans, and discussing what we could do to further the growth of the ministry.

At a moment of convivial laughter, the door opened and Nancy looked in. She saw me there with the staff in a very intimate conversation—to which she was not privy—and quickly closed the door. Slowly realizing what it must have meant to her, I jumped up and ran to intercept her, but she was in the car and gone.

That evening when she came home I tried to mollify her by telling her what was happening. She would have none of it. I had been basking in the glory of "my ministry," accepting the accolades of "my staff," getting my strokes of appreciation and affection—and she had no part of it. Our worlds were getting further apart.

That episode made me realize I had great respect for what I was doing, and little for what she was doing for the family. It started long periods of intense thought and prayer on the status of my marriage, ministry, and family. Thinking the ministry and marriage could be separated, and both be successful, I had believed a lie. As a result, I had become more intimate with my church staff than I was with my own wife and family. Though I had the respect of the congregation, I had lost Nancy's through neglect.

I also had to face the truth that I had encouraged Nancy to augment our income instead of going before the church to ask for a raise. Cowardice on my part, courage on hers, and now I was having to face my character defects and masculine inadequacies.

Jesus told us to go and make things right with others before we could come and offer our gifts upon the altar (Matthew 5:23-24). It was my responsibility to make right what I had made wrong.

To this day I wince as I think about those days. That is why I write as I do, to encourage other men to do right so they won't have to reinvent the wheel.

Wife and family come before business, ministry, or career. God comes before wife and family. I had it inverted and had to be converted. Conversion is a constant, not only instant, process. Our freedom from wrong believing is dependent upon our discipline to receive truth. Only truth makes us free (John 8:32).

Once I accepted the truth, accepted responsibility for my actions, asked forgiveness of my wife and family, things began to change dramatically. Nancy and I agreed on a specific date when she would stop work and God honored the date by blessing our income. We then took a family vacation and began to live again as God intended—and the ministry never suffered one iota for the time I spent with my family!

—Edwin Louis Cole

Diminished Revival

While growth is not the sure measure of success, neither should lack of growth be a sign of failure. Take the case of Brian, a young pastor of a small Baptist church in Southern California. I first met Brian when he drove me to the airport after a speaking engagement. As we were cruising along the freeway, I asked my standard question, "How are things going in your church?"

He hesitated for a moment then said, "we've cut our membership in half," glancing at me quickly, as if expecting me to be disappointed."

"What happened?" I asked.

"We had 220 members, but the place was dead, and no matter what I preached, nothing changed. So one day the deacons and I prayed. 'Lord, bring only Your people here. We want those who are ready to repent and give themselves wholly to You.' We stood at the door of the church silently praying this prayer as people filed in."

Brian glanced at me several times to see if I was questioning his sanity. Who in this age of church growth, in California of all places, would pray for people to stay away from their church?

"An amazing thing happened," he explained. "God answered the prayer. People began dropping out, one by one. We went from 220 to about 100. Then the place began to change. We almost went broke, but people got serious with God, they got involved—and now membership is creeping back up."

And then he grinned and added, "I think we may be going to have revival."

Brian might be right. Often before revival there is a drop in church attendance. When the Holy Spirit convicts, people confess their sins and repent. Those who are hardened of heart usually flee. Separating the chaff from the wheat signals that the church is becoming pure and holy.

—Charles Colson

Miracle Vehicle

There had been many months of preparation to serve as missionaries in Taiwan and finally the day had come for us to actually go. We arrived in Taiwan safely, but exhausted from the long journey. Morrison Academy has several English language schools for missionary children in Taiwan, and my wife and I had been assigned to work as teachers in Taichung at the main campus. Taichung is a lovely city nestled in a beautiful valley in the heart of Taiwan's farming country. Teachers' housing is provided on campus and there is good bus transportation to the city center. We were confident we could get by without a car, so we hadn't made arrangements to have one before leaving the States.

It was a delight to be met at the airport by Morrison's superintendent. But our hearts sank when he said, "Welcome, Grant and Miriam. We are so glad you're here. I'm sorry to have to break this news to you so soon, but Grant, because of your experience, you have been reassigned to be principal at our Kaohsiung campus. You will stay here with us tonight and tomorrow we will arrange for transportation to your new location."

I queried God, "What have you done to us? Taichung is such a pleasant city, but Kaohsiung? (It was Taiwan's largest industrial center, and isolated near the southern tip of the island.) Kaohsiung is dirty and smoggy with heavy air pollution. It's the last place in Taiwan we would choose to live, I can't believe You would allow this to happen."

We were to spend our first few days in Kaohsiung with missionaries who were assigned to help us get settled and interpret for us when necessary. Other missionaries were leaving on furlough within a week, and we were to move into their house as soon as they left. The problem was, the house was several miles from the school campus. Poor connections made the trip there by bus extremely difficult and time consuming, taxi fare was prohibitive, and there was absolutely no way we could arrange to secure a vehicle of our own. We felt panic-stricken. Here we were in a foreign land, neither being able to speak the language nor even read the street signs; and now this insurmountable problem.

When we went to see the house where we were to live, we learned that the missionaries who were leaving had a three-year-old car they had not yet been able to sell at a bargain price of $2,500. Not sure how I would get the money, I asked excitedly, "Would you take twelve monthly payments so it will be paid in full by the time you return?"

"I'm sorry, Grant, I wish we could, but we need the cash now for traveling expenses," came his quick reply.

My heart sank. Again my wife and I wondered what we were going to do. We felt so stranded, so helpless. We reminded the Lord that we desperately needed transportation to carry on the work we had been assigned to do for Him. "Lord," we pleaded, "There is no visible way that we know to provide for it." With uncertain faith, we asked that He either miraculously provide us with $2,500 within the next few days to buy the missionary's car, or provide us with another means of transportation.

The following day we were surprised to receive three letters from the U.S. that had been forwarded from Taichung. We had not expected mail from home so soon. Our surprise turned to amazement when we opened the first letter and found a sizable check enclosed. When we opened the second letter and found another sizable check, we were absolutely speechless. We could not believe our eyes when upon opening the third letter we found still another check.

We added them all up and the total was exactly $2,500, all of which was completely unexpected. Upon looking at the postmarks, we found the letters had been mailed in the United States about the same time our flight left there.

We were reminded of Isaiah 65:24, *Before they call I will answer; while they are still speaking I will hear.* The Lord knew before we left America what assignment He would have for us in Taiwan and had acted to meet our financial need before we ever knew it existed. Numerous times in our lives we had seen the Lord answer prayer and supply our needs, but never before could we remember such a dramatic and specific solution coming so quickly. Our "Miracle Vehicle" opened the door to numerous ministry opportunities and strengthened our trust in the Lord who truly cares.

—Grant Sickles

Bringing Home Strays

My sister has always been a great lover of animals. While growing up together, she constantly brought home stray dogs, cats and an assortment of other creatures.

I, on the other hand, brought home stray people. Surely it must have driven my mother nuts at times. I pretty well covered the whole gammit, from the young mother with a newborn, to the man without work. But Mom was great. She always made sure they were well-fed and cared for and had a comfortable place to sleep.

One of my strays was particularly memorable. This young teen was beautiful and articulate. She captured our hearts with a deeply-impassioned story. She explained how she had run away from her loving home in the Pacific Northwest to indulge in a prodigal lifestyle. After much grief and disappointment, she now proclaimed she had seen the error of her ways and needed our assistance to return home. We put her up for the night and bought her a train ticket to return home.

Several months later I received a letter from our runaway friend. With great anticipation, I opened the envelope, convinced that there would be waiting the tale of a blissful family reunion. As I read through the letter, my elation turned to profound disbelief and then complete despair. Our reformed runaway had really been a con. She confessed to using us to actually help her run away. Her real home was near ours. We had been lied to and taken advantage of. She was writing to claim repentance again. Hopefully, this second time was sincere.

Nevertheless, the whole experience was at best a tremendous lesson. Why didn't we make a simple phone call to her parents to verify her story? We could have avoided the entire incident if we had. We spent our hard-earned money to fund a fruitless and possibly life-threatening endeavor. Good intentions aren't always good enough.

Over the years, I've determined to become more shrewd in how I give. Not selfish, not greedy, but shrewd. When's the last time you heard a sermon on "Snake-Like Shrewd": Key to Christian Maturity "or" The Spiritual Benefits of Becoming as "Shrewd as a Serpent!" Nobody likes to talk about it, but it's what Jesus taught and lived.

—Kevin Downing

11

Purity

Blessed are the pure in heart; for they shall see God.

Matthew 5:8

Selective Witnessing

I was walking with my pastor and another Christian brother in the corridors at the Promise Keepers conference in Indianapolis, 1994. We were checking out the booths before the sessions started. We met a teenager with his head completely shaven except for a little blond pony-tail on the very top of his head. In less than a second I had formed my opinion that this kid is a loser, a punk, and a jerk. The very next second I'm hit with the thought that this is someone's son. His face shows his hate for being there, and perhaps hatred for his father. As the other two kept walking, I stopped in my tracks, feeling hurt for this boy and his father's relationship. Immediately, I started praying for them—something I felt impressed to do.

An "altar call" was given near the end of the first session. I sat there in my aisle seat, giving thanks for the Holy Spirit's working, when I was brushed by someone going forward to the altar. It was the very same youth I had prayed for earlier. PRAISE THE LORD!

Men are most affected at these conferences by having met their Savior, becoming better husbands, better fathers, etc . . . but I came home knowing I had been judgmental and guilty of "selective witnessing."

—Keith Nash

Grabbing The Bait

Once upon a time I was an avid fisherman. Then I caught "the big one"—a nine-pound, thirteen-ounce smallmouth bass. (I had it stuffed to prove I did it.) After that, fishing never turned my crank like it did before. Here's how it happened . . . .

It was a warm, muggy Memorial Day morning. My wife and two small children took advantage of the holiday and slept in. Not me, though. I was out on the lake early. Ordinarily, my little johnboat would slip across the water at the slightest breeze. But this still day it sat like it was frozen in concrete. I hit the battery-powered trolling motor and glided another few yards around the shoreline.

I positioned myself about fifty feet from shore—the perfect distance to cast the oil-colored plastic worm on a weedless hook that I was using for bait. On each cast I carefully selected what looked like the place I would wait for a worm if I were the Loch Ness Bass.

On my first pass around the lake I didn't get a single strike. I had just passed by our dock when I heard the water ripple slightly on the other side of my boat. As the good hand of Providence would have it, I was just completing working my plastic worm in from the shoreline. Bored, I gave it a little flick of the wrist. I was surprised to see the worm land on the other side of the boat precisely where the water had rippled.

Immediately, something akin to King Kong with fins grabbed my bait and started to run. My heart stopped beating. The reel whirred wildly as my line ripped through the water. *Could this be my day?* I wondered.

The number one rule for catching bass is that you let the fish run with the bait. If you try to set the hook too soon, the bass will simply spit out the bait and, with it, the hook. What you want to do is make sure the fish feels no resistance so that it will think it has the worm, no "strings" attached. You want that bass to get lulled into a false sense of confidence—to feel safe enough to swallow the whole bait. So you let it run, count to ten or twenty real slow, then give a strong yank, and set the hook. After that, all you do is reel her in—there's no way for her to get off the hook.

That's how I caught my big one. And that's exactly how Satan works too. He lets us grab the bait, but he doesn't try to set the hook right away. Instead, he lets us run a while until we lull ourselves into a false confidence. Then, just when we are sure it's safe, he sets the hook, and it's too late. All that's left is to reel us in.

—Patrick M. Morley

Walk A Little Plainer, Daddy

"Walk a little plainer, Daddy," said a little child so small. "I'm following in your footsteps, and I don't want to fall. Sometimes your steps are very plain, sometimes they are hard to see; so walk a little plainer, Daddy, for you are leading me. I know that once you walked this way many years ago; and what you did along the way, I'd really like to know. For sometimes when I'm tempted, I don't know what to do; so I walk a little plainer, Daddy, for I must follow you. Someday when I'm grown up, you are like I want to be; then I will have a little child who will want to follow me. And I would want to lead just right, and know that I was true; so walk a little plainer, Daddy, for I must follow you.

Guardrails

Lindy and I were headed north through Italy's Alps during a time when we were stationed in Europe. At the edge of the Swiss Alps, in the Simplon Pass, we got caught in a savage blizzard. It was bad enough that a work crew along the road actually stopped us. There was serious concern that the road was not only hazardous, but actually impassable.

However, one wizened old toughie on the road crew scoffed at his fellows' fears. I can still hear him saying, "Bah! Road is *goot*! Yah, goot!"

That was all this soldier needed to hear. I got out, chained up our little Mustang, and we headed up the pass. We were going to conquer those mountains. After all, we were young, and had grown up driving on snow in eastern Washington. We thought ourselves invincible. At least, I did. Lindy wasn't so sure. Oh well, as they used to say at Ft. Benning, "Drive on, Ranger!" So I did.

But the blizzard got worse. The banks piled higher. The road narrowed. The snow was beyond belief. I found myself thinking, *Well Stu, this sure isn't Yakima!* By the time we had climbed high into the Alps, we found ourselves in a virtual whiteout. Every once in a while, the swirling winds would create a tiny break in the blizzard and we could see where we were—and that's when it got really scary!

The road was a tiny, icy ribbon climbing the steep flanks of enormous mountains. Just a few inches off the pavement, it was straight down. A sheer drop-off of thousands of feet. If you left the road, it meant certain death. And in Europe, evidencing that typical European disregard for public safety, guardrails were almost nonexistent.

Even so, there seemed little sense in stopping. We were, quite literally, in the middle of nowhere—and it was freezing cold. *Drive on, Ranger!* But by that time, all the smiles and bravado were gone. I had my wife and unborn baby in this dangerous mess. This was life and death.

As we rounded yet another white-knuckle turn, Lindy said, "Stu, you're going a little too fast!"

"We're only going seven miles an hour," I replied. And just as I said those words we began to slide. I tapped the brakes. As I feared, that only made it worse. We were sliding faster, out of control, and there was nothing I could do. This was crazy. It wasn't supposed to end this way! But there we were, shooting toward the edge of eternity.

I gripped the wheel. Our bodies tensed. We closed our eyes, waiting for the inevitable. But just when we thought we'd launch over the cliff into a white abyss, we heard a loud crack and found ourselves jerked around by a violent impact. Our necks snapped forward, then sideways, as the Mustang spun to the right and careened toward the other side of the road before plowing into a soft snowbank.

We blinked, glanced at each other, and simultaneously shouted in our wonder and relief, "What was that?"

Still trembling, I crawled out of our only slightly-damaged car, walked through the blowing snow to the point of impact, and bent down. There, mostly buried beneath the snow, was the now exposed metal of a guardrail! (I thought about kissing that thing, but didn't want to leave my lips in Switzerland!)

It was only a short piece of guardrail—one of a few over the entire pass. But it was at just the right spot for Stu and Linda Weber! To our minds, a divine Providence had installed that one stout little length of metal on that treacherous road just for us. Just when we needed it.

It was time for worship! And gratitude! We thanked God for a life-giving, life-saving, future-preserving guardrail. Something so simple had literally saved our lives. Were it not for that guardrail, neither of us would be here today. And that little one in Linda's womb (now in graduate studies at Oxford) would not be here, either. Nor our other sons. An entire family . . . a beautiful heritage . . . whole generations would have been destroyed . . . were it not for that guardrail.

Today when we drive through the Cascades, Oregon's spinal mountain range, we see a lot of guardrails. And we see them differently than most people. Most are "oohing" and "aahing" over the wildlife or mountain scenery. But you may catch us saying something like, "Look at that wonderful guardrail. Have you ever seen anything so beautiful in your life?" Guardrails have come to mean the world to us. The fact is . . .

Life
without
guardrails
can kill you!

Life is a risky prospect. Physical dangers abound. Spiritual dangers threaten the life of your soul—the life that matters forever. You can't even imagine how high those stakes are. Your personal future, your family's heritage, and the generations to come will feel the impact of how you stand up to those dangers. It's a far more dangerous passage than weathering a blizzard in the Alps.

The great and living God, who invented life, knows just how treacherous this earthly trip can be. That's why, from the very outset, He placed guardrails at strategic points alongside the road. His strong counsel? It is not good for man to be alone. No one should travel by himself. Every man needs a friend. Friends are divinely placed guardrails.

—Stu Weber

Climb Higher

British aviation pioneer Frederick Handley Page was once flying across Arabia when he heard the sickening sound of gnawing in his small plane. Unknown to him, a huge rat had been attracted by the smell of the food put in the cargo hold of the airplane and had managed to get aboard.

Page's heart began to pound when he realized the damage this rodent could do to the plane's control mechanisms. If the rat gnawed through certain critical lines, it would cause a great problem.

Page didn't know what to do. He was flying solo, and there was no such thing as an automatic pilot on those early planes. But then he remembered something he learned in school: Rats can't survive at high altitudes.

So Page began to climb higher, so high that it became difficult even for him to breathe. But he listened intently and after a while the gnawing stopped. When he arrived at his destination, he found the rat lying dead behind the cockpit.

Too many of us have the rat of sin gnawing at our lives. We have the rat of immorality nipping at us, the rat of improper language biting us, the rat of marital destruction chewing on us. Our spiritual planes are about to crash.

But there is something you can do. You can climb higher. Increase your altitude! It may get a little tough to breathe up there, because you haven't been used to climbing that high before. But just keep climbing. The Holy Spirit will keep you alert and awake. Keep climbing until you don't hear the rats gnawing anymore. Keep climbing until God brings victory where you didn't think there could be any.

Climb to an altitude you never thought your spiritual airplane could reach, and you'll discover a freedom you never thought possible. Know, reckon, yield, be free!

—Tony Evans

12

Spiritual Life

. . . that I may know Him, and the power of His resurrection and the fellowship of His sufferings, being conformed to His death.

Philippians 3:10 NKJV

Yonggi Cho—An Unlikely Star

Yonggi Cho graciously invited me to be his guest in Seoul, Korea. I was to speak to the largest church congregation in the world. With 700,000 members, they were still growing rapidly toward the astronomical one million mark.

On several occasions through the years I had welcomed Pastor Cho to my pulpit in North Hollywood. Now I was totally embarrassed to think how casually we had treated him. In Korea he is a towering giant; a royal potentate receiving and dispatching powerful emissaries to represent both the church and himself. He is a national and international influence.

Yet he still impressed me as a simple and sincere man who remembers his humble beginnings and is very much aware that he must give account to the one who gifted him and called him to this lofty position.

When I first knew Cho in the 1950's, he had recently been converted from Buddhism and saved from an early death bed. Abandoned by his doctors to die with terminal tuberculosis, his family cast him out after he was miraculously healed and converted to Christianity. Only the loving care of American missionaries kept him from suicide.

Trained in the mission school, Cho soon took to the city streets and began fervently telling his remarkable story. Not only relatives and neighbors, but strangers heard what he had experienced and learned. Cho eventually came to North Hollywood as our invited guest to tell of his conversion and healing story.

"While lying on my death bed without hope, a total stranger came to tell me about another God called Jesus. I cursed and taunted this uninvited and unwanted young person who happened to be a woman. In our culture she was doubly inferior: a woman and a Christian. I was a life-long Buddhist, *and* a man. Still, she faithfully returned to my bedside for five successive days. I was weak and dying. She gave me a Bible, showed me scriptures to read, and then mysteriously disappeared without my knowing who she was, where she came from or where she vanished to."

Cho was then divinely led to a nearby missionary who also prayed for him and for his healing. Doctors soon pronounced him cured. Through that missionary, a friend of mine, I first heard of an emerging force in Seoul, Korea.

In the war-torn slums, Cho soon began ministering to ever-growing multitudes. Like their new-found leader, thousands and thousands more were converted to Christianity. With help from the missionaries and another lady, his mother-in-law, the former Buddhist founded a church. A Christian Church. Now the greatest church in the world.

Is there a key to gathering and pastoring a flock of almost a million Korean believers? Cho told the rest of the story.

"Yes," he explained. "Knowing from experience the power of prayer, I secured a remote mountain near the well-known demilitarized zone, the DMZ. There I send my members by the bus load to fast and pray. Hundreds are there twenty four hours a day, seven days a week. I also retreat there regularly to a special cave. Day and night, without stopping, our church members pray for Korea and for the world. That is our power source for evangelizing our nation."

Of course when I was invited to be Cho's guest, I made sure that I was taken to the mountain and especially to his private prayer cave. There I found a simple rug spread out to cover the bare, cold ground. A stark light bulb was hanging over head. There he cannot be disturbed. One of his favorite prayers is the first one he prayed as a Buddhist: "Jesus, I want to meet you and have a consultation about my future." The prayer still brings results. When I visited Cho's cave-retreat, this thought surged into my mind: perhaps we would have more churches like Full Gospel in Seoul, if we had more prayer mountains frequented more often by both pastor and people.

—D. Leroy Sanders

Eager To Get Home

When I was at Multnomah School of the Bible, Dr. Willard Aldrich served as its president. At the time, his mother was almost ninety-six and Dr. Aldrich would visit her every day at noon to feed and talk with her. Mrs. Aldrich dearly loved Jesus and was waiting for Him to come.

One day, when Dr. Aldrich went to feed his mother, she did not want to eat. She felt her time had come, and asked Dr. Aldrich to pray that the Lord would allow her to go to be with Him.

"Mother, I can't ask God to take you home," Dr. Aldrich explained. "That's His business. Why don't I feed you a little soup, instead? After all, you can't go to heaven on an empty stomach."

"No, Willard," she answered. "They will feed me some as soon as I get there."

That evening, she went to be with the Lord.

What confidence! That's the way I'd like to go. I want to talk about going to be with Jesus with the same assurance I have when I discuss any activity I've planned. If we live in the power of the indwelling Christ, we have an absolute assurance of the future. We know where we are going when our life on earth is over.

Mrs. Aldrich isn't the only Christian to have known with certainty where she was going. Reading the biography of F. B. Meyer, I learned that one of the last postcards he wrote before he died, read, "Dear Brother: I have raced you to heaven. I am just off. See you there. Love, F. B. Meyer."

—**Luis Palau**

It All Adds Up

Like most men, my first act upon entering the house at the end of a work day has always been to empty my pockets. Receipts, paper clips, scratch paper, car keys and a few coins was a typical collection. One day, I decided to get organized—partially, at least. I placed a small wooden bowl on the desk. Each day, I would still make the pile, but the coins would go in the bowl. When the bowl filled up, I would empty it into a cardboard box in the closet. Over a period of months, that bowl filled up several times.

My 14-year old son, Tim, walked into my office one day. "Dad, can I roll those coins for you?"

I hated rolling coins. That's why I had put it off for so long. So I responded, "Tim, that'd be great. I'd really appreciate it."

His next question reminded me of his entrepreneurial spirit. "Can I keep ten percent for my fee?"

I should have known that he had thought this through—much more carefully than I had. I figured there was about $40 or so collected. Was it worth four dollars to have him roll those coins? "No problem, Tim, the ten percent is yours."

He disappeared for an hour or so. Then I heard him enter the room. "Dad, I finished."

"That's great, Tim. Did you take your fee?"

"Sure did," he replied.

"How much did you get?" I asked.

"About thirty dollars," he announced.

I was aghast. "Tim, I told you to only take ten percent."

"I did," he countered.

Quick math. Quick shock. "You mean I have three hundred dollars in that box?" I questioned.

"Nope, now you have $270."

Ask me for three hundred dollars today, and I'd probably be

hard-pressed to come up with it. But with a minimum of effort, just a few coins a day, I ended up with a surprising result.

Walking with God is like that. It's important to spend time with God in an extended, quality session. But I can't overlook the benefits of quick contacts with Him during the day. Casual prayers in the car, reviewing a verse or two while standing in line, making contact quickly throughout the day as situations arise—things that seem almost too minimal to count. But when carried out over time, the results are surprising. It can turn a routine with God into a relationship.

—Michael Bechtle

Lessons Learned Early

At eighteen I struck up a friendship with the assistant manager of a fast-food place. He was a bright-eyed, open sort of a guy. Spiritual things never came up, but I looked for openings.

One day his face was lit up like noon in June. "Have I got something to tell you! It's the greatest thing I've ever heard of, and I'd be no friend if I didn't share it with you. You've got to come with me to a meeting tomorrow night."

"Well, sure, but what?"

"Just say you'll come."

I was convinced he had become a Christian, and I was depressed. Not for him, of course, but for me. This guy was more excited than I had ever been.

I told my dad—a police chief—and asked if he'd go with me. "I think I'd better," he said. "It's as likely a scam as anything. This guy naive? Interested in getting rich quick?"

"Probably, but Dad, he was as excited as a new believer."

"He *is* a new believer. But in what?"

We rode with my friend. And Dad was right. It was a pyramid selling scheme. Your average Joe, with a little work, a little luck, a little investment, and enough relatives could make a shade under $105,000 a year selling gyroscopes that would keep your car from fishtailing. Honest.

It sounded so good, such a sure thing, that I didn't know how anybody could pass it up. I wondered where I would come up with the money and how many my dad would buy. I could see why my friend was so excited. These people put Christians to shame.

When the pitch was over, the sales force took over. "How many would you like, sir?"

Dad was masterful. "None for me, thanks," he said.

The young salesman thought he had been prepared for every

objection. "If you have any questions about the product, I can answer them."

"No questions."

"If you need financing, we can arrange that. Let me start you with one on a no-risk, fully-guaranteed, money-back basis." He slid the order form under Dad's nose.

"No, thank you."

"You don't want to make $105,000 a year?"

Dad looked him in the eye and smiled. "I'm not motivated by great amounts of money."

Now there was one he hadn't heard before. "You're not? How about just the one for yourself? Do your family a favor and keep yourself safe. Keep your own car from fishtailing."

"My car doesn't fishtail. I drive slowly in bad conditions."

That valuable lesson has protected me against irrepressible sales people ever since. When they learn I'm not motivated by money, they have nowhere to go, unless their product truly is more important than the money we can both make off it.

On the way home in a steady drizzle I learned another lesson. My friend's car was equipped with "the product."

"Watch this," he said, gunning the accelerator as he turned a corner. The car spun completely around in the street.

He was red-faced, and we were silent for the next several minutes until my friend spoke. "Chief Jenkins," he said, "if you're not motivated by money, what are you motivated by?"

What an opening.

—Jerry B. Jenkins

God's Discipline

The story is told of a little boy who was floating his boat on a pond when the boat floated away. A man came by, saw the boat out on the pond, and began throwing stones on the far side of the boat. The boy asked, "What are you doing?"

But then something very interesting happened. As the stones hit the water beyond the boat, they created ripples which pushed the boat back toward the boy. Even though the stones disturbed the smooth water, they achieved the desired result.

That's how God's discipline is. When we drift away from Him on the "Sea of Sin" or the "Pond of Unrighteousness," He throws the disturbing stones of His loving discipline out beyond us in order to push us back to the shore of our first love.

—Tony Evans

A Son's Death

A short while ago I was speaking at a series of meetings in Belgium. One night my interpreter, Wilfred, was driving me to my engagement in the city of Ghenk at the border of Germany, very near the now well-known city of Maastricht, where the historic treaty was signed for European unity. I really did not know Wilfred well, so our initial communication was introductory and general. There was something about his demeanor, however, that endeared him to me as a gentle individual who had experienced some of life's pains and who had been scarred by carrying its heavier burdens. The hour was late, and the darkness of the night created a setting of stillness and aloneness that was perfect for a memorable interchange. We came from two different parts of the world—he from a small country that would have fit into one of India's smaller cities, I from a country too vast to measure by any typical ways of generalization. He came from a country still remembering the sounds of Nazi feet on its sidewalks; I came from one where the warfare has been more of the soul. With all that separated us, the next few moments would dramatically bring incredible closeness of heart and mind.

He began to tell me how it was that he came to commit his life to the person of Jesus Christ and how extremely this commitment had been tested. The many pauses during the narrative and the moving tone of his voice revealed how intensely he felt about what he was saying. He told of how he had been attending a conference in a rather Edenic setting somewhere in Switzerland some years ago. He described the unfolding events of one fateful day: "The hymns resounded all day on the reality of heaven, and the speakers expounded on it. I was basking in the greatness of this hope and enjoying the promise of such a destiny. Quite unexpectedly, my name was called during the meeting to go immediately to the office as there was an urgent call awaiting me. I did just that and picked up the phone to hear the somber and sobbing voice of my wife, Faith, informing me that our nine-month-old baby had, without warning, died in his crib a short while ago."

He recounted that the news brought him to the lowest point in his life. The devastation defied description. The anguish and anger built up within his heart to volcanic proportions, threatening to spew out his uncontainable grief. A cry within him wanted to sue God for contempt of human life—so ran the litany of emotions that spelled one basic feeling, that of absolute bewilderment. He packed his bags, bought himself a train ticket, and sat alone in his seat looking out through the window where nothing seemed to ease the ache.

Across the aisle from him sat a man reading his Bible, opposite whom sat two young people who did not try to hide their disdain toward so-called religious books. Their taunts were finally responded to by the man holding the Bible, and their discussion took on some heavy philosophical jousting. Finally, one of the young men, anger unmasked, leaned over and said to the man, "If your God is as loving and kind as you say He is, tell me why He lets the innocent suffer? Why does He permit so much warfare? Why does He allow little children to die? What kind of love is that?"

The questions, especially the last two, stabbed Wilfred in a way he had never felt before, and he caught himself on the verge of blurting out, "Yes, you religious zealot! Answer them and me, and tell us why He lets children die. What sort of love is that?" But a strange mental transformation took place in Wilfred's own mind. He awaited the other man's answer, and then he looked at the two young men and found himself saying, "Do you mind if I enter into your conversation? I'll tell you how much God loves you; He gave His only Son to die for you."

The young men abruptly interrupted him and argued that it was easy for Wilfred to make such platonic pronouncements disconnected from the concrete world of death and desolation.

Wilfred waited for the appropriate moment because he needed every ounce of courage and conviction to say it once, but to say it clearly. "No, no, no, my dear friends," he said. "I am not distanced from the real world of pain and death. In fact, the reason I am on this train is because I am heading home for the funeral of my nine-month-old son. He died just a few hours ago, and it has given the cross a whole new meaning for me. Now I know what kind of a God it is who loves me, a God who willfully gave His Son for me."

—Ravi Zacharias

According to an Associated Press account, in September 1994 Cindy Hartman of Conway, Arkansas, walked into her house to answer the phone and was confronted by a burglar. He ripped the phone cord out of the wall and ordered her into the closet.

Hartman dropped to her knees and asked the burglar if she could pray for him. "I want you to know that God loves you and I forgive you," she said.

The burglar apologized for what he had done. Then he yelled out the door to a woman in a pickup truck: "We've got to unload all of this. This is a Christian home and a Christian family. We can't do this to them."

As Hartman remained on her knees, the burglar returned furniture he had taken from her home. Then he took the bullets out of his gun, handed the gun to Hartman, and walked out the door.

Praying for our enemies is incredibly disarming.

—Scott Harrison

Searching For A Purpose In Life

I got an opportunity to go to the University of Missouri on a football scholarship. I was so proud when they put that in the paper. I thought that everyone in Riverview, Michigan would realize that surely Bill McCartney has arrived and he's a guy that everyone can look to with respect and admiration. That was important to me. It wasn't long after I got to Missouri that I realized most of the guys there were every bit as talented, or more talented than I was. I knew that if I was going to have their respect and admiration, I had to do something significant. At first, I just wanted to make the team. Then I wanted to get in the game. Then, that wasn't enough, I wanted to be a starter. Once I became a starter, I wanted to earn honors. You really couldn't satisfy me.

My attempts to earn self-esteem carried over into my coaching career. As a high school coach, I began to discover that the more games we won, the better I felt about myself and the better I was received in the community. That fueled an initiative that drove me long and hard trying to achieve and accomplish things as a coach. Then the really big break came.

In 1974, at the age of thirty-three, I got the opportunity to go to the University of Michigan and be on that great football staff. I was the only high school coach Bo Schembechler ever hired. That was important to me. I knew that once I walked into that big stadium of 100,000 and rubbed elbows with the winningest football coach in the country, everybody would recognize, once and for all, that Bill McCartney had arrived. But it wasn't long after I got there that I discovered everybody there knew more football than I did. I again realized that if I was going to get their attention, affection, or esteem, I would have to achieve great things.

Then I met Chuck Heater. I was thirty-three years old and there was a guy on our team who was nineteen. He was a sophomore, fullback-running back and I noticed a quality to his life, a dimension to him, that was very attractive to me. So, I approached him. I said, "Chuck Heater, I see in you a dimension that I know I don't have. You're such a great competitor. You're so fiery and yet there's a peace and a serenity to you that's so beautiful. What is it about you?" Chuck stood back for a second and sized me up. He wasn't used to being approached by a coach on the Michigan staff quite like that. He said, "I'll tell you what, Coach. In two weeks eighteen Michigan athletes from all sports are having a conference in Brighton, Michigan. I'd like for you to come. Then, I'll try to answer your question."

What I heard at that conference changed my life; and it has never been the same. For the first time I was confronted with whether or not I had actually surrendered control of my life to Jesus Christ. I understood that if I would submit to Christ, Almighty God would take dominion in my heart and take over the direction in my life. Then, my life would start to gain some real satisfaction and fulfillment. That really appealed to me because in my work I had just entered into an arena where it was extremely competitive and I wasn't feeling good about myself.

I remember going home that day being excited because I had made a decision to give my life to Jesus Christ. It was something I had never done before. My wife, Lyndee, was in the living room with a lady from the neighborhood. I came busting in the front door and told her what happened. I then excused myself and left the room. The neighbor reached over and tapped Lyndee in the ribs and said, "I've seen it before. Don't worry about it. It blows right over." But it didn't blow over.

One of the reasons it didn't blow over was because I immediately started getting together with other men—for encouragement, fellowship, prayer, and Bible study.

—**Bill McCartney**

The Faith Of A Child

The park usually provided a serene refuge where I could just sit and pull myself together. I was in a secluded spot that day, but when the park was invaded by a group of gradeschoolers on a field trip, I couldn't escape the sounds of unrestrained joy as the children unleashed their boundless energy on the playground equipment.

The exuberant mood of the children was in sharp contrast to my own. I had been out of a job for nearly a month—with nothing more than anxiety to show for my persistent efforts at finding work. Lack of a formal education and a felony prison record were enough to insure job applications were dismissed almost out of hand.

I was discouraged. Reflecting on my own childhood didn't help. The son of divorced parents, raised by an absentee mother and emotionally- and physically-distant father, I felt hopeless by my 16th birthday. Suicide seemed the only way out.

When I failed in my attempt to end my life, my depression deepened. The Marine Corps seemed like a good idea but with the help of drugs and drink, I managed to rack up a number of infractions by the end of my tour of duty and was discharged under less than honorable conditions. With a full-blown addiction to alcohol and drugs, my criminal actions resulted in a 17-year prison sentence for armed-robbery.

Sixteen months of imprisonment dragged by before I reached my rope's end and cried out to God for help. I admitted my condition and my need, owning up for the first time to just what a mess I had made of my life. Through the influence of a Christian inmate, I received Jesus Christ as my personal Lord and Savior.

The next three-and-a-half years were filled with studying the Bible and seeking the counsel of mature believers, including prison chaplains and fellow Christian inmates. I recall one prisoner in particular, who had prior to his incarceration been a deacon for twenty years. God used Harold to mold and shape my Christian character. Playing the devil's advocate, he would often take the opposing side in an effort to make me wrestle with the newfound truths I was experiencing. Our many "theological debates" resulted in those truths becoming a vital part of my Christian walk.

Eventually, I was entrusted with a job at the Governor's Executive Mansion, which resulted in a commutation of my sentence and early parole.

Almost immediately, my faith was put to the test. A fellow resident and I decided to share an apartment. We were into the six-month's lease by only a few weeks, however, when my room-mate decided the responsibility was too much for him and jumped ship. Adding insult to injury, my lawn maintenance job ended. Penniless, and with bills coming in and the rent due, I was on the verge of despair.

Then I discovered, in-between efforts at job-hunting, one of the city's lovely parks. As I listened to the children at play, I was struck by the amazing qualities they possessed. To them, every-one and everything is a marvelous adventure, every setting a perfect opportunity to play. They waste precious little time holding grudges or planning revenge, choosing instead to live and enjoy life as fully as possible.

I was reminded that Jesus Christ, the greatest teacher who ever lived, commanded that His followers possess childlike faith. And I desired the kind of faith that trusts implicitly and loves unceasingly. Only with such faith could I experience true health and strength.

I left the park that day with a renewed sense of God's presence. I could see more clearly the need to let go of the past and trust Christ for today—and tomorrow. I was beginning to understand that I am called to live a life of simple trust in Him.

God proved faithful to my renewed faith. An associate pastor at the church I was attending learned of my plight and took a personal interest in my situation. He petitioned the church and they paid my rent for the month. He spoke with the president of the company he had co-founded and I was given an opportunity to prove myself on a job. He reached into his own pocket and helped me to finance a used car so I'd have transportation. He took a chance on me, and in so doing modeled the childlike faith I had so recently been reminded of.

Today makes more than five years since my release from prison. I work part-time and attend North Carolina State University, where I am preparing for a career in Marriage and Family Counseling. My wife of two years, Sharon, is a committed Christian and holds a post-doctorate position at N. C. State.

From the day I opened my heart to Christ, He has continued to bring compassionate and caring people into my life. Their presence reminds me that only God knows for sure what the future holds; mine remains only to trust in His perfect love and guidance . . . with the faith of a child.

—Greg Williamson

Getting Permission From Mom

When my eldest, Dallas, was six, my wife and I overheard him giving instructions to one of his tiny soldiers.

"You may die in this mission," he said, "but if you're a Christian, you'll go to heaven. In heaven you can ask Jesus for anything you want, and if it's all right with your mom, He'll give it to you."

—Jerry B. Jenkins

Love Enacted

Loving God would be impossible if God had not loved us first, and loved us so deeply. It is hard for us to imagine the God of the universe caring so deeply for each of us individually and uniquely, but He does. I saw a human display of this type of love when I was traveling on a business trip to the remote town of Fairbanks, Alaska.

After checking into my hotel room, I set out to find the dining room for a long overdue dinner. As I ate, an affluent-looking man walked past me. He was a man who appeared to be quite wealthy. A huge gold watch hung loosely from his arm. His feet were attired in Italian loafers that make men's feet look about two sizes smaller than they really are. The brass buttons on his navy blazer stood out against the darkness of the room. I had a hunch that I was looking at a man who wanted for little.

As he passed me, he made his way up a few steps and was taken to his table on the eating level next to me that was about three feet above the floor I was on. As I listened to him order, I heard him ask the wine steward for a bottle of the best red wine in the house. This request confirmed my belief that he was a man who had it all. The wine steward turned to retrieve the prize with great anticipation.

I watched the wine steward and the wealthy man go through a rather lengthy and drawn-out ritual of bottle opening and tasting. The cork was removed from the bottle and placed in front of the man who picked it up and waved it back and forth closely to his nose. It must have smelled quite good to them because they proceeded to the next step. The wine taster poured a little into a glass for the man and a little into the silver "baby rattle" hanging from his neck. The man took a sip and seemed to gargle with it. He must have liked it as he nodded to the steward and tapped the glass to signal a pour was in order.

While all of this was going on, I just happened to observe

another diner of very different means. Across the room I noticed an elderly woman come in and sit down after draping her hole-ridden coat and scarf across the opposite chair. Her hair was matted and no one would have been surprised to find some type of vermin living there. Her face was deeply-creased and her leathery skin revealed a woman who had lived in the cold much of her life. She ate alone, isolated in sadness, as a direct contrast to the man who looked like he had it all. I was saddened by the obvious plight of this old woman.

I glanced back up at the wine steward and the man of means. The wine steward was leaning over listening to the request of the man. The steward responded by picking up the expensive bottle of wine and a glass and placing them on his tray. He turned around and walked back through the crowd of diners, many of whom would have enjoyed the attention of this man. He passed them all up and went directly to the table of the old woman. He spoke with her and after she made a faint nod, he set the wine bottle down next to the glass and then poured her a glass of red wine from the best bottle in the house. With what might have been her first blush in many years, she grasped her glass and held it high in the air as she glanced toward the wealthy man. He stood with his glass in the air, in a saluting toast to the woman. In an amazing moment of compassion and connection, I watched as they shared a glass of wine from the best bottle of wine in the house.

I began to weep for I had seen played out before me a human enactment of the love God has for each of us. In the midst of a world of beautiful people, God has chosen each of us to share the best he has to offer. It is better than any bottle of wine. Sadly, rather than experience God's love, too many people are afraid to pick up the glass and drink it in. Amazingly, experiencing God's love begins when we decide to give to God what he deserves and demands, our time, our money and our heart.

—Stephen Arterburn

A Street Vendor Named Contentment

Ahhh . . . an hour of contentment. A precious moment of peace. A few minutes of relaxation. Each of us has a setting in which contentment pays a visit:

- Early in the morning while the coffee is hot and everyone else is asleep.
- Late at night as you kiss your six-year-old's sleepy eyes.
- In a boat on a lake when memories of a life well-lived are vivid.
- In the companionship of a well-worn, dog-eared, even tearstained Bible.
- In the arms of a spouse.
- At Thanksgiving dinner or sitting near the Christmas tree.
- An hour of contentment. An hour when deadlines are forgotten and strivings have ceased. An hour when what we have overshadows what we want. An hour when we realize that a lifetime of blood-sweating and headhunting can't give us what the cross gave us in one day—a clean conscience and a new start.

But unfortunately, in our squirrel cages of schedules, contests, and side-glancing, hours like these are about as common as one-legged monkeys. In our world, contentment is a strange street vendor, roaming, looking for a home, but seldom finding an open door. This old salesman moves slowly from house to house, tapping on windows, knocking on doors, offering his wares: an hour of peace, a smile of acceptance, a sigh of relief. But his goods are seldom taken. We are too busy to be content. (Which is crazy, since the reason we kill ourselves today is because we think it will make us content tomorrow.)

"Not now, thank you. I've too much to do," we say. "Too many marks to be made, too many achievements to be achieved, too many dollars to be saved, too many promotions to be earned. And besides, if I'm content, someone might think I've lost my ambition."

So the street vendor named Contentment moves on. When I asked him why so few welcomed him into their homes, his answer left me convicted. "I charge a high price, you know. My fee is steep. I ask people to trade in their schedules, frustrations, and anxieties. I demand that they put a torch to their fourteen-hour days and sleepless nights. You'd think I'd have more buyers." He scratched his beard, then added pensively, "But people seem strangely proud of their ulcers and headaches."

May I say something a bit personal? I'd like to give a testimony. A live one. I'm here to tell you that I welcomed this bearded friend into my living room this morning.

It wasn't easy.

My list of things was, for the most part, undone. My responsibilities were just as burdensome as ever. Calls to be made. Letters to be written. Checkbooks to be balanced.

But a funny thing happened on the way to the rat race that made me slip into neutral. Just as I got my sleeves rolled up, and the old engine was starting to purr, and getting up a good head of steam, my infant daughter, Jenna, needed to be held. She had a stomachache. Mom was in the bath, so it fell to Daddy to pick her up.

She's three weeks old today. At first I started trying to do things with one hand and hold her with the other. You're smiling. You've tried that too? Just when I realized that it was impossible, I also realized that it was not at all what I was wanting to do.

I sat down and held her tight little tummy against my chest. She began to relax. A big sigh escaped her lungs. Her whimpers became gurgles. She slid down my chest until her little ear was right on top of my heart. That's when her arms went limp and she fell asleep.

And that's when the street vendor knocked at my door.

Goodbye, schedule. See you later, routine. Come back tomorrow, deadlines . . . hello Contentment, come on in.

So here we sit, Contentment, my daughter, and I. Pen in hand, note pad on Jenna's back. She'll never remember this moment and I'll never forget it. The sweet fragrance of a moment captured fills the room. The taste of an opportunity seized sweetens my mouth. The sunlight of a lesson learned illuminates my understanding. This is one moment that didn't get away.

The tasks? They'll get done. The calls? They'll get made. The letters? They'll be written. And you know what? They'll get done with a smile:

I don't do this enough, but I'm going to do it more. In fact, I'm thinking of giving that street vendor a key to my door. "By the way, Contentment, what are you doing this afternoon?"

—**Max Lucado**

"Girls are called the opposite sex 'cause they always want to do the opposite of what we want to do."

Free As A Bird

It didn't make sense to me. The criminals were as free as a bird and the birds were in jail. It probably doesn't make sense to you either. Let me explain.

When I was first transferred to the zoo health center, I found myself caring for a cage full of red-tailed hawks. There were fifteen of them, and they were crowded together in a pitifully small cage. To my eye, they looked to be very depressed. I inquired as to the reason why we might be caring for fifteen red-tailed hawks off exhibit and the answer really frosted me.

The senior keeper, an extremely jovial Mexican-American man by the name of Johnny Torres, said, "Eeeeeeh, those hawks are evidence for court trials. These guys caught them illegally and we keep them here until their trial is over."

"What happens when the court trials are over?" I asked.

"I don't know," he answered. "We never hear. Some of these birds have been here a long time. We don't even know which bird goes with what trial. So they'll probably die here."

"That doesn't make sense to me," I protested.

"Richmond, did somebody lie to you and tell you things make sense around here? It's best not to ask too many questions about this either. The guys down below, down in administration, they don't like to know that they got problems. So my advice is to drop it."

Well, to tell you the truth, it just wasn't in my nature to drop it. After all, it was the sixties and this was a cause. It seemed to me that the poor, the children, and the animals needed help. This was injustice pure and simple. The poachers were free and the poachees were being punished.

I inquired gently and became convinced that the birds were in trouble. Nobody cared about their plight, and the red tape to get them released was so sticky that no one would wade through it.

There was only one answer. They must be let go. But it must

look like an accident. The punishment for letting low-risk animals out was nothing more than a notice to correct a deficiency. I had never received one before, but it would be a small price to pay to right this wrong.

I decided that I would let them go on a Tuesday afternoon when the supervisors were at the animal health committee meeting. They would be out of the area for about two hours, more than enough time to accomplish my mission.

Tuesday came and the supervisors left the hospital area. I made my way out to the cage, slipped the lock out of the hasp, and left the door wide open. I looked around. There was no one in sight. I slipped back into the health center and set about my duties with a profound sense of fulfillment, an abiding feeling of satisfaction. It was not to last.

After one hour I decided to check the cage. Astonishment, disbelief, wonder, and confusion reigned supreme as I beheld all fifteen birds still in the cage relaxing. There was still time. Perhaps the red-tails just needed some inspiration. Well, I knew what would be inspirational. I ran into their cage waving my arms and growled like a bear. That inspired them, all right. They flew out of the cage and landed not ten feet from the cage door. The look that they gave me was pitiful. They were confused and it was clear to me that they wanted back into the cage. "Don't you see the sky?" I pleaded. "That's what you were meant for." I began feeling a little self-conscious inside the cage so I stepped out to finish my address. "What's wrong with you? You're not chickens. You're majestic birds of prey. You hunt your food. God gave you a purpose, now go fulfill it." I decided to go back to the health center. Maybe their instincts would take over and they would feel some primal urge to command the wind. I left for fifteen minutes and then returned. Not one bird had felt any urges. In fact, some had walked back into the cage. With fifteen minutes to go, I gave up. I don't mind telling you I was more than a little deflated. I ended up herding the birds back into the cage like goats. Where had I gone wrong?

I had approached their problem "anthropomorphically," which

is a fancy way of saying I was projecting my thoughts into the minds of the birds. The birds had not been sitting in the cage longing to be free. Those were my thoughts. They had long since become satisfied with just waiting to be fed. No famines to suffer. No droughts to survive. No territorial battles to enjoin. It wasn't all bad. I felt bad, but they didn't. The reason I felt bad was because by caging them we had taken something from them that they needed to be noble—their purpose. God had created the red-tailed hawks to hunt rodents and reptiles. Few birds can equal their elegant flight or fearless pursuit of prey. This group of birds had been robbed of their ecological purpose. And we weren't even letting the zoo patrons appreciate them. That's what was bothering me.

I thought a bit more about freedom as I finished my responsibilities that day. I concluded that freedom was the ability to fulfill the purpose for which you were created. I further reasoned that man had an interesting distinction. Unlike the animals, man can never be kept from fulfilling his purpose. He is always and in every circumstance free to perform the function for which he was created. Man's purpose is to love and to serve God. The more difficult the circumstances, the greater the opportunity to achieve that purpose. We are now and will always be free to be what we were meant to be, that creature designed to glorify God and enjoy Him forever.

Are you fulfilling the purpose for which you were created? Or have you become satisfied with the ways of the world? You have the freedom to choose.

—Gary Richmond

13

Success

Now thanks be unto God, which always causeth us to triumph in Christ, and maketh manifest the savour of his knowledge by us in every place.

II Corinthians 2:14

The Great Adventure

My Dad was one of those one-of-a-kind men. He had no trouble sharing his love and giving me a hug or one of those "straighten-up-boy" looks. He was always fun to be with and talked to me like I really mattered. He was the same with everyone.

One summer we went to eastern Washington to visit the family home. I was about seven or eight years old at the time. I was all ears when Dad told me about the "Fort" he and his brother and friends had built. It was on a hill across a wheat field in back of their home.

With one of those faraway looks in his eyes, Dad told me about the cowboy and Indian games they had played up there. We walked to the back sitting porch and Dad pointed out the rock wall of the fort that still stood 25 years later; a true engineering feat for 12-year-olds. One thing led to another and we decided to go on an adventure—to climb the hill for a closer look at the fort.

It was a long, hot climb that seemed to take forever. But we finally made it. All the way to the fort Dad continued to tell me his boyhood stories of adventure and daring. Standing in the fort, my father began to play cowboys and Indians with me. We fought off every attacking tribe for the better part of an hour. Tired but victorious, he reminded me that we needed to head for home because dinner would soon be ready.

Then my father did something that made an incredible impact on my life. (I can still remember the feeling some thirty-seven years later.) Dad said, "Let's run home!" He grabbed my hand and we started racing down that steep hill. Soon my little legs gave out and he said, "Hold on," and he ran even faster. My feet left the ground and I literally flew all the way down the hill, the two of us laughing all the way. It was the most wonderful adventure I ever had with my father.

Years later reflecting on that experience, I have to say that it prepared me for my relationship with my Heavenly Father.

Twenty-nine years ago I gave my life to Jesus Christ and became part of God's forever family. And quite literally, as I hold onto the Father's hand, my life flies in His adventure. God has taken me places I never even dreamed I could go: places like India, Afghanistan, Iran, Lebanon, Egypt, Ethiopia, and Israel. I have met with world and Christian leaders and common street beggars and have seen the imprint of God's love on them.

I learned that you lose nothing in the surrender of your will to the Father; you only gain an adventure that is directed by God and empowered by His Holy Spirit.

—**Randy Yenter**

The Myth Of Money

In 1923, an important meeting was held at the Edgewater Beach Hotel in Chicago. In attendance were eight of the world's most powerful financiers:

1. the president of the largest independent steel company
2. the president of the largest gas company
3. the greatest wheat speculator
4. the president of the New York Stock Exchange
5. a member of the president's cabinet
6. the greatest "bear" on Wall Street
7. the head of the world's greatest monopoly
8. the president of the Bank of International Settlements

By all accounts these men had ascended to the upper reaches of success. They had discovered the secrets of making money. As they left the hotel, life took them in different directions. What happened to them? Twenty-five years later:

1. The president of the largest independent steel company, Charles Schwab, died bankrupt, having lived on borrowed money for the last five years before his death.

2. The president of the largest gas company, Howard Hopson, became insane.

3. The greatest wheat speculator, Arthur Cotton, died abroad, insolvent.

4. The president of the New York Stock Exchange, Richard Whitney, went to Sing Sing Penitentiary.

5. The member of the president's cabinet, Albert Fall, was pardoned from prison so that he could die at home.

6. The greatest "bear" on Wall Street, Jesse Livermore, died a suicide.

7. The head of the world's greatest monopoly, Ivar Krueger, died a suicide.

8. The president of the Bank of International Settlements, Leon Fraser, died a suicide.

David was right when he said, *The sorrows of those will increase who run after other gods* (Psalm 16:4).

Money makes a wonderful servant but a ruthless master.

The Confidence Factor

Lack of confidence demolishes many Americans who want to cruise the road of success. A successful person is one who believes in himself. That does not negate Christ nor suggest that we can go it alone. We can't. But it also means confidence is an essential tool in our mental kit of drives and emotions. An example is Roger Staubach, at one-time a star Navy quarterback who, as a junior, won the Heisman Trophy. He also played for the Dallas Cowboys in the '70s, and quarterbacked the team in four Super Bowl outings—two to victory.

Starting out as a Plebe at the Naval Academy can be rough. Hazing is the rule of the hour; making Plebes look ridiculous is the name of the game. For Staubach it was no different. He arrived at summer football camp with high expectations. At a Sunday breakfast, one of the upperclassmen began verbally pummeling Roger about his aspirations. The upperclassman was the backup quarterback for the varsity Navy offense. He knew that soon this Plebe would be in competition with him.

"Hey, Staubach," he shouted. "I hear you're going to take my job away. Is that right?"

"No, sir," Roger answered. He was going to be courteous about it anyway.

"That's strange," the upperclassman replied. "I'm sure that's what I heard."

Staubach looked the bruiser in the eye and said, "What is your job, sir?"

"Number two quarterback!"

"I'm not going to take your job away, sir," Roger said with a smile.

The upperclassman grinned thinking all was well until Staubach added, "It's the starting quarterback job that I'm going to take, sir."

And it was not long before he did just that.

Now that is confidence. Rip-roaring, in your face, pull no punches, take no prisoners CONFIDENCE.

I've found that it's the kind of confidence that comes from a relationship with Christ. He's there with you, beside you, around you, ahead of you. Where you are, He is, and you can't go anywhere that He isn't.

That gives me confidence to keep on going, keep on trying, keep on keeping on.

—**Mark R. Littleton**

Ordinary Scales

My friend, Mark, was on weekend business in a distant city. Since he had no Saturday responsibilities, he spent the day working in his hotel room. In the next room, he heard someone playing the cello. The practice session continued for six hours. Mark was surprised to hear this excellent musician playing scales, over and over, for the first two hours of his practice.

That evening as he visited with business associates in the hotel, Mark learned that his hotel neighbor was one of the premier cellists in the world and had been practicing for a solo performance with the local symphony that night.

Mark observed that this virtuoso cellist knew the importance of reviewing the basics—ordinary scales—on the night of a major concert.

That's true in my spiritual life as well. The longer I walk with God, the more I need to practice the presence of God through the basic, ordinary disciplines of prayer, Bible study and meditation. It's the simple key to spiritual success.

—**Michael Bechtle**

First Things

When I was a kid growing up, I knew a man who loomed bigger than life to me. His name was Edwin E. Bailey, and he ran the astronomical observatory at the Franklin Institute in Philadelphia. I would go to the Franklin Institute most Saturdays just to spend time with him. His encyclopedic mind fascinated me. He seemed to know something about everything.

I was friends with Ed Bailey right up until he died several years ago. When he was in the hospital, after a serious stroke, I went to visit him. In an effort to make small talk, I told about all the places I had been to speak and how I had come to his bedside right from the airport.

He heard me out and then said with a slightly sarcastic manner, "You go all over the world speaking to people who, ten years from now, won't remember your name. But you haven't time left for the people who really care about you."

That simple sentence hit me hard and changed my life. I have decided not to let my time be used up by people to whom I make no difference, while I neglect those for whom I am irreplaceable.

A friend of mine recently got a call from the White House asking him to consult with the president of the United States. He said no because it was to be on a day he had promised to spend with his granddaughter at the seashore. The nation survived without him, the president didn't miss him, and his granddaughter had some precious time with her "Pop-Pop." First things ought to be put first.

—Tony Campolo

Lou Holtz—A Winning Star

In 1988 Lou Holtz led his Notre Dame team to their historic twelve-to-nothing record. It was a remarkable turnaround for the fighting Irish after only three seasons of coaching by Holtz. Recounting their amazing triumphs, he didn't take too much of the credit for himself.

Holtz explained, "I have three simple rules for my athletes. First: the 'Do-Right Rule.' And if you don't know what is right, read the Bible. Number two: 'The Do-The-Best-You-Can Rule.' Not everyone can be an all-American, but everyone can do the best he can. Number three: 'The Golden Rule.' Treat everyone as you want to be treated."

"There are three questions I ask my players. They are basic questions for winning in marriage, business, sports, and in general. Number one. Can I trust you? Number two. Are you striving to be the best you can be? Number three. Do you care about me?"

That formula worked for Notre Dame. That once-losing team rallied to post a record of thirty-three to three.

Holtz says that he is proud of strong football giants who can cry. "As National Champions, we went to Washington on January 18, 1989, at the invitation of President Reagan, and we really celebrated! I've never seen happier guys. But twenty-four hours later our team was in deep mourning—weeping openly. Bobby Satterfield, a second-string player died suddenly of a congenital heart defect. He was no star, but he was one of the family. We really cared for each other. That's what set us apart."

"At the end of our team meetings I would always ask, 'who has a problem?' And some of our team members always had an answer. We proved that when people care, we can win. That's my simple formula."

Holtz says, "I was turned away from Notre Dame as a young interested student. Not good enough. Not qualified. But many years later I was sought out by that very same Notre Dame. Now they needed me, of all things, as a teaching coach."

What made the difference? Lou Holtz had discovered some secrets to winning. Now Notre Dame, as an institution of higher learning, rolled out the red carpet, because they believed that the Lou Holtz formula was well-worth the learning.

—D. Leroy Sanders

Places, Everybody!

Palm Sunday was a special day of celebration for our church as we looked forward to hearing "Messiah: True and Faithful," a musical drama presentation. Here I was, fifty years old, trying to remember thousands of lines. Well, it seemed like thousands. This was my first major attempt with drama. I had been picked to play the part of a fictitious character, a contemporary of Jesus, to help retell the wonderful story of Easter.

Three times a day I listened to the recorded script, read the words silently and aloud only to be frustrated with memory loss at the first rehearsal. Then came words of encouragement and hope from others. More than once I found myself committing it all the Lord. Practice continued. On the eve of Palm Sunday my wife, Bobbie, ran lines with me until my brain turned to mush.

Waking up on Sunday morning after about five hours of sleep, I rejoiced in His creation, His love, His blessing, His hope! Yes! This is the day the Lord has made and I will rejoice in it.

Later after a preliminary welcome and a few announcements, the overture sounded the beginning of a magnificent score. I sat behind a partition and continued to pray.

Then I felt an overwhelming sense of God's presence. Please understand that I am not one given to hearing the audible voice of God, but on this Easter morning I heard Him speak to this nervous heart: "I will be with you. You are doing this for My glory. I will speak through you and others who celebrate My life during these moments."

The performance went smoothly and I saw again how God had proved Himself the "Messiah: True and Faithful!"

—Charles Brown

Mickey's Legacy

By age 14, a shy Mickey Mantle was already superior in baseball, basketball and football. At 19 he joined the Yankees and for 18 years was the envy of all major league players—2401 games played, 8102 times at bat, 536 home runs and a record-breaking home run of 565 feet. In his prime nobody was better. A Hall of Fame American Hero.

Sadly, however, his 42 year run-in with alcohol was as legendary as his runs on the baseball diamond. Just before his recent death, he spoke candidly of his life, his family and his regrets. *First,* Mickey found his niche. He discovered his special abilities and honed them until he became a champion. The deepest desire in every person is to find his purpose and place and to make his unique contribution. Also, Mickey faced his own failure. No excuses, no scapegoats, no playing the victim or the blame games, he took personal responsibility. "I've been a poor husband to my wife and a neglectful father to our four sons. It seems to me all I have done is take . . . have fun and take. God gave me a great body to play baseball . . . gave me everything and I wasted it. Don't be like me." He knew the difference between a hero and a role model.

Finally, he found his God. Though he often talked religion with his drinking buddies, it had never become a personal matter. Bobby Richardson, his Yankee all-star teammate, now at Mickey's bedside, spoke to him about God's love and Christ's sacrifice. A few days before his death, he exclaimed, "I've given my life to Jesus Christ." In Yankee Stadium, amid the hundreds of signs in his memory, one banner, obviously a child's work said, "Dear Mick, we miss you down at earth, but have a nice new life in heaven." Because of Mickey's commitment and God's dependable promise, I believe that has come true for him.

—J. Allan Petersen

Going Out Of Business Sale

One day the devil was contemplating going out of business, and he decided to sell all his tools to whomever would pay the price. On the night of the "fire" sale, all his favorite tools were attractively displayed. Malice, Hate, Envy, Jealousy, Greed, Sensuality and Deceit were among them. To the side, though, lay a harmless wedge-shaped tool which had seemed used more than the rest.

Someone asked the devil, "What's that?" (pointing to the wedge-shaped tool). "It's priced so high."

The devil answered, "That's Discouragement."

"But why is it priced so much higher than the rest," the onlooker persisted.

"Because," replied the devil, "With that tool I can pry open and get inside the person's consciousness when I couldn't get near it with any of the others. Once discouragement gets inside, I can let all the other tools do their work."

Remember, we probably confront some form of discouragement every day. How we handle this emotion determines whether we succeed or fail in reaching our goals. Discouragement is only a pit-stop, it's not the pits unless you allow it to be.

—**Eric Scott Kaplan**

How Turkeys Can Fly

Ever since I was a kid building model airplanes, I dreamed of the day I'd fly my own plane. I'd hang around an old dirt airstrip in the farm town of Mansfield, Washington, soaking up the smells and sounds of 1940 vintage planes used for spraying.

For my high school graduation in 1955, a spray pilot friend took me up in his Supercub. We did rolls, loops and spins right over my folks' house. He told me he'd teach me to fly that summer. I could hardly wait.

Just a few days before my first lesson I came down with what I first thought was the flu. It got worse—fast. Within two weeks I was stiff as a board, one of the last polio cases in the nation.

Rehabilitation finally got me walking again on legs that were 80 percent paralyzed. My right arm was useless and my left arm only 50 percent functional. As much as I wanted to "soar on wings like eagles," it seemed I was destined to stay grounded with the turkeys except for the times I flew as a passenger.

I went to college and, despite paralysis, became a physical education teacher. But I couldn't forget my dream of flying. I'd hang around airports, watching planes take off and land. I talked to people about flying, but they told me my legs were too weak to operate the rudders, or that one half-good arm wasn't enough for the rest of the controls. "It's too dangerous," they warned. "You'll kill yourself."

One day I nearly drove off the road near our local airport, because I was distracted watching a plane take off. My wife Judy knew I still had the dream. "Go for it, Dan," she said.

On May 26, 1975, barely twenty years after polio, I took my first 30-minute introductory lesson—one I'd bought at a fund-raising auction in town. My teacher, Cormac Thompson Sr., was a 68-year-old veteran who'd gotten his license in 1929. Mr. Thompson (I was too much in awe of him to call him "Cormac") helped me into the left pilot's seat of the Piper Cherokee. After a brief overview of buttons and controls, he had me taxi the plane to the end of runway two-five.

I soon found out planes weren't like cars. What I thought was the steering wheel was called the "yoke" and reserved for flight. The rudder pedals were tied into the nose gear to turn the plane. We went through the runup check list, then pulled onto the runway.

He said I could do the takeoff. Excitedly, I advanced the throttle and in a few seconds we had an airspeed of 60 mph.

"Rotate," Mr. Thompson ordered.

"What?"

"Pull back on the yoke!"

I eased back on the wheel (yoke)—and the plane floated into the air. I was flying! Taking over the controls, he flew us to a practice area and turned the plane back over to me. It was awful! I had to reach across my body for the flaps, throttle, and trim. Every time I'd reach for them, the plane would dip, tip and do everything but fly straight and level. I went all over the sky. When we landed, I wondered if others were right—that somebody like me shouldn't be flying.

But I couldn't give up. God had helped me achieve many other dreams once thought impossible after polio. Why not this one? I went back to the airport and tried again, but with me in the instructor's seat so that my good left arm could better grab the controls. Our next flight was better. I had hope.

From then on we flew once or twice a week. I felt like a one-man band as I found my legs and arm doing a hundred things at once (or it so it seemed). Half a year of lessons later, Mr. Thompson got out of the plane as we ended one session.

"You're ready," he said, "Take it up by yourself this time."

Mixed emotions swirled inside me. This was the moment I'd dreamed of. But could I really do it? I taxied to the end of runway two-five, said a hurried prayer, and radioed Unicom. Then I pushed the throttle forward and took off. Wow! I was flying alone! I wanted to keep going, leaving my instructor standing by the runway for a few hours while I cruised the hills and valleys.

But he was expecting me back in five minutes, so I went through all the landing routines, touching down perfectly. I did it!

In time, with more lessons and tests, I was signed off by a FAA flight instructor. I flew to my home airport where my wife was waiting. She climbed in—my first passenger. As we started our first flying adventure together, we both cried. Well, she cried and my eyes just sweated a bit. There's nothing like flying to get you close to heaven. Take it from a turkey-turned-eagle.

—Dan Miller

DON'T QUIT

When things go wrong as they sometimes will,
when the road you're trudging seems all up hill,
when the funds are low, and the the depts are high,
and you want to smile, but you have to sigh,
when care is pressing you down a bit,
rest if you must, but don't you quit.

Life is odd with it's twist and turns,
as everyone of us sometimes learns
and many a failure turns about,
when he might have won
had he stuck it out.
Don't give up
though the pace seems slow,
you may succeed with another blow.

Success is failure turned inside out,
the silver tint of the clouds of doubt,
and you never can tell how close you are.
It may be near when it seems so far.
So, stick to the fight when you're hardest hit.
It's when things seem worst
that you must not quit.

The Pain is Gone—I Have The Gold

The intense competition of the Olympic Games never fails to elicit outstanding examples of courage, dedication, and commitment to a goal.

The 1976 summer Olympics were no exception. A young Japanese athlete was leading the gymnastics events. Tragedy struck when, during the floor exercises, Shun Fujimoto broke his knee. Of course, no one expected him to appear the next day for the finals, in the rings.

But appear he did. The immense crowd was hushed as Fujimoto lifted to grasp the suspended ropes and rings, his knee heavily taped.

Flawlessly, the gallant competitor executed a beautiful routine of twists, turns and somersaults, but then the drama mounted. The crucial dismount seemed impossible for Fujimoto to land upright on a broken knee. No one moved as he flipped silently into the air, and then land, his face tensed but somehow he stood straight and threw his hand victoriously into the air!

Afterwards, reporters asked how Fujimoto could stand the pain. "Yes," he said, "it was so bad that it brought tears. But now the pain is gone and I have the gold!"

—Harold P. Hazen

Colonel Sanders—The Un-retired Star

Colonel Harland Sanders was ensconced at the luxurious Beverly Hills Hotel and invited us to join him for some old-fashioned Southern hospitality. When business discussions were concluded I asked, "Colonel, while you are here in California, would you be my Sunday guest at the church?" I knew that he had recently been "born again." He agreed to my request. So we stood together in my pulpit on Sunday morning.

"I un-retired and began a new business when I was 65. But better still, I began a completely new life when I was almost 80," the aging but still vibrant Colonel from Corbin, Kentucky told us. "I discovered that my millions of dollars could not buy inner peace. Among other obnoxious things I did, I cussed almost non-stop. My cussing didn't solve anything. It only showed how frustrated and miserable I felt. I knew, I needed to be saved from my lifetime of sins. I needed a miracle from God.

"On a Wednesday night I was tormented and felt desperate. I got in my car and started driving and praying. Finally, I saw a church with the lights on and cars in the parking lot. I parked and walked in. When the Pastor closed with prayers, I went forward, got down on my knees and prayed to God for his mercy and help. Simple as that, I had my miracle. I found peace, forgiveness and assurance of God's love for me at that altar. I haven't cussed since that Wednesday night."

We all laughed and the crowd applauded as they thronged to meet the Kentucky Miracle Man. Only now we all knew from his own mouth that the franchising miracle he performed wasn't nearly so great as the "born again" miracle he received. That was the miracle that cured the Kentucky Colonel of his non-stop cussing.

—D. Leroy Sanders

Pressing Forward—Looking Back

Athletes from all over the world who bring years of preparation and training compete for the ultimate prize in each Olympics: a gold medal distinguishing them as the best—uniquely unbeatable in their chosen sporting event.

A dramatic moment occurred during the 1954 British games, when the world's two greatest milers met to answer the same challenge: who was best?

As John Landy and Rodger Bannister (both of whom had broken the once insurmountable barrier, the 4 minute mile) pressed toward the last quarter mile, something happened that bears noting and may be worthy of application in our own lives.

Shoulder-to-shoulder, the two strained to gain an edge as the finish line approached. In an unforgettable split second, Landy looked back to see where Bannister was, and in that eyelash of time, Bannister streaked ahead to win the race.

Think of it! One man looking back and one looking ahead . . . on to victory. In that snapshot, who are you today?

—Harold P. Hazen

A Surprising Encounter

Little did I realize when I opened the gate that something was set in motion that would have such a profound impact on my life. At fifteen years of age, I was engaged in some home missionary work in my community. I approached a particular home and, once beyond the gate, entered into a big yard. The house was quite a distance away and when I was approximately halfway to the house I met with a terrifying surprise: two Doberman pinchers rushed toward me, barking wildly. They looked vicious and I was terrified. Fortunately, I was carrying a briefcase so I quickly thrust it upward and held it between me and them as we circled round and round.

After what seemed like an eternity, a lady came out of the house and called off the dogs. Her tone of voice scolded me as she asked, "Don't you know what you did was very dangerous?"

I felt ashamed for my lack of observation as I explained that I had not seen the "beware of dogs" sign. Once I had profusely apologized for causing the disturbance, she asked me to come inside.

The eyes of this lady I had just met soon told me that kindness had replaced her stern greeting. She prepared me a snack and asked, "Now, young man, what brought you to my house today?" She listened intently as I described my mission and allowed me to leave some Bible study material.

As I was preparing to leave she said, "Come, I want to show you something." When we rounded a corner and approached the living room, I noticed pictures of a boxer all over the walls. "Do you know who this is?" she asked.

Of course I did—it was Jack Dempsey. Then came the second surprise. "I am Jack's mother," she proudly proclaimed. She told me about the tough environment Jack had grown up in. While he was a child she ran a boarding house near the construction of the Moffett Tunnel for the railroad. She was a small lady and very feisty. She took the stance of a boxer with her clenched fists raised and said, "I taught Jack all he knows about taking care of himself."

We had a wonderful visit! I was reaching for the door to leave when I received the third surprise. She wrote a small check and handed it to me as she stated, "15-year-old boys always need socks."

Over a period of time I visited her several more times and brought her the Good News of God's love and salvation from His Word. Yes, she had touched my life, and somehow I seemed to fill a need for friendship in her's as well.

About a year later I was on my own. If I had food, clothing and shelter, it was up to me to provide it. I believe God used Mrs. Dempsey to instill in me some of the wonderful and practical information she had taught Jack so that I, too, could take care of myself. That surprise encounter over 50 years ago remains as vivid in my mind as if it only happened yesterday and its benefits remain precious to me to this day.

—Harvey Price

Love To Win More Than You Hate To Lose

On January 21, 1991, ABC News reporter Bill Redeker was interviewing an unidentified Marine general in the Persian Gulf. In response to Redeker's questions as to how to handle the shock of battle, the general asked his marines to remember one word, a word marines don't use very often. The word was *love*.

. . . And love is what you use to overcome the feelings of fear which are natural. Sometimes I've got to prompt guys. What would cause a woman, a mother of ninety-eight pounds, to run out and pick up an automobile off her child? Love. What would cause a marine to jump on a hand grenade, killing himself in order to save his fellow marine? Love. They don't fight because they hate the enemy. They fight for their buddies. They fight for love . . .

I've never talked to a true combat veteran who said he fought because he hated the enemy. I've never spoken to an athlete who said he won by hating his competitor. I've never spoken to anyone who said he or she stayed happily married simply by hating divorce. You must love to win more than you hate to lose.

Love to win more than you hate to lose. If you want to move toward a goal—any goal—you have to desire it. You have to love it. Don't attempt to motivate yourself by avoiding loss. That will only set you up for failure. Love to win. Want to achieve your goal. Have a compelling desire to excel. It's a positive force and will attract success to you. If the driving force in your life is fear of failure, you will focus on and experience fear. Ultimately, you will fail as a result of the negative energy created by obsessing. Identify an area in your life where you've experienced undesirable results because you've been afraid to lose. Change this around by being "for winning." Do something positive in this area each day for a week and observe the results. *Love to win more than you hate to lose.*

—**John Q. Baucom**

Credits

The Messiah Is Among You from *Carpe Diem*, Tony Campolo, Word, Inc., Texas, 1994. Used by permission of publisher.

Playing the Game for Someone Else from *What Makes a Man?*, Bill McCartney NavPress, Colorado, 1992. Used by permission of publisher.

Just Wait! from *Returning to Your First Love*, Tony Evans, Moody Press, Illinois, 1995. Used by permission of publisher.

Weathering Life's Storms from *Storm Warning*, Billy Graham, Word, Inc., Texas, 1992. Used by permission of publisher.

A Case in Chile from *The Secret Kingdom*, Pat Robertson, Word, Inc., Texas, 1992. Used by permission of publisher.

The Test of Endurance from *Storm Warning*, Billy Graham, Word, Inc., Texas, 1992. Used by permission of publisher.

Broken Promise from *The Hidden Value of a Man*, Gary Smalley and John Trent, Focus on the Family, Colorado, 1992. Used by permission of publisher.

The Myth About Work from *The Seven Seasons of a Man's Life*, Patrick M. Morley, Thomas Nelson Publishers, Tennessee, 1995. Used by permission of publisher.

Building Our Kids from *The Seven Seasons of a Man's Life*, Patrick M. Morley, Thomas Nelson Publishers, Tennessee, 1995. Used by permission of publisher.

Wake Up Call (adapted) from *As Iron Sharpens Iron*, Howard Hendricks, Moody Press, Illinois, 1995. Used by permission of publisher.

My Mother's Prayers from *On Becoming A Real Man*, Edwin Louis Cole, Thomas Nelson Publishers, Tennessee, 1992. Used by permission of publisher.

"He Ain't Heavy, He's My Brother" from *Locking Arms*, Stu Weber, Multnomah Books, Questar Publishers, Oregon, 1995. Used by permission of publisher.

A Red Rose for Rachel from *Point Man*, Steve Farrar, Multnomah Books, Questar Publishers, Oregon, 1990. Used by permission of publisher.

Availability Versus Structure from *Walking With Christ in the Details of Life*, Patrick M. Morley, Thomas Nelson Publishers, Tennessee, 1992. Used by permission of publisher.

"He Was A Saint!" (adapted) from *Can Man Live Without God?*, Ravi Zacharias, Word, Inc., Texas, 1994.

"Did What Again?" from *A Man's Confidence*, Jack Hayford, Thomas Nelson Publishers, Tennessee, 1992.

No Instant Maturity from *If I'm Not Tarzan and My Wife Isn't Jane, Then What Are We Doing in the Jungle?*, Steve Farrar, Multnomah Book, Questar Publishers, Oregon, 1991. Used by permission of publisher.

"Are You God?" from *Improving Your Serve*, Charles R. Swindoll, Word, Inc., Texas, 1981. Used by permission of publisher.

The Old You from *Returning to Your First Love,* Tony Evans, Moody Press, Illinois, 1995. Used by permission of publisher.

Greatness of Life from *On Becoming A Real Man,* Edwin Louis Cole, Thomas Nelson Publishers, Tennessee, 1992. Used by permission of publisher.

Take Time for the Moment from *Walking With Christ in the Details of Life,* Patrick M. Morley, Thomas Nelson Publishers, Tennessee, 1992. Used by permission of publisher.

Measuring the Value of Life from *The Hunger for Significance,* R.C. Sproul, Regal Books, California, 1983, 1991. Used by permission of publisher.

Final Word, Final Acts from *No Wonder They Call Him the Savior,* Max Lucado, Multnomah Books, Questar Publishers, Oregon, 1986. Used by permission of publisher.

The Journey from *You Are Never Alone,* Charles L. Allen, Revell, a division of Baker Book House Company, Michigan, 1978. Used by permission of publisher.

"Shoooooooppping" from *The Hidden Value of a Man,* Gary Smalley and John Trent, Focus on the Family, Colorado, 1992. Used by permission of publisher.

A Woman's Desire for Security from *The Hidden Value of a Man,* Gary Smalley and John Trent, Focus on the Family, Colorado, 1992. Used by permission of publisher.

Passion from *Tender Love,* Bill Hybels, Moody Press, Illinois, 1993. Used by permission of publisher.

Meeting Needs from *The Hidden Value of a Man,* Gary Smalley and John Trent, Focus on the Family, Colorado, 1992. Used by permission of publisher.

Patience from *Walking With Christ in the Details of Life,* Patrick M. Morley, Thomas Nelson Publishers, Tennessee, 1992. Used by permission of publisher.

A Plan from *Point Man,* Steve Farrar, Multnomah Books, Questar Publishers, Oregon, 1990. Used by permission of publisher.

The Child Who Stumbles from *When You Can't Come Back,* Dave Dravecky, Zondervan Publishing House, Michigan, 1993. Used by permission of publisher.

In the Belly of the Whale (condensed and adapted) from *The Seven Seasons of a Man's Life,* Patrick M. Morley, Thomas Nelson Publishers, Tennessee, 1995. Used by permission of publisher.

Surprised and Encouraged from *The Hidden Value of a Man,* Gary Smalley and John Trent, Focus on the Family, Colorado, 1992. Used by permission of publisher.

Compliments from *The Hunger for Significance,* R. C. Sproul, Regal Books, California, 1983, 1991. Used by permission of publisher.

Being Called A Man from *The Hunger for Significance,* R. C. Sproul, Regal Books, California, 1983, 1991. Used by permission of publisher.

She Believed in Me from *As Iron Sharpens Iron,* Howard Hendricks, Moody Press, Illinois, 1995. Used by permission of publisher.

Ten Marks of a Mentor from *As Iron Sharpens Iron,* Howard Hendricks, Moody Press, Illinois, 1995. Used by permission of publisher.

"I Knew You'd Come" (adapted) from *Locking Arms,* Stu Weber, Multnomah

Books, Questar Publishers, Oregon, 1995. Used by permission of publisher.

Fellow Soldiering from *Locking Arms*, Stu Weber, Multnomah Book, Questar Publishers, Oregon, 1995. Used by permission of publisher.

A Simple Comment from *Men and Women*, Larry Crabb, Zondervan Publishing House, Michigan, 1991. Used by permission of publisher.

Knowing the Sheep Individually from *The Hunger for Significance*, R. C. Sproul, Regal Books, California, 1983, 1991. Used by permission of publisher.

The Motive for Good Deeds from *The Seven Seasons of a Man's Life*, Patrick M. Morley, Thomas Nelson Publishers, Tennessee, 1995. Used by permission of publisher.

Priorities from *On Becoming A Real Man*, Edwin Louis Cole, Thomas Nelson Publishers, Tennessee, 1992. Used by permission of publisher.

Diminished Revival (adapted) from *The Body*, Charles Colson with Ellen Santilli Vaughn, Word, Inc., Texas, 1992. Used by permission of publisher.

Grabbing the Bait from *The Seven Seasons of a Man's Life*, Patrick M. Morley, Thomas Nelson Publishers, Tennessee, 1995. Used by permission of publisher.

Guardrails from *Locking Arms*, Stu Weber, Multnomah Books, Questar Publishers, Oregon, 1995. Used by permission of publisher.

Climb Higher from *Returning to Your First Love*, Tony Evans, Moody Press, Illinois, 1995. Used by permission of publisher.

God's Discipline from *Returning to Your First Love*, Tony Evans, Moody Press, Illinois, 1995. Used by permission of publisher.

A Son's Death from *Can Man Live Without God*, Ravi Zacharias, Word, Inc., Texas, 1994. Used by permission of publisher.

Searching For A Purpose In Life from *What Makes a Man?*, Bill McCartney NavPress, Colorado, 1992. Used by permission of publisher.

A Street Vendor Named Contentment from *No Wonder They Call Him the Savior*, Max Lucado, Multnomah Books, Questar Publishers, Oregon, 1986. Used by permission of publisher.

Free As A Bird from *There's a Jungle Out There*, Gary Richmond, Harvest House, Oregon, 1996. Used by permission of publisher.

First Things (adapted) from *Carpe Diem*, Tony Campolo, Word, Inc., Texas, 1994. Used by permission of publisher.

The Pain Is Gone—I Have the Gold, Harold P. Hazen, Ark Multimedia Publishing, Inc., 1995.

Pressing Forward—Looking Back, Harold P. Hazen, 1996.

Contributors

Stephen Arterburn is co-founder and Chairman of Minirth-Meier New Life Clinics. He is author of 18 books. Stephen lives in Laguna Beach, California with his wife Sandy and daughter Madeline.

Stanley Baldwin is an author and speaker based in Oregon. His books have been translated into ten languages and four of his 19 titles have sold over 200,000 copies each.

David H. Baty was born into a family of 11 children. He and his wife, Virginia, have 5 children and 13 grandchildren. His life's work was in construction and sales. Presently, he is owner and operator of David Baty's Sharpening Service in Olathe, Kansas.

John Q. Baucom is the author of nine books, including *Baby Steps*™ *to Happiness* (Starburst Publishers). He specializes in helping people prolong their SuccessCycle™ through books, speeches, tapes, and consulting. Contact: Human Resource Center, 7433 Preston Circle, Chattanooga, TN 37421. (423) 954-1074

Michael Bechtle is a speaker and seminar leader helping people balance their time and life. He has spent 20 years in college classrooms, church ministry and corporate training. Mike lives with his wife and two children in Brea, California.

Tim Bechtle lives with his family in Brea, California, where he is a sophomore at Brea Olinda High School. His free time finds him either in the ocean or on the soccer field. Tim is involved with the youth group at his church.

Lewis Boore is a 1981 graduate of West Point. He is the director of marketing for a national high-tech firm. Actively involved in lay ministry in San Diego, Lew and his wife, Danna, welcome opportunities to speak to Christian men, women and couples. Contact: (619) 444-3400.

Charles Brown and his wife Bobbie have four children and one grandson. Charlie serves on the elder team with Bible Fellowship of Riverside, California. He writes material used in worship, devotionals and serves on the board with The Inland Empire Christian Writers Guild. Contact: 6929 Morningside Ave., Riverside, CA 92504. (909) 689-2440.

Paul Budd is a Chaplain at John Knox Village Retirement Community. He is married to Kim and they have one son, Aaron. Paul is an ordained Elder in the United Methodist Church. Contact: 400 NW Murray Rd., Lee's Summit, MO 64081. (816) 524-8400 ext 2245.

Laurence A. Davis is 73 years old, and had his first work published in 1938. He is a widower and his activities include lay preaching, biking, camping, and reading. Contact: 9215 Belview, Wichita, KS 67209. (316) 722-1870.

Gene "Rob" DeShores is Protestant Chaplain at California Institute for Women at Fontera, California. Rob oversees 600 volunteers, and on Sundays he monitors nine church services. Contact: (909) 597-1771 ext. 6366.

Kevin Downing, Ph.D., is a popular radio host and marriage counselor in the Los Angeles area. He frequently speaks on "People Pleasing" and other topics. Contact: Turning Point Counseling, 620 N. Diamond Bar Boulevard., Diamond Bar, CA 91765. (800) 99-TODAY.

Clay Ellis has been married for 22 years and is the father of 3 children. He and wife Gloria are involved in counseling and ministry with youth and adults. Contact: 13550 Soper Court, Chino, CA 91710.

Bill Farrel is a senior pastor, co-director of Masterful Living Ministries, and co-author of *Pure Pleasure: Making Your Marriage a Great Affair* and *Marriage in the Whirlwind: Seven Skills for Couples Who Can't Slow Down*. Bill resides in San Diego, California, with his wife, Pam, and three sons. Contact: (619) 727-9122.

Dave Fite lives with his teenaged children, Dan and Bekah, and his wife, Karin. David has worked for an insurance company for over 23 years. He and Karin are active in marriage ministries of their church. Contact: 3823 Requa Ave., Claremont, CA 91711. (909) 593-3304.

Charles R. Flowers is a management consultant, information professional and human resource motivator. He also is a recognized expert in employee and customer relations. Contact: 2050 Pacific Beach Dr. #205, San Diego, CA 92109. (619) 581-9247.

Vernon Garten is retired from ownership/operation of a crane construction business. He has served as Deacon, Elder, and Sunday School teacher and works with adult literacy programs. Vernon plays golf and travels with his wife in their 5th wheel trailer. Contact: 401 Oak Ridge Ct., Valley Springs, CA 95252. (209) 772-2521.

Dave Getz is a freelance writer. His current writing project is a Christian novel for boys (ages 8-12) set in the Arizona mountains. Contact: 323 E. Auburn Drive, Tempe, AZ 85283. (602) 838-7169.

Todd Gordon is a fifth grade teacher and aspiring writer. He has Bachelor Degrees in English and Religious Studies. His hobbies include computers, cartoons, theology, toy collecting, and bicycling. Todd lives with his wife and cat in San Bernardino. Contact: 540 E. Weir Rd. #131, San Bernardino, CA 92408. (909) 799-1434.

Wayne Gordon is the husband of Anne and father of three children. Wayne is pastor of Lawndale Community Church, located in the 15th poorest neighborhood in the United States. Wayne authored *Real Hope in Chicago* and was named the 1995 "Chicagoan of the year." Contact: 3848 West Ogden Ave., Chicago, IL 60623. (312) 762-6389.

Richard "Dick" Hagerman has had numerous magazine and newspaper articles published. He is the author of *Eat, Drink, and Be Especially Joyful.* A dentist of 37 years, Dick has also been a lay preacher and elder in the United Presbyterian Church. Contact: P.O. Box 365, Wendell, ID 83355. (208) 536-2187.

David Hahn currently serves as Music Pastor at CMA church in Lancaster, Pennsylvania. His ministry has taken him to Japan, Germany, Holland and Africa. David has studied at Nyack College, Syracuse University, and most recently completed his Masters Degree at Temple University. Contact: 400 Ashford Dr., Lancaster, PA 17601. (717) 560-9434.

Mike Hayes has lived in the San Fernando Valley, California since 1958. For 26 years he has been married to author Judith Hayes. They have two daughters, Sasha and Annabelle. Contact: 10056 Fullbright Ave., Chatsworth, CA 91311. (818) 701-9775.

Sam Hinman has lived in various parts of the world—compliments of the United States Navy. Sam is married and has two daughters and three grandchildren. He currently resides in Southern California.

Ed Horton is a Business Analyst for the Information Technology division of a major corporation. He primarily writes fiction and devotionals. Ed and his wife are members of the Orangewood Church of the Nazarene in Phoenix, Arizona. Contact: 5652 W. Pontiac Dr., Glendale, AZ 85308. (602) 561-6789.

Timothy L. Hudson was born and raised in Georgia. He was schooled in Theology and self-taught in Powerlifting. Timothy has been Campus Minister at the University of Georgia since 1982. He is also the Athlete Chaplaincy Director for the Athens Venue of the 1996 Olympics.

Jerry B. Jenkins, former vice president for publishing and now writer-in-residence for Moody Bible Institute of Chicago, is the author of more than 100 books, including the bestseller, *Left Behind.* Jerry is a frequent guest on Dr. James Dobson's Focus on the Family radio program. He lives with his wife and boys at Three Son Acres, west of Zion, Illinois.

Karl Joy completed his fourth semester at Fullerton College in May, 1996. He is also taking an apologetics class at Simon Greenleaf University. Karl enjoys playing the piano and making the most out of life. Contact: 1808 Viola St., Anaheim, CA 92807. (714) 779-6650.

Eric Scott Kaplan is the author of *Dr. Kaplan's Lifestyle of the Fit and Famous* (Starburst Publishers). As a dynamic and motivating speaker, Eric has also been seen extensively on television and heard on radio. Contact: BigScore Productions, P.O. Box 7341, Lancaster, PA 17604.

Tim Kimmel is the husband of Darcy, father of four, and President of Generation Ministries. He is author of four books, such as *Little House on the Freeway.* As a speaker, Tim is known for being "the most predictably unpredictable family advocate for your audience." Contact: Generation Ministries, 10214 N. Tatum, Street B300, Phoenix, AZ 85028. (602) 948-2545.

Richard "Dick" J. Lindholtz is a retired optometrist. He and wife Barbara have three children. For the past twenty-five years, they have served in a ministry of premarital counseling for their church. They currently function as church ministry staff associates. Contact: 1025 Miller Drive, Davis, CA 95616. (916) 753-2245.

Mark R. Littleton has written for *Reader's Digest, Chicago Tribune, Moody Monthly* and *Leadership.* He is the author of more than 15 books and is a graduate of Dallas Theological Seminary. Contact: 5350 Eliot's Oak Road, Columbia, MD 21044. (410) 995-0831.

Jack Martin was born in San Francisco, California, and is a career postal employee. He dreams of qualifying for the Senior PGA Tour after retirement.

D. Larry Miller is best-selling author of *God's Vitamin C for the Spirit* series with his wife, Kathy Collard Miller. As a police sergeant in Huntington Beach, California and a professional speaker, his moniker is "The Sarge." Contact: P.O. Box 1058, Placentia, CA 92871. (714) 993-2654.

Dan Miller shares his inspirational story to churches, businesses, associations, schools, and students. Focus on the Family has broadcast his story in English and Spanish. Dan and his wife do seminars on Attitude and how to be Dreammakers, not Dreambreakers! Contact: 2485 Alaska Ave. East, Port Orchard, WA 98366-8214. (360) 871-TGIM.

Keith Nash is a telephone service/technician, husband of Kendra, and father of Kenneth, Kyle, and Karsten. Keith is a farmboy from Colfax, North Dakota. Contact: Route 1, Box 448, Warroad, MN 56763. (218) 386-2909.

Craig A. Nell is married to Deborah. They have a daughter Sophia. Craig's ministry includes social worker, home group church leader, and Bible-study teacher. Contact: 1300 N. Clinton St., Space 10, Santa Ana, CA 92703. (714) 265-1364.

Michael Vincent Obar was born in the Philippines and raised north of Dallas, Texas. He now resides in LaCrosse, Wisconsin, where he works at Shepherd's Voice Christian Bookstore. Michael is worship leader for Rivers Harvest Church. Contact: Questar Publishing, 205 W. Adams, Sisters, OR 97759.

Richard A. Osborn is the husband of Susan. Richard is an assistant editor for *The Christian Communicator*. He enjoys keeping his verbal skills sharp by solving the daily crossword puzzles in the newspaper. Contact: 3133 Puente St., Fullerton, CA 92835. (714) 990-1532.

Luis Palau is in his third decade of mass evangelism and has spoken to hundreds of millions of people in 95 nations through radio and television broadcasts. He has spoken face-to-face to 11 million people in 63 nations. Contact: Luis Palau Evangelistic Association, P.O. Box 1173, Portland, OR 97207-1173. (503) 614-1500.

J. Allan Petersen is nationally-known as a marriage and family life specialist. His eight best-selling books have sold over two million copies and are translated into a dozen languages. Peterson publishes *Better Families,* a monthly family information bulletin. Contact: Family Concern, P.O. Box 900, Morrison, CA 80465-0900. (303) 697-1202.

Harvey Price earned his M.Ed. degree at Colorado State University and, as a college Dean of Instruction, has spent many years touching the lives of young people. Harvey and wife, Betty, co-authored ABC's *of Abundant Living*. Contact: P.O. Box 151115, San Diego, CA 92175-1115. (619) 466-9136.

Darren Prince, 21, is finishing his undergraduate studies at Wheaton College with degrees in Christian Education and Literature. Afterwards, he intends to pursue his calling to minister God's grace among the urban poor. Darren enjoys writing songs, stories, and poems. Contact: 301 Rainier Circle, Placentia, CA 92870.

D. Leroy Sanders has been an evangelist and pastor. He founded the Los Angeles Mayor's Prayer Breakfast in 1973 and is chaplain at the Motion Picture Home in Woodland Hills, California. Contact: 80 Flintlock Lane, Bell Canyon, CA 91307.

Grant Sickles is a man of many talents. His varied career has included being a pastor, educator, psychologist and business executive. After early retirement, he and his wife served as short-term missionaries in a number of different countries.

Don Tofel is married to Joyce and is dad to Marnie and Alison, both in college. Don is a sales representative, selling equipment to hospital OR's, and enjoys writing about "the lighter side of life." Contact: 546 Harvest Lane, Verona, WI 53593. (608) 845-5591.

Bob Treash is the assistant editor for Wycliffe Bible Translators in California. His plans for the next year include teaching English as a second language in China. Contact: 50 Laurie Rd., Trumball, CT 06611.

Carl Westling (a.k.a.) Cuyler W. Wenberg is self-employed and single with four married children and seven grandchildren. Carl served in the Marine Corps and graduated from Washington State University. Contact: 1500 E. Warren St. #151, Santa Ana, CA 92705. (714) 541-4974.

Philip Wiese is a business consultant and owner of Cable Express. He is married to Patricia and has three children. Contact: 10 Firestone Court, Madison, WI 53717. (608) 831-2818.

Alan Willcox, ACSW, is a professional social worker with nearly 30 year's experience in the mental health field. He enjoys counseling, teaching, and public speaking. Contact: 101 East Park St., Paola, KS 66071-1987. (913) 294-3324.

Greg Williamson is a freelance Christian writer working toward his B.S. degree in psychology at North Carolina State University. He lives with his wife, Sharon. Contact: 3505-203 Palm Court, Raleigh, NC 27607-3440.

Randy Yenter is senior pastor of Trinity Church in Spring Valley, California. He is married to Kathie and they have one son who is also discovering "The Great Adventure."

Jeffry R. Zurheide, married to Karen, is father of Molly and Andrew. Holder of M.Div. and D.Min. degrees, Jeffry, since 1988 has been pastor of Wilton Baptist Church, Wilton Connecticut. He is also an Adjunct Professor of pastoral care with a 1997 book due on that subject.

Books by Starburst Publishers
(Partial listing—full list available on request)

God's Vitamin "C" for the Spirit of MEN
—D. Larry Miller

Subtitled: *"Tug-at-the-Heart" Stories to Encourage and Strengthen Your Spirit.* Compiled in the format of best-selling *God's Vitamin "C" for the Spirit*, this book is filled with unique and inspiring stories that men of all ages will immediately relate to. True stories by some of the most-loved Christian speakers and writers on topics such as Integrity, Mentoring, Leadership, Marriage, Success/Failure, Family, Godliness, and Spiritual Life are sure to encourage men through the challenges of life. Contributors include Bill McCartney, Tony Evans, Larry Crabb, Tim Kimmel, Billy Graham, and R. C. Sproul, to name a few.

(trade paper) ISBN 0914984810 **$12.95**

God's Chewable Vitamin "C" for the Spirit of DADs

Subtitled: *A Dose of Godly Character, One Bite at a Time.* Scriptures coupled with insightful quotes to inspire men through the changes of life. This little "portable" is the perfect gift for men of all ages and walks of life. It provides the encouragement needed by Dad from time to time.

(trade paper) ISBN 0914984829 **$6.95**

God's Vitamin "C" for the Christmas Spirit
—Kathy Collard Miller & D. Larry Miller

Subtitled: *"Tug-at-the-Heart" Traditions and Inspirations to Warm the Heart.* Written in the same spirit as best-selling *God's Vitamin "C" for the Spirit*, this collection will rekindle new and old traditions for celebrating the Christmas season. This keepsake includes a variety of heart-tugging thoughts, stories, poetry, recipes, songs and crafts. Christian writers and speakers, such as Pat Boone, Cheri Fuller, Gloria Gaither, Joni Eareckson, and Michael Card combine their talents to produce a book that is sure to encourage a time of peace, relaxation, and the building of your own cherished Christmas memories.

(hardcover) ISBN 0914984853 **$14.95**

God's Vitamin "C" for the Spirit
—Kathy Collard Miller & D. Larry Miller

Subtitled: *"Tug-at-the-Heart" Stories to Fortify and Enrich Your Life.* Includes inspiring stories and anecdotes that emphasize Christian ideals and values by Barbara Johnson, Billy Graham, Nancy L. Dorner, Dave Dravecky, Patsy Clairmont, Charles Swindoll, H. Norman Wright, Adell Harvey, Max Lucado, James Dobson, Jack Hayford and many other well-known Christian speakers and writers. Topics include: Love, Family Life, Faith and Trust, Prayer, Marriage, Relationships, Grief, Spiritual Life, Perseverance, Christian Living, and God's Guidance.

(trade paper) ISBN 0914984837 **$12.95**

Books by Starburst Publishers—cont'd.

God's Chewable Vitamin "C" for the Spirit

Subtitled: *A Dose of God's Wisdom One Bite at a Time.* A collection of inspirational Quotes and Scriptures by many of your favorite Christian speakers and writers. It will motivate your life and inspire your spirit. You will *chew* on every *bite* of **God's Chewable Vitamin "C" for the Spirit.**

(trade paper) ISBN 0914984845 **$6.95**

Baby Steps to Happiness —John Q. Baucom

Subtitled: *52 Inspiring Ways to Make Your Life Happy.* This unique 52-step approach will enable the reader to focus on small steps that bring practical and proven change. The author encourages the reader to take responsibility for the Happiness that only he can find. Chapter titles, such as, *Have a Reason to Get Out of Bed, Deal with Your Feelings or Become Them, Would You Rather Be Right or Happy?,* and *Love To Win More Than You Hate to Lose* give insight and encouragement on the road to happiness.

(trade paper) ISBN 0914984861 **$12.95**

Little Baby Steps to Happiness —John Q. Baucom

Inspiring, witty and insightful, this portable collection of quotes and affirmations from **Baby Steps to Happiness** will encourage Happiness one little footstep at a time. This book is the perfect personal "cheerleader."

(trade paper) ISBN 091498487X **$6.95**

The World's Oldest Health Plan —Kathleen O'Bannon Baldinger

Subtitled: *Health, Nutrition and Healing from the Bible.* Offers a complete health plan for body, mind, and spirit, just as Jesus did. It includes programs for diet, exercise, and mental health. Contains foods and recipes to lower cholesterol and blood pressure, improve the immune system and other bodily functions, reduce stress, reduce or cure constipation, eliminate insomnia, reduce forgetfulness, confusion and anger, increase circulation and thinking ability, eliminate "yeast" problems, improve digestion, and much more.

(trade paper-opens flat) ISBN 0914984578 **$14.95**

Dr. Kaplan's Lifestyle of the Fit & Famous —Eric Scott Kaplan

Subtitled: *A Wellness Approach to "Thinning and Winning."* A comprehensive guide to the formulas and principles of: FAT LOSS, EXERCISE, VITAMINS, NATURAL HEALTH, SUCCESS, and HAPPINESS. More than a health book—it is a lifestyle based on the empirical formulas of healthy living. Dr. Kaplan's food-combining principles take into account all the major food sources (fats, proteins, carbohydrates, sugars, etc.) that when combined within the proper formula (e.g. proteins cannot be mixed with refined carbohydrates) will increase metabolism and decrease the waistline. This allows you to eat the foods you want, feel great, and eliminate craving and binging.

(hard cover) ISBN 091498456X **$21.95**

Books by Starburst Publishers—cont'd.

Grapes of Righteousness   —Joseph H. Powell

Subtitled: *Spiritual Grafting Into the True Vine.* Dr. Powell uses an analogy that compares and contrasts our development into God's kingdom under His hands, to the cultivating and nurturing of a vineyard by a gardener. He explores grafting, pruning, nutrition, and dormancy to illustrate the basic Biblical principles necessary to spiritual birth and subsequent growth and maturity.

(trade paper) ISBN 0914984748 **$10.95**

Winning At Golf   —David A. Smith

Addresses the growing needs of aspiring young golfers yearning for correct instruction, positive guidance, and discipline. It is an attempt not only to increase the reader's knowledge of the swing, but also sets forth to inspire and motivate the reader to a new and rewarding way of life. ***Winning At Golf*** relays the teachings of Buck White, the author's mentor and a tour winner many times over. It gives instruction to the serious golfer and challenges the average golfer to excel.

(trade paper) ISBN 0914984462 **$9.95**

Home Business Happiness   —Ann Tuites

Subtitled: *Secrets on Keeping the Family Ship Afloat/From Entrepreneurs Who Made It.* More than 26 million people in the U.S. work at home businesses and the number is growing. ***Home Business Happiness*** offers invaluable advice from inventive and pioneering entrepreneurs in the country who have made it, and gives the secrets of their success. This book provides a network for success in a reader-friendly style and covers such topics as time-management, legal issues, publicity, filing taxes, and avoiding pitfalls.

(trade paper) ISBN 0914984705 **$12.95**

Migraine—Winning the Fight of Your Life   —Charles Theisler

This book describes the hurt, loneliness, and agony that migraine sufferers experience and the difficulty they must live with. It explains the different types of migraines and their symptoms, as well as the related health hazards. Gives 200 ways to help fight off migraines, and shows how to experience fewer headaches, reduce their duration, and decrease the agony and pain involved.

(trade paper) ISBN 0914984632 **$10.95**

The Crystal Clear Guide to Sight for Life   —Gayton & Ledford

Subtitled: *A Complete Manual of Eye Care for Those Over 40.* ***The Crystal Clear Guide to Sight For Life*** makes eye care easy-to-understand by giving clear knowledge of how the eye works, with the most up-to-date information available from the experts. Contains more than 40 illustrations, a detailed index for cross-referencing, a concise glossary, and answers to often-asked questions. This book takes much of the guesswork out of eye problems, alleviating the fear and apprehension often experienced by patients when medical problems develop.

(trade paper) ISBN 0914984683 **$15.95**

Books by Starburst Publishers—cont'd.

Parenting With Respect and Peacefulness —Louise A. Dietzel

Subtitled: *The Most Difficult Job in the World.* Parents who love and respect themselves parent with respect and peacefulness. Yet, parenting with respect is the most difficult job in the world. This book informs parents that respect and peace communicate love—creating an atmosphere for children to maximize their development as they feel loved, valued, and safe. Parents learn authority and control by a common sense approach to day-to-day situations in parenting.

(trade paper) ISBN 0914984667 **$10.95**

Beyond The River —Gilbert Morris & Bobby Funderburk

The first novel of *The Far Fields* series, ***Beyond the River*** makes for intriguing reading with high spiritual warfare impact. Set in the future and in the mode of *Brave New World* and *1984*, ***Beyond The River*** presents a world that is ruined by modern social and spiritual trends. This anti-utopian novel offers an excellent opportunity to speak to the issues of the New Age and "politically-correct" doctrines that are sweeping the country.

(trade paper) ISBN 0914984519 **$8.95**

Angels, Angels, Angels —Phil Phillips

Subtitled: *Embraced by The Light...or...Embraced by The Darkness?* Discovering the truth about Angels, Near-Death Experiences, and other Spiritual Awakenings. Also, why the sudden interest in angels in this day and age? Can we trust what we read in books like *Embraced By The Light?*

(trade paper) ISBN 0914984659 **$10.95**

Nightmare In Dallas —Beverly Oliver

The hard-hitting account of the mysterious *"Babushka Lady,"* Beverly Oliver, who at the age of seventeen was an eyewitness to the assassination of President John F. Kennedy. This is only the second book to be written by one who saw the event first-hand. Beverly was a personal friend of Jack Ruby and was married to a member of the Mafia. Beverly's film of the event (the only other known motion picture) was confiscated by two men who called themselves FBI agents. To this present day, neither she nor any other known person has been permitted to view the film. Why? This book tells the story.

(hard cover) ISBN 0914984608 **$19.95**

POW/MIA–America's Missing Men —Chimp Robertson

Subtitled: *The Men We Left Behind.* Raises questions and relays the thoughts and feelings of more than 75 soldiers, ex-soldiers, senators, congressmen, entertainers, and media members about the *POW/MIA* issue on whether America left its soldiers in Southeast Asia. Quotes and comments include those from: Gen. William C. Westmoreland, Senator John Kerry, Oliver North, American Legion Magazine, and the National League of Families of Missing Americans.

(hardcover) ISBN 0914984640 **$19.95**

Books by Starburst Publishers—cont'd.

Common Sense Management & Motivation   —Roy H. Holmes

Teaches the principles of motivating subordinate personnel via good human relations. It is written from practical "how-to" experience rather than classroom theory. Specific subjects covered include: Basic motivation psychology, Effective communication, Delegating, Goal-setting, Confronting, and Leadership qualities. A must book for all existing or aspiring supervisors, managers, business leaders, and anyone else interested in managing and motivating people.

(hardcover)   ISBN 0914984497   **$16.95**

Stay Well Without Going Broke   —Gulling, Renner, & Vargas

Subtitled: *Winning the War Over Medical Bills.* Provides a blueprint for how health care consumers can take more responsibility for monitoring their own health and the cost of its care—a crucial cornerstone of the health care reform movement today. Contains inside information from doctors, pharmacists, and hospital personnel on how to get cost-effective care without sacrificing quality. Offers legal strategies to protect your rights when illness is terminal.

(hardcover)   ISBN 0914984527   **$22.95**

On The Brink   —Daymond R. Duck

Subtitled: *Easy-to-Understand End-Time Bible Prophecy.* Organized in Biblical sequence and written with simplicity so that any reader will easily understand end-time prophecy. Ideal for use as a handy-reference book.

(trade paper)   ISBN 0914984586   **$10.95**

Purchasing Information:

Listed books are available from your favorite Bookstore, either from current stock or special order. To assist bookstores in locating your selection be sure to give title, author, and ISBN #. If unable to purchase from the bookstore you may order direct from STARBURST PUBLISHERS. When ordering, enclose full payment plus $3.00 for shipping and handling ($4.00 if Canada or Overseas). Payment in US Funds only. Please allow two to three weeks minimum (longer overseas) for delivery. Make checks payable to and mail to STARBURST PUBLISHERS, P.O. Box 4123, LANCASTER, PA 17604. **Prices subject to change without notice.** Catalog available for a 9 x 12 self-addressed envelope with 4 first-class stamps. 7-96